D1506416

Sherlock
Bones

KITCHENER PUBLIC LIBRARY

SH
Kea

Sherlock Bones

Tracer of Missing Pets

John Keane

Discarded From
Kitchener Public Library

J. B. LIPPINCOTT COMPANY

PHILADELPHIA AND NEW YORK

*The names and identifying circumstances
of the people in this book have been
changed to protect their privacy.*

Copyright © 1979 by John Keane
All rights reserved
2 4 6 8 9 7 5 3 1
Printed in the United States of America

U.S. Library of Congress Cataloging in Publication Data

Keane, John, birth date
Sherlock Bones: Tracer of missing pets.

1. Animals, Treatment of.   2. Pets.
I. Title.
HV4708.K4   363.2'33   78–31850
ISBN–0–397–01335–3

This book is dedicated to my mother,
God rest her soul

Contents

Acknowledgments

I WANT TO THANK, first of all, my brother Bill for his constant personal, and occasional financial, support—and for having seven young sons to serve as Uncle Sherlock's unofficial "pet posse."

To Virginia Barber, my literary agent, I owe a debt of gratitude for the belief in Sherlock that inspired her efforts in my behalf. The same goes for my attorney, Don Parris, whose professional competence and personal friendship I value most highly. Barry Schwenkmeyer helped me wrestle my Irish gift of gab into the paragraphs and chapters that make up this book, and I thank him for that.

Then I want to thank my hundreds of clients, all the owners and their pets. Working with them has taught me the depth and complexity of people-pet relationships.

To my dog Paco I owe perhaps the greatest debt of all, for he opened me up to the feelings that have made Sherlock Bones more than just a business, no matter how hard I tried to pretend otherwise.

JOHN KEANE

Oakland, California
September 25, 1978

9

Sherlock Bones

1
Sasha

No MATTER WHAT you may have heard, San Francisco can get colder than the nose on a polar bear—especially when you're parked on the street in an unheated VW van at five in the morning, numb with exhaustion and shot through with doubt. Did I really think Sasha would show her face here, this morning? I peered once more at the unfinished restaurant across the street, clutching my Styrofoam coffee cup for any vestiges of warmth it could give me. Wisps of the city's famous fog wafted through the half-open window. Better cold air than steamy windows, I told myself, but better yet was my nice warm bed across the bay in Oakland. Was this any way for a grown man to make a living? If this case hadn't been special. . . . But who was I trying to kid? Sooner or later all my cases become special.

Paco shifted in his sleep on the seat behind me, toasty warm under the gray and white mop of fur that covered him like a great hairy tea cozy. Lucky guy. He could lie there dreaming of white woolly flocks in lush green pastures—or whatever Old English sheepdogs dream of—while I had to stay alert and man my canine stakeout. For a moment I considered crawling back and curling up with him, but I knew he would take it as an invitation to a romp—and I was in no mood for a romp now. Time was running out, and I was getting worried. In fact, to tell the truth, I had been worried ever since I took this case.

Four days earlier I had gotten a call from an electrical contractor by the name of Ned Taylor who wanted me to help him find his dog Sasha. As he told his story I could hear the anxiety and fear that had driven him to seek help. Sasha, he told me, was his sidekick. Every morning she would ride with him in his truck to his various jobs and keep him company while he worked. If she wasn't lying patiently at his side, she was out exploring the interesting smells and crannies of the neighborhood. Over the years Ned had taken to packing two lunches, one for himself and one for Sasha, and when noontime came they would repair to his truck and relax together over the contents of their respective brown bags. He loved having Sasha around, even if she wasn't with him every moment; just knowing she was nearby made him feel good. She added continuity and companionship to his frequently solitary work. Sasha had, in short, become a special part of his life as only a treasured pet can. They were fast friends, and now she was gone.

There seemed to be nothing special in the circumstances of her disappearance. Ned was working on a restaurant in San Francisco. At the end of one day, he had packed up his truck to head home but couldn't find Sasha. At first he hadn't been worried because she often took off around the neighborhood, but when the minutes stretched into an hour and she still hadn't returned, he became concerned. He asked some shopkeepers and people on the street if they had seen her, but no one had anything to report. By this time it was getting dark, and he knew he had to get home to his family back across San Francisco Bay in Walnut Creek. Reluctantly he drove across the Bay Bridge and through the tunnel that runs under the Berkeley hills to the communities to the east, telling himself that surely she would be waiting for him the next day at the restaurant in San Francisco. The following morning he packed two lunches as usual and set off for work, avoiding the emptiness in the truck by imagining the happy reunion at the end of the ride.

But Sasha was not there. Nor did Ned have any time to look for her, for this was his last day at the restaurant and he had a lot of work to do in order to meet his deadline. He tried to put her out of his mind by throwing himself into his work, but every few minutes he caught himself looking up, expecting to see her cheerful, loving presence. He tried not to think what might have happened. When other workmen noticed her absence, he put them off by saying she had been gone overnight before—although she never had. By the end of the day, however, when Sasha still hadn't appeared, he could no longer avoid a sick feeling in the pit of his stomach. Maybe she was gone for good.

"I'd look for her if I had the time," Ned told me, with more than a trace of guilt in his voice, "but I've had to start a new job on the other side of town. Anyway, she's got tags on. That should make it pretty easy, shouldn't it? I mean, don't you think someone will find her and turn her in?"

"That happens a lot," I replied, trying to provide him with the reassurance he was so desperately looking for. "Now, when exactly did you lose her?"

"Just a week ago today."

A week ago! My heart sank. For the hundredth time I cursed whatever makes people wait so long. Do they really believe their pets can execute those marvels of navigation we read about in the paper from time to time? Do they have such total faith in the dedication of animal shelters? Don't they know the dangers a pet faces when it is loose on the street? Don't they know that each day a pet is missing decreases the chances that it will be found?

I knew Ned didn't want to hear any of this, and it wouldn't help him get Sasha back. We needed to start moving. "The first thing I'll need is a description," I said. "What does Sasha look like?"

"Look like?" he replied. "Oh, she's beautiful, a German-shepherd mix. Sort of a medium-brown color, you know, with dark-brown eyes. She's got a very expressive face, everybody says so. People really take to her, even perfect strangers."

Ned was in love with his dog. I could appreciate his love and his eagerness to contribute, but he wasn't giving me very much to go on. A medium-brown lovable dog with an expressive face —how many animals in San Francisco would match that description? Hundreds, if not thousands. I needed more information.

"Is there anything unique about her appearance?" I asked. "Something special, a distinguishing feature of some sort, maybe?" I was not feeling at all hopeful.

"Something special?" And then he laughed. "Yeah, sure there is! My God, how could I have forgotten! She's only got three legs."

"Three legs!"

"Yeah, three legs. Her right rear leg is missing. I don't know how it happened—it was already gone when I got her. But I never notice it any more. She gets around just fine on the legs she's got. Hey, that's going to be a big help, isn't it?"

For the first time in our conversation I felt a surge of hope —not much, but some. Having only three legs certainly cut down on the number of possible suspects. Ironic for a dog's safety to be tied to a disability, but in this case that seemed to be the only bright spot on the horizon.

As Ned had been talking, I had been turning over possibilities in my mind. He said he had checked out the animal shelter, but I would have to retrace his steps. Unfortunately, dealing with some animal shelters calls for more guile and skepticism than most pet owners realize. And I couldn't fool myself with thinking Sasha might return home. Cross the Bay Bridge? Get through the tunnel? No way, not in the real world. Ned had told me she was wearing tags. That was a good sign, but it was also possible that someone could have removed her collar. If so, she could already have been picked up by a shelter and maybe destroyed. There were other, more grisly possibilities I didn't even want to entertain. One of the things you learn in my business is that there are many sick people in the world who take out their twisted feelings on innocent animals.

I put these possibilities out of my mind. If we were going to find Sasha, we had to generate some positive energy and act on the supposition that she could be found. A three-legged dog was bound to have a lot of visibility. Maybe that would offset the time that had passed since she disappeared. My hunch was that, if

Sasha was alive, she was somewhere in San Francisco looking for her master. And the places she would look would be recent work sites, starting with the restaurant.

I told Ned my hunch and asked him to drop off an article of his clothing at the restaurant, something with his scent that might attract her and make her stay until we could pick her up.

"And leave some food," I added. "Is there anything special she likes?"

"Yeah, chicken," he said. "Any kind. She's a real chicken freak."

"OK," I said. "You leave the chicken and a shirt or something, and I'll check it tomorrow morning early. That's the time lost animals are most likely to come out of hiding." I also made a mental note to ask around at nearby Kentucky Fried Chicken restaurants—an outside chance, to be sure, but I didn't have a lot to work with.

Before Ned hung up, I got all the information I needed to go ahead: a detailed description of the dog and the addresses of his recent jobs in the city. I could tell he was feeling a lot better already. OK, Sherlock, I said to myself, the ball's in your court now.

The next two days I devoted to the basic routine I've developed for putting the word out and generating leads. I checked the animal shelters. Nothing. Ned had put ads in the paper, so that was one thing I didn't have to worry about. I took the description of Sasha to my local instant printer and had a thousand posters made up—not the pale, handwritten notices on three-by-five cards or the Xeroxed posters that fade so quickly, but bold, clear sheets with my distinctive logo, REWARD stamped in big black letters, and THREE-LEGGED DOG prominently featured. I would have liked to insert a black-and-white photograph but, like a surprising number of pet owners, Ned only had color snapshots of poor quality for a poster. They wouldn't reproduce well, but they would be helpful for me to have, so I asked him to drop off a few at my office.

The next morning I stopped at the restaurant. There was

Ned's shirt, tied to a post, and an empty plate I assumed had held chicken—but no Sasha. Hoping that whoever had eaten it needed a meal, I set out for the neighborhoods Sasha was familiar with. I put posters in all the special places I have learned are most effective and talked to those people most likely to be aware of new animals in the vicinity. I asked workmen at Ned's projects to keep their eyes open; they were only too happy to oblige. Sasha, I began to realize, was a special dog, and a lot of people would be disappointed if I couldn't find her. This realization helped carry me through the legwork phase of this case—buttonholing merchants, knocking on doors, checking out possible hiding places—the kind of time-consuming, discouraging, and frequently boring activity that never shows up on TV detective shows. The only thing that keeps you going is the knowledge that the next poster you put up or the next person you talk to could mean the difference between success and failure.

Of course, as Sherlock Bones I had an additional handicap. "A pet detective? Yeah, sure. What are you, some kind of nut?" I get lots of responses like that. Then there those who buttonhole *me* and want to know everything about my job. Generally, I try to spend some time with these people, no matter how frantic or rushed I am, on the same theory that makes me welcome any exposure in newspapers, radio, or television: the more people who know about what I do, the more people will be on the lookout for my posters and for any stray animal.

In the case of Sasha, I had to take a lot of ribbing I hadn't really expected. I remember pulling up to a bus stop in front of a newsstand. I could see the bus coming and knew I had only a few seconds, so I handed the news dealer a poster and said, "I don't have much time, but I'm Sherlock Bones, tracer of missing pets, and I'm looking for a three-legged dog. I'd appreciate it if you could put up this poster for me."

"A three-legged dog!" His face broke into a big smile. "Hey, man, you be sure and give a twenty-five percent discount, you hear?"

I laughed as I got back in my van—you really need a sense

of humor to survive in my business—but there was a part of me that wasn't laughing, and I realized how close I was to this case. "Case," indeed. Sasha was Ned's sidekick, his buddy, just as Paco was mine. I knew how I would feel if something happened to old Pac. What would I ever do without him? I decided I'd rather not dwell on it. Back to generating positive energy.

By the end of the second day I had done all I could. Now I had to force myself to sit back and wait. When I first started out, waiting was the hardest part, but I gradually came to realize that anything more at this point was wheel spinning. First I had to have leads.

This time there was no wait at all. Almost immediately the phone calls started to come in. People all over San Francisco had sighted Sasha and wanted to claim the reward. (The motivational value of a financial reward is another aspect of dealing with people who claim to love animals that I've had a hard time coming to terms with, but that's another story.) Near Fisherman's Wharf, in the elegant heights of Russian Hill, deep in the Mission district —San Francisco apparently had far more than its fair share of three-legged dogs. They couldn't all be Sasha, but I wouldn't know unless I chased them down.

With Ned's color snapshots in my pocket, I set out in my van with Paco. By ten o'clock that night, with frequent calls to my answering service, I must have checked out five "no shows" and four three-legged dogs. None of them was Sasha; in fact, only one of them was even brown.

It was close to midnight when I got back to my flat in Oakland. Too exhausted to give Paco a walk (he didn't seem tired at all), I found a piece of cheese in the refrigerator, heated up some coffee, and collapsed on the couch. I had the feeling I might not make it as far as the bed that night. It wouldn't have been the first time.

The phone rang. Damn, I thought, not another one. Maybe it's a wrong number, maybe it's another over-eager bounty hunter, maybe it's— I answered on the second ring.

"Hey, Sherlock, where you been?"

"Where do you think?" It was Flo. Dear old Flo. Saying she works for my answering service doesn't even begin to tell her story. Flo is . . . I guess *involved* is the word. With other services I've had, it's just a job—"Hello, Sherlock Bones. . . . You lost your what? Your *bog?* . . . Oh, your *dog*. One moment, please." Flo cares, she really does. An unmarried woman in her middle years, she always has several dogs and cats of her own that she dotes on. Unlike a lot of her peers, however, she doesn't do much hand wringing. She wants action. She's got an incredible memory for my unfinished cases and a blind faith in my magical powers to solve every one of them.

I wasn't at all sure I wanted to talk to her now.

"Come on, Sherlock," she said. "It's not as bad as all that. Anyway, I've got some good news."

"Did somebody find Sasha?" I was too tired to register much enthusiasm.

"Could be, could be. I was talking about her to my girl friend tonight, and she said she thinks she saw her early this morning, about six thirty."

"Her and half the rest of San Francisco." Fatigue had gotten to me.

"Will you listen? It was on her way to work, right where Sasha was lost at the restaurant. Don't you remember? Come on, Sherlock, get with it."

I shook off my torpor. Maybe Sasha had come back for more chicken. Maybe my hunch was right after all.

"OK, thanks, Flo," I said, trying to sound like the supercool sleuth she assumed me to be. "I'll check it out."

"Tomorrow morning, first thing?"

"What do you think?" I replied. Flo never lets up. "Anyway, it already *is* tomorrow morning."

"Right," she answered, satisfied she had gotten me back on the track. "I'll leave the whole matter in your capable hands. You're a good boy, Sherlock. But you'd better find that dog."

With that threat echoing in my weary head, I crawled into bed, set the alarm for four o'clock, and tried not to get my hopes up. Flo's lead seemed the best so far, but in my present condition I didn't trust my judgment. It wouldn't have been the first time Flo had galvanized me into action by the simple force of her own conviction—plus the unspoken message that a quitter would not be a friend of hers for very long. Dear old Flo, she knew just what I needed. Sleep? That was for pantywaists, not the intrepid Sherlock Bones.

So it was that I happened to be sitting in my van on a San Francisco street at five in the morning with Paco, the cold, and my tepid cup of coffee. It was still dark. Streetlights picked up the glistening fog on the pavement and the quickening early morning traffic. I saw a few poor souls making their way on foot. No one looked very happy. I was not exactly delirious with joy myself.

I was just considering making a quick run to the all-night diner for another cup of coffee when a face appeared at my window.

"Can I help you?" It was a policeman. Automatically I checked my rearview mirror and saw his squad car pulled up behind me, his partner in the passenger seat. "You got a problem or something?"

Oh no, officer, I wanted to say, I'm just lying low for a three-legged dog. Not the best response, I realized, but cops do that to me sometimes. There's a lot the public doesn't know when it comes to the police finding missing animals.

"No, everything's OK," I said. Hoping he may have heard of me, I added, "I'm Sherlock Bones and I'm on a stakeout for a missing dog."

"You're Sherlock Bones." His voice had that flat, don't-think-you-can-surprise-me-I've-heard-everything tone. His eyes swept the van, no doubt checking for hidden weapons. I had said the wrong thing. A vision of being yanked from my seat and patted down flashed in my head.

"Actually, I just go by the name of Sherlock Bones," I said quickly, handing him one of my cards. "My real name is John Keane."

Without removing his eyes from me he managed to look at

my card. Not in the least reassured, he said, "And what are you doing out at this hour of the morning?"

I could see I was not getting through. Thinking a display of expertise would convince him of my identity, I said, "This is the best time to look, from five to eight in the morning."

"Oh, really?" he replied, still humoring me but unable to keep an edge of sarcasm from his voice. By this time Paco had roused himself from his reverie and, unaware of the moment's gravity, was doing his level best to kiss the cop. The cop remained unmoved.

"That's right," I replied, digging myself in deeper. "And this particular dog's only got three legs. Maybe you've noticed her hanging around here."

"Uh," he said. "Could I see your driver's license? Just take it out slowly and hand it to me."

He took my license, walked back to his car, and conferred with his partner for what seemed a long time. In my depleted state, all sorts of horror stories flashed in my head. Did I have any unpaid parking tickets they could lock me up for? Could they arrest me for loitering? Even taking me to the station for further questioning would put an end to this morning's search for Sasha, and I was convinced that this morning would decide the case, one way or another. Ten days is a long time for a pet to be missing and then be found. Too long, I feared.

When the cop returned, I could sense that nervousness had been replaced by the bored distaste of public officials forced to deal with harmless cranks. "Well, you're in luck, buddy," he said. "My partner read an article in the paper about you last week, so I guess it's OK. Lotsa luck."

I breathed a sigh of relief, handed him a poster, and resumed my stakeout. By this time it was getting light and the tempo of the street was picking up. With each minute that Sasha did not appear I felt my optimism fading.

At eight o'clock I saw some workmen open up the restaurant. Once again I checked with them and went over the premises looking for an out-of-the-way corner she might have made into a lair, but there was no sign that she had been there. I trudged back to the van, leaned on the wheel, and tried to decide what to do next.

It was Saturday morning, and Ned would be at home. The best thing seemed to be to call him and tell him the bad news. I saw no way to justify dragging the search on any longer; there didn't seem to be any reason to continue. I hated to disappoint him. I hated to think about what might have happened to Sasha. Animals used to loving care can survive on their own, but that's what it is—survival, nothing more. I started the van and drove around until I spotted a phone booth, struggling to convince myself that I had done all I could and that as a professional I wasn't supposed to get involved. Sasha, after all, had already been gone a week when I took the case. What could I do?

It didn't work. With the dime in the phone, I changed my mind and called the answering service. Maybe some more leads had come in. Maybe Flo was on duty. Maybe she had an idea or two.

"Sherlock Bones." It was Flo.

"Hi," I said. "Well, I went to the restaurant at five o'clock, but—"

"Sherlock!" she shouted. "Am I glad to hear from you!"

"Not when you find out what happened," I said. "She wasn't there. I guess we'd better—"

"No, no, it's OK," she said. "I just got a call from a guy that's got Sasha. He had her for a couple of days before he saw your poster."

"What about her tags?" I asked, feeling my hopes rise in spite of myself.

"Well, he was a little vague about that, but he said she had some. Look, he described her perfectly: same coloring, same missing leg, the whole thing. And he said she had really nice eyes. Come on, Sherlock, get a pencil and I'll give you the address."

It was on the southern edge of San Francisco, almost ten miles away. Flo's enthusiasm once again proved infectious, and by the time I reached the street she had given me I was ready for anything. The neighborhood was one of larger, once-elegant older houses that had long since been broken up into apartments. At first glance it looked respectable enough, but a closer inspection revealed the losing battle it was fighting with urban blight. Not far away, fast-food franchises and gas stations were creeping up. One more decade and it would give up any remaining pretensions to its former glory and slip quietly into shabby decay. I made a mental note that the man who had called quite probably needed the reward money.

He lived on the top floor of a faded-yellow frame house. As I climbed the stairs, I wished that Flo had been able to tell me more about him. Rewards bring out all kinds of people—some well-meaning, some not so nice. I knocked on his door and tried to prepare myself for any eventuality, but all I could think of was how much I wanted Sasha to be on the other side of that door. This time, my intuition told me, I had found her. Or was my intuition just giving me what I wanted to hear?

The first thing that hit me when he opened the door was an enormous American flag that completely covered the opposite wall.

"Hello," I said, handing him one of my cards. "I'm Sherlock Bones and I understand you've got a dog I'm looking for."

"Oh, yeah," the man replied. "So there really is a Sherlock Bones. I was wondering. Come on in."

Except for the flag, the room was totally nondescript—the usual pieces of furniture, a rug, maybe a lamp or two—perfectly ordinary. The man struck me the same way. Of some indeterminate age under forty-five, he could have been anything—student, clerk, gas-station attendant. The flag provided the only touch of the bizarre, all the more for its completely pedestrian surroundings.

This was the moment of truth. Dear God, I prayed, don't let him be a member of the lunatic fringe—or if he is, at least let him have Sasha. "Could I see her?"

"Sure. Just a sec." He disappeared into a back room and in a moment emerged with the saddest, most forlorn creature I had ever seen. I checked Ned's snapshots. Was this the same dog? The dog in the pictures looked happy, well-fed, *alive*. This dog was dirty, with grease spots on her back and a sunken stomach. She was so sad. I know some people say dogs don't experience human emotions, but this dog was sad. I knelt to pet her, but she just stood there, tail down, head lowered, resigned to whatever I would do to her. I lifted her face with one hand and with the other stroked her head, trying to elicit some response. Her eyes just stared straight ahead.

With no idea of what I would find, I checked her tags. They matched. This was Sasha.

"Hello, Sasha," I said, rubbing her velvety brown ears. "Hello, Sash, old girl. It's OK, it's all over now. I'll take you home." She didn't stir; she seemed to have given up completely. I wished desperately that there was some way I could reassure her, but she was beyond hope. How many times in the past ten days had people petted her and called her by name? How many times had she wagged her tail at strangers in the hope that they would take her back to her master? How long had it taken for apathy to consume a lively, lovable dog? How much longer would it have been before she wasted away completely? I put my face next to hers and stroked her head, but she didn't seem to notice me.

"She was hanging around the house two days ago when I came home from work," the man said. "I gave her some food, but she threw it up. Now she just lies there."

I felt a tremendous surge of gratitude for this man's kindness and was ashamed of my initial suspicions. So what if he *is* crazy, I thought. What's crazy? And who am I, of all people, to judge? He had the compassion to take a lost dog off the street and help her find her master, and that's what counts. There was just one thing that puzzled me.

"Why didn't you call her owner?" I asked. "His name is right here on her tag."

The man shifted uneasily. "Well, if you want to know the truth, I wasn't sure he deserved her back. I mean, just look at her, she's a mess. I thought, Who would treat a dog like that?"

"But she's been lost ten days," I replied. "She didn't look like this two weeks ago."

"How was I supposed to know that?" the man countered defensively. "Anyway, she's a nice dog, and I thought I might keep her. But she just lies there. She won't do anything. Well, then I saw your poster, and I figured that if the owner went to all that trouble he must really miss her, so I gave you a call. Not him—you."

"He's going to be very grateful to you," I said. "If you saw my poster then you know he's offering a reward."

"I don't *want* the damn reward!" the man shouted.

For the first time I took a good look at him. His face was flushed. It suddenly occurred to me that Sasha had triggered an emotional response in this nondescript man, stirred feelings that had lain dormant before, feelings that he would have to stifle now that her owner had been found. What had it cost him to make that call?

He looked away from Sasha. "She's a nice dog, but she just lies there. That's not right, I know it."

There was nothing I could do except thank him profusely and take Sasha home. I picked her up in my arms and carried her down the stairs to the van. She made such a tiny bundle, lying right where I put her on the back seat, not even responding when Paco took an exploratory sniff. He seemed to know something was wrong and solemnly took his place on the seat next to mine.

I couldn't get back across the bay to Walnut Creek fast enough. I didn't even stop to call her owner. The only medicine that would cure Sasha was familiar turf and the sight of Ned. How I wished I spoke the language of dogs so that I could let her know her long ordeal was over. What had happened to her in the last ten days? How in the world had she traveled all those miles of densely populated San Francisco to end up in front of that man's house? Now that she had been found, I wanted to know how she had gotten lost, but I realized that was a story only Sasha would know.

All this time, riding in the van, Sasha had lain motionless on the back seat. I checked over my shoulder as we got onto the bridge and thought I detected a flicker of life in her eyes, but I couldn't be sure. Soon, however, she stood up and started looking out the window as she sensed the familiarity of a route she had traveled twice a day for most of her life. And when we entered the tunnel under the Berkeley hills she went crazy. I suppose the noise and smells of the engines magnified by the tunnel were all she needed to realize where she was going. She started jumping around the van, bounding up and down from the seat, leaping into my lap, and licking my face. And crying! I swear to God that's what it was—not barks or yelps or howls but great sobs. There is no other way I can describe it. She knew she was going home at last. I couldn't help myself; tears started running down my face—tears of relief, of joy, of knowing that she knew she was safe. I was laughing and crying at the same time. Paco joined in the melee, and by the time I pulled up in front of her house the three of us had lifted each other to a fever pitch of anticipation.

Ned was standing on the front lawn. Before he had time to register what was happening, Sasha leaped from the car and literally threw herself into his arms, licking his face and crying and twisting her body in paroxysms of unadulterated joy. She just couldn't get close enough to him. Ned did not look like the kind of man much given to emotional displays, especially in full view of his neighbors, but you wouldn't have known it to see him join in the crying and the tears and the laughing. In a few moments his wife came out, holding their baby, and Sasha almost knocked them down with her leaps and contortions. I could see why Ned had forgotten about her missing leg. Sasha was forty pounds of perpetual canine motion, totally transformed from the pathetic creature I had found just over an hour ago.

The last member of the family to be greeted was their second dog, a dignified hound. The two dogs approached each other with prancing little steps, touched noses, and then set off tearing around the lawn. Paco added his bulky presence to their carryings-on, and I admit that I was glad for the confusion that prevented anyone from having to say anything. My cheeks were wet as I took in the whole wonderful sloppy reunion, right there on the lawn in front of God and everyone. It was the best possible ending I could have imagined, and I felt on top of the world.

After we had all regained our composure and rehashed the whole affair over a big pot of coffee, Ned turned to me and said, "I used to think it was cruel not to let a dog run free, but no more. I don't think any of us could go through the experience of the last two weeks again, especially not Sasha. I'll just have to keep her close by when she's with me, that's all there is to it."

Later, driving home with Paco snoozing in the back, I gave myself time to savor the joy of what I had just witnessed and to appreciate my part in it. That may sound a little strange, but unless you can find ways to replenish your energy and confidence, you can burn out fast. I believed Ned when he said he would make sure Sasha never ran away, but it wouldn't surprise me if one day I get a call asking me to help find her again. I have to keep reminding myself that we are only human and can frequently lose sight of our best intentions. Two years ago, when I started out as a pet detective, I would never have dreamed I was running the risk of becoming a true believer. Burning bushes were not part of my plan. The whole idea was supposed to be a lark, not a deeply felt personal commitment.

But that was two years ago.

2
Is This Any Business for a Grown Man?

SINCE I'M SO OFTEN ASKED how I happened to become a pet detective, I wish I had a short answer—part of my lifelong involvement with animals, perhaps, or the result of careful career planning. The truth of the matter, however, is that I've only had one pet in my life, and I didn't get him until I was over thirty. And as for careful career planning, my metamorphosis into Sherlock Bones has felt more like Toad's wild ride than anything else. I suppose you could say it all started one afternoon in the sauna at the Oakland Athletic Club, where I happened to spot an ad in the paper offering $1,000 for the return of a Chihuahua. But to understand the power of that ad to turn my life around— especially since I never even managed to reach the owner, let alone find the dog—you'd have to know why I was in the sauna in the first place.

The simplest explanation is that I was unemployed—but unemployed with a difference, at least for me. After a lifetime of false starts—dropping out of high school to join the marines, trying my hand at one job after another—I'd just turned my back on my first job triumph: four successful years as an insurance salesman. At last I'd gotten all the goodies I thought were measures of success—a lovely girl friend, nice clothes, a racy sports car, and an elegant houseboat moored in an estuary of San Francisco Bay. But the job was killing me. I hated talking to people about dying, I hated the paperwork, I hated the office politics.

29

Perhaps only another underachiever can appreciate how hard it is to give up the first good thing you've ever had going, no matter how much you hate it. Of course, by the time I bit the bullet things weren't all that good any more. My girl friend and I were going through a slow process of breaking up, my sales were falling off, and I had eaten myself into overweight and general bad health. "If you don't make some changes in your life now," my doctor said, "you might not be around to make them later."

The sauna was part of my program to get myself back in shape, in every sense of the word. Thanks to a couple of big commissions, I had some time to research the job market and find something that really fit me. I traded my sports car in on a used VW van, moved into a modest apartment, and went on a diet. I started working out afternoons at the gym and spent my mornings exploring new careers. I read books. I took tests. I visited employment agencies. This flurry of organized activity whittled away at my waistline, but to my dismay it produced very little in terms of a job.

At each employment agency a dismal scenario repeated itself. A counselor would take a look at my sketchy education and scattered work experience and pull out the same set of jobs. Did I want a truck route selling salami to grocery stores? No? Well, then, how about cleaning windows? Oh, you want something unique, he (or, more frequently, she) would say with thinly veiled sarcasm, something off the beaten track?

"But Mr. Keane," one woman told me, tapping my folder with her pencil, "frankly, there isn't a lot here for me to work with. If I were you, I'd reconsider my decision to leave the insurance business."

Enter Paco, my first and only pet. As an antidote to these daily doses of rejection, I had started going to the movies. One of them was *Serpico*. As you may remember, Serpico had an Old English sheepdog he came home to after fighting corruption in the New York City police department. That's just what I needed, I decided—a loyal dog to befriend me in my battles against the world. I'd call him Paco, the nickname Serpico took when he became an undercover cop, and we'd take long walks on the beach together. In the evenings we'd sit before a roaring fire, me with a good book, Paco snoozing on the hearth. It was a wild fantasy —I didn't even have a fireplace and could ill afford to buy an expensive pedigreed dog—but I couldn't get it out of my head.

I made some inquiries and discovered a kennel in Sacramento with some sheepdog puppies for sale, but even as I made the long drive to the kennel I had no real intention, or so I told myself, of getting a dog. When I was growing up in the Archie Bunker section of Queens, New York, pets were creatures other families had. Our family didn't engage in many open displays of affection, even among ourselves, and to waste them on a pet was deemed rank weakness. Once, when I was about six years old, my brother and I set up a cage behind some bushes in our backyard and ran a secret hostel for some cats we found following the neighborhood garbage truck. (It never occurred to me then that cats belonged to people. Even today I sometimes wonder.) But as soon as my father found our cageful of cats, he closed down the operation.

That was the sum total of my experience as a pet owner, but when I got to the kennel and saw that little bundle of black and white fur rolling around on the front lawn, I had to have it. In a matter of minutes I was the proud parent of a ten-week-old Old English sheepdog, and my whole life took a turn for the better. Feeding, walking, and brushing Paco made me feel more like a mother hen than the Jack London character I had fantasized, but it took my mind off my troubles. Even as a puppy, his presence had a soothing effect on me; he helped fill the spaces in my single life that creeping panic had occupied before. I wouldn't have admitted it at the time, but I suppose what happened is that I fell in love a little, and maybe a lot.

Even so, I wasn't yet aware of the plight of missing animals. My interest in the ad in the sauna had nothing to do with the Chihuahua's welfare. I thought it would be a quick way to make some money and perhaps even the beginning of a career as a pet bounty hunter. I wasn't getting very far with my standard job-hunting efforts, so why not give this a try?

After I showered and dressed, I called the number several times. There was no answer. That's funny, I thought, they care enough to offer a big reward, but not enough to sit by the phone. By this time the idea was beginning to intrigue me, though, so I called another number in an ad that offered an unspecified reward for the return of a white toy poodle lost in San Francisco. A man answered.

"Hello," I said. "I see in the paper you have lost your dog, and I—uh, my name is John Keane and I have a business helping people find missing pets."

"Really?" he replied. "That's odd. I've never heard of such a thing."

"Oh yes," I said with what I hoped was assurance. "And I'm calling to see if you'd like some help."

There was a pause. "What do you charge for this service?" he asked warily.

I hadn't given that one blessed thought. "Charge? Well, I don't charge anything if I don't find it," I ad-libbed, "and if I do . . . how does fifty dollars sound to you?"

It sounded fine. He had no time to look for the dog, and his wife and kids were driving him crazy. He gave me a description of the dog, told me where it had been lost, and we hung up. I was in business! Good-bye, salami truck! Hello, adventure! I swung by my girl friend's apartment, and the two of us sped off across the Bay Bridge to San Francisco.

Not having the slightest idea of what to do, we started at the scene of the crime, a doughnut shop on a busy street where the man's daughter had left the dog while she went inside. There we learned that a woman had come into the shop carrying a white poodle, claiming the dog had almost been hit by a car and wanting to know where its owner was. By this time the little girl had left by a rear door, so the woman said she would take the dog home and place an ad in the paper. She hadn't left her name, no one remembered seeing her before, and she had never placed an ad. We spent four hours looking that afternoon—talking with people, driving up and down streets, standing on corners and whistling—but we never found the dog.

I tried to pretend the whole experience had just been a lark, an entertaining way to kill an afternoon, but underneath my bravado I was sorely disappointed. This was to have been my ticket to an exciting new life. During the next few days I tried to put it out of my mind, but it wouldn't go away. I had been too impatient, I decided. I needed to give myself more time, devise a plan of attack.

That brought up another problem: I didn't know what the hell I was doing. If I was going to be a pet bounty hunter, I had better learn how. On an impulse I called the Oakland police for advice, but they brushed me off like dandruff. Finding pets was clearly not on their list of priorities, despite all the newspaper photographs I'd seen of burly cops retrieving kittens from trees and window ledges. "Check the pound, buddy," the desk sergeant told me brusquely.

In Oakland the pound—or animal shelter, as it is officially known—happens to be run by the police department. Rather than risk another brush-off, I got in my car and drove there myself. Located in a down-at-the-heels part of town, it is housed in a low, utilitarian building that looks as if it had been hastily erected as a temporary structure sometime during World War II. I entered a well-lighted, official-looking room with a counter that divided the reception area from an office with three or four desks. The sergeant in charge, fortunately, was not there. In his place was a man I'll call Charlie, a guy in his late thirties who told me he was a supervisor but sometimes went out on the truck as well.

Taking a deep breath, I told him what I wanted to do. "I know it sounds a little strange," I said, "but I think there might be a need for such a service. My problem is I don't know the first thing about missing pets, and I thought you could fill me in."

"Sounds interesting," he said. "Let's go in the back room and talk. It's a good excuse to take a break."

I'll be forever grateful to Charlie. He could have given me the cold shoulder. Many animal-shelter people have, especially those who see me as a threat rather than a help, but not Charlie. He led me into the room that functions as the sergeant's office and employee lounge.

"Fix yourself a cup of coffee," he said. "I'll be back in a minute."

While I was waiting, I could hear dogs barking from behind another door in the office. I opened it tentatively and found myself in the shelter itself, the room with the cages, where the stray animals that had been turned in or picked up were kept. Not sure I was supposed to be there—not sure, suddenly, I wanted to be there—I took a few steps forward into a cacophony of barking. The fear and anxiety were so strong you could almost touch them. I had an instantaneous impression of a prison—harsh lighting, cement floors, cages everywhere, and an incredibly high noise level. Wishing I had never come in, I walked past one row of cages. In the first an old golden retriever was lying in the corner, looking as if he'd given up. Next to him a little terrier was yapping his head off, desperately trying to get my attention; then a black mongrel, just standing there, slowly wagging his tail. In the corner was a bank of smaller cages full of cats. They appeared to be in shock. Who wouldn't be, I thought, taken off the street, set down in these surroundings, not knowing what was going to happen next? In the last cage was a little puppy, a shepherd-collie mix who couldn't have been more than four months old. I knelt and put my hand against the cage and he licked it greedily.

"I see you've found a friend." It was Charlie.

"Yeah, I guess so," I said, standing up. "Some nice dogs here," I added, too dazed to know what else to say.

"Some of the best," he said, "but you'd better look quick, because most of them will be gone in a few days."

I was having trouble focusing my attention. "You mean, back with their owners, or adopted?" I asked.

Charlie gave me a long look. His face wore the expression of a would-be seducer who discovers at the critical moment that he's got a virgin on his hands. "What I mean," he said after a pause, "is that they'll be gone. Period."

"Oh," I replied lamely, the truth suddenly sinking in. "You mean put to sleep." I looked at the puppy. "But not all of them, right? Like this little puppy. . . ."

"Come on, John," he said evenly, as he led me back to the office. He took one chair, I another. No one else was in the room. "OK," he said finally, "what can I tell you?"

I didn't answer for a moment. What I had just experienced had obliterated the questions I had prepared. "Well, for starters," I began, "I guess I'd like to know how many of the dogs that come in here are—uh, put away."

"Seventy percent." His face betrayed no emotion.

"Seventy percent!" I couldn't believe what I was hearing. I was prepared to accept a few—old dogs, sick dogs, street animals —but seventy percent! That was seven out of every ten animals. "What about the others?" I asked.

"Maybe ten percent get adopted, and another twenty percent are picked up by their owners. They're almost always the ones with tags." His voice remained even; he could have been giving a weather report.

"But . . ." I didn't know what to say. I had come here to pick up a few tricks of the trade and had been assaulted with a horror story instead. I could feel my insides churning with feelings I didn't know what to do with. I was angry at the animal shelter, at the pet owners, and, irrationally, at Charlie, sitting there with his cool-as-a-cucumber attitude. Didn't the man have any feelings? Why was he dumping this information on me? What was I supposed to do about it? (I didn't know it then, of course, but this anger was to become my constant companion in the weeks and months ahead.)

"Hey, John," Charlie said, "if you get in this business, you'd better wise up."

"Yeah, well, that's why I'm here, to—"

"No," he interrupted, "I mean wise up about pet owners. You probably think they're all dedicated animal lovers, right?"

"Well, maybe not all of them, but . . . I don't see what you're getting at."

"Look," Charlie said patiently, "we're in the middle of a pet explosion in this country. Everybody and his brother's got one. Take a good look at the sidewalks and you'll see what I mean. Then the owners get bored or it's too much trouble or they don't keep them in, and they end up here. Lots of people bring their pets here. They turn 'em in like library books. We always say we'll try to find them a home—that's what the people want to hear—but what I told you is the real truth. And by the way, if you quote me, I'll deny it."

"But what about the dogs that are actually lost?" I was thinking of Paco. If he were lost, I'd be haunting the pound, and I was sure most other pet owners would do the same. I wasn't buying Charlie's cynical view of the pet-owning public.

"Some get returned, that's true," he said calmly, ignoring my rising voice. "But you'd be surprised how lazy people are. They'll make a phone call but won't take the time to come down here and check for themselves. If the dog's not wearing tags, we can't make a positive identification over the phone. And if dogs are here more than five days, we put them away."

"That's how long you keep them? Only five days?"

"That's right," he said. "Official policy. As a taxpayer, you ought to be glad. Do you know how much it costs to feed and board animals?"

"And then you kill them." I felt sick to my stomach—at the bureaucracy, at "official policy," at the harmless-sounding euphemisms that hid an awful truth. They said they put animals to sleep—as if they would later wake up.

"Look, pal," Charlie said testily, finally nettled. "You were the one that asked. Don't get on my back. I just work here."

I was to return again to Charlie and learn more from his off-the-record remarks, but I had had all I could take for that day. I came to appreciate his need for a hard shell, but I didn't have one. Driving home, I had no room in my head for any high-flying fantasies. Charlie had brought me down with a thud. After what he had told me, I could never again think of finding missing pets as bounty hunting. A missing animal was in real danger, and if what Charlie said was true, the official agency responsible for helping wasn't doing enough. Was this something I really wanted to get involved in? I was looking for something lighter, more fun. I had gotten out of insurance so I wouldn't have to talk about dying any more. But there were those dogs and cats back at the shelter, their lives literally ticking away. Was I going to sit by and do nothing? What could I do, anyway?

What I did, at first, was more research, the results of which put a slightly different slant on what Charlie had told me—and, if anything, painted an even bleaker picture. Perhaps it was true that many pet owners were too lazy and unconcerned to look for their pets, but it was also true that the Oakland Animal Shelter was only open during business hours. Granted, it was open Saturdays, but, as I had learned from Charlie, a lot can happen to an animal between Monday and Saturday. I also found out that in the East Bay alone there were at least six official public or private animal shelters—all operating more or less independently, all with slightly different policies and procedures, and all likely way stations for lost or unwanted pets.

I started talking to friends about what I was learning, and they contributed experiences of their own. One woman nearly missed finding her cocker spaniel, even though she visited the pound every day, because it had been locked up in a special quarantine room by mistake. Another man called a private shelter in search of his cat, only to be told that it accepted only those animals surrendered by their owners. When he decided to check the place in person, he found his cat—and also the name of the woman who had turned it in. She was sorry, she told him when he phoned her, but she had found his cat and taken it there, saying she was its owner, because she thought it stood a better chance of finding a good home than if she had turned it over to the city pound. I heard of animals with tags whose owners were assured over the phone that their pets were not in the pound—when the truth was someone had incorrectly copied the license numbers into the pound's animal registry. One man told me he hadn't been too worried when he lost his dog, since it had up-to-date tags, but when it hadn't turned up after four days, he went to the pound and retrieved it at the last possible moment—without tags or collar. Some kids, he decided, must have taken the collar off.

I went to the library and did some reading. I found out that Charlie was right: we *are* in the midst of a pet explosion. "It took us over fifty years to register our first million dogs," said the president of the American Kennel Club, "but since 1970 we have been averaging over one million dogs a year." In 1975 it was estimated that there were over thirty-four million dogs and forty-six million cats in the United States, giving us the highest ratio of pets to people of any country on earth. National studies of the problem talked in terms of cost ($500 million a year for "animal control" programs, much of that going for killing and disposing of unwanted animals), disease (over forty diseases are transmitted to people by pets), and filth (New York's half-million dogs drop an estimated fifty-two tons of feces in public places *every day*, a state of affairs which has produced a city law requiring owners to clean up after their pets). According to one source, Charlie's seventy-percent figure was low: fully *ninety* percent of the fifteen million animals that pass through shelters and pounds are destroyed, most as a result of having been abandoned or turned in by their owners. And Charlie was not alone in his cynical view of the pet-owning public. One highly placed director of a national animal welfare agency was quoted as saying, "When people tell me they're going to breed a dog so their kids can watch 'the miracle of life,' I invite them over here to watch the miracle of death."

My brain reeled. I read of accusations against the pet-food industry that their advertising fuels an unwanted boom in pets and takes food from the mouths of the world's poor—and counterclaims that a market for by-products helps keep down the price of food raised for human consumption. The problem was enormous, far greater than I had ever supposed, and everyone seemed to be pointing the finger of blame somewhere else. This wasn't my cup of tea. Crusading wasn't my style, and I had no interest in becoming one of those professional animal lovers who try to organize the world around animal welfare and whose holier-than-thou attitude never fails to turn me off. The whole affair struck me as too hysterical, too emotional—too unmanly, if you want to know the truth.

Or was this all some sort of cop-out? Maybe I was just scared of failing, afraid to make a commitment. Back and forth I went, but always there hovered in my mind the specter of that ticking clock at the animal shelter. So I got back on the phone and started calling lost-pet ads. I avoided facing the issue of a long-range commitment. I just wanted to tell owners what their pets might be up against and offer my help. Maybe they weren't aware of the diligence required to track down missing pets or of the slipups that can occur.

I didn't get to first base. Reactions ranged from distrust to out-and-out anger. "Look, buddy," one man said, "I don't know what your game is, but you've got no business preying on people when they're desperate. That's extortion."

With responses like that, I might be back slogging away at the insurance business today, clock or no clock. After all, if it was rejection I was after, I could have gone to the employment agencies; at least they were polite about it. Two events intervened, however, to push me over the edge into the world of animals.

First, I came up with the name Sherlock Bones. Despite the horror stories about the plight of missing pets I'd been bombarded with, I still wasn't through with my fantasy of becoming a pet detective, and one evening the name Sherlock Bones just sort of floated into my consciousness. Without stopping to think, I sketched out a logo and a business card, complete with Paco in the Sherlockian deerstalker hat, which is the same design I use today. There was no effort involved; it was as if the name had simply been waiting offstage for the right time to present itself. It seemed inevitable, a perfect encapsulation of my fantasy, a canine twist on the name of literature's most famous detective.

That night, just before I fell asleep, something else floated into my brain—a piece of my past I had completely forgotten about. I was about four and had gotten myself lost in some undergrowth in a park near our house. It was late on a winter day and the sun was sinking, but just before total panic set in I spotted Lassie, a neighborhood dog, making her rounds. She came up to me and sniffed my face, and I threw my arms around her neck, never before so glad to see a familiar nose. She gave her tail a couple of wags and started to walk away. I fastened my hand in the fur on her back and hung on as she made her way out of the park and back onto familiar turf. I suppose you could say Lassie was just going home, but as far as I was concerned, she had delivered me to safety.

That did it. The next morning I quit pussyfooting. I had some cards printed, registered the name, took out the proper license, found an answering service, put an ad in the paper—and before I had time for any second thoughts, I was in business. God knows why I thought my luck would be better this time around, but Sherlock Bones had assumed a life of his own, and I was determined to go with it, wherever it took me.

Where it took me, at first, was back to the animal shelters. Thanks to my ads and a couple of short articles about my services in local papers, I gained a degree of legitimacy—enough, at least, to get a few requests for help and over seventy calls from people who had found dogs and cats and wanted me to locate their owners. Without any advance planning I was becoming an informal clearinghouse. I charged owners of missing pets ten dollars the first week and five dollars a week thereafter. For this fee I'd get a photograph of the missing pet and would make daily "pound rounds," trying to match the photos with the pets in the cages. It was slow going. I'd stand paralyzed in front of a cage. Was that yellow dog Pepper or wasn't it? I didn't dare make a mistake, so if I thought there was the slightest chance, I'd call my client and tell him or her to come down and check.

It didn't take me long to realize that this was a job better left to owners, who usually (but not always, as I later learned) can pick out their own pets when they see them. However, even owners can often be amazingly ignorant when it comes to a knowledge of their pets' most salient features, including gender. Once I was in the back room at a shelter where a well-dressed matron was having a terrific argument with one of the employees about a cat.

"That's my Jennifer!" she was shouting in a tone of voice I'm sure she rarely used.

"Lady," the man replied patiently, "that there's a male cat."

"It certainly is not!" she retorted. "Don't you think I can recognize my own cat? Just look at that white spot on her nose. Now take her out of the cage this minute."

"Suit yourself," the man replied, rolling his eyes at me. As soon as he opened the cage door, the cat sprang into the woman's arms and held on for dear life. It was obviously her cat.

"You see?" she said triumphantly, scratching Jennifer's ears. "This is Jennifer, my *female* cat."

The man, outraged at this challenge to his professional skills, lifted the cat's tail and pointed out two round furry appendages, irrefutable evidence of masculinity. "See them things, lady?" he said, enjoying his moment of vindication. "Them's balls. Like I said, this here's a male cat."

The woman, too furious at being proved wrong to speak, took her cat and huffed out. I wouldn't be surprised if she never accepted Jennifer's instant sex change; to some people, all cats are female. One thing was certain, though. If she'd been one of my clients and had given me *her* description of Jennifer, I'd never have found the animal.

The second event, the one that truly sealed my fate, occurred just when my initial momentum as Sherlock Bones was slowing down. Three weeks into my new career, all I had to show for my efforts was a long list of pets people had picked up and a growing sense of frustration and hopelessness. Then one Saturday morning I saw a poster announcing a dog show at the Oakland Coliseum. That's where I should be, I thought, talking to all those owners of pedigreed dogs! They're the ones who could really use my services! The only problem was that the show was scheduled for Sunday, the very next day. When I called the organizer, he told me it was too late to get a booth at the show. He liked the idea, though, and suggested I might want to pass out fliers in the parking lot. Twenty-four hours later I'd scared up some posters, deputized my brother Bill's seven young sons as Sherlock's official "pet posse," and gotten us all to the Coliseum parking lot. While my posse stuck fliers under windshield wipers, I stood at the entrance to catch people as they drove in and out. I had just gotten started when a car wheeled up next to me on its way out.

The driver was in a hurry. Rolling down the window, he blurted, "Hey, you haven't seen a greyhound around here, have you? One just got loose from the show, and I've got to find it."

"You're not going to believe this," I said, handing him a flier, "but I happen to be in the business of—"

"OK, thanks anyway," he said, grabbing the poster and driving off.

"Hey, wait a minute!" I shouted, but he was already out of earshot. Damn, I thought, why didn't he let me finish? Maybe I could have helped him.

That evening, having delivered my pet posse back home in time to do their homework, I was sitting in my brother and sister-in-law's living room rehashing the day's events. In the background a local TV news show was flogging away at a dull weekend: ". . . lost today at the Oakland Coliseum's dog show," I heard the newscaster say.

"What's that guy talking about?" I asked.

"I don't know," my sister-in-law said. "Something about the world's most expensive greyhound."

"Hey!" I shouted. "I met the guy that lost that dog today! I even gave him a flier!"

"No one ever reads those things," my brother replied. Bill has always been one of my greatest supporters, but at that point even he had a hard time mustering enthusiasm.

"Yeah? Well, who knows?" I said. "I think I'll check my service. Maybe he called."

Sure enough, someone had left a message about a greyhound. I called the number he left and reached the man in the parking lot, who turned out to be not the dog's owner but its handler. He was from out of town and had to leave in the morning, but the owner was on his back, and he was desperate. We agreed that I'd search the pounds, since that was all I did in those days. He was greatly relieved to have someone helping him.

"Must be some dog," I said. "How much is the world's most expensive greyhound worth, anyway?"

"Let's just say she's a hell of a high-priced dog. I thought I stood a better chance of getting the papers and TV interested if I said she was *the* most expensive. She sure is slippery, though. God knows where she's got to by now."

"Try the parks and cemeteries," I suggested, remembering something I'd read recently. "When lost animals are really scared, they will sometimes hide out in dark, quiet places during the day."

The next morning I hit the pounds with renewed vigor. The fact that I had a famous client helped counteract the attitude many of the shelter employees took toward my work. (Later on, when I became more effective, they became either more supportive or more hostile, but at the time they looked upon me with benign contempt, the way you might regard a distant relative who had taken up flagpole-sitting.) I didn't see anything resembling a greyhound, though, and by early afternoon, when I arrived at the Oakland shelter, I was beginning to get discouraged. My friend Charlie was in the front office reading the newspaper.

"Hey, Sherlock," he called. "I see you're on the greyhound case."

"That's right," I replied. "How did you know?"

"Right here in the paper, buddy. You're hot off the presses."

There it was, an article about the greyhound, with a quote from the handler saying he had retained the services of Sherlock Bones, tracer of missing pets, Oakland's famed pet detective.

"Fantastic!" I shouted. "Don't you think that's fantastic, Charlie? I mean, you helped get me started."

Charlie wasn't about to give me any satisfaction. "Big deal," he said. "Two lines in the paper and you're bouncing off the ceiling. All I have to say, John, is don't forget us little people now that you're a superstar."

But it was a big deal to me. Maybe dubbing me "Oakland's famed pet detective" was a bit much, but it felt good to get some official recognition and acclaim for a crazy idea I had taken from a fantasy and made real.

When I got home later that day, there were messages from newspapers and TV stations that were following the case. Did I have any more news on the greyhound, and by the way, what was it exactly that a pet detective did? In the next few days, a local TV show did a short segment on me, and the following Sunday the *San Francisco Examiner* ran an article on my business. I talked about how I got started and the long list of homeless pets I had gathered. Maybe, I thought, their owners will read the article and claim their animals.

As things turned out, though, I had no time for missing pets in the next few days. Monday morning my phone started ringing and didn't stop for a week. The wire services had picked up the *Examiner* story and sent it all over the world, and now everyone wanted to know more about this strange person who called himself Sherlock Bones. Had I said I wanted to get the word out on the plight of missing pets? Had I said I wanted recognition? Well, I got it, all right—from all over the country and overseas as well. Producers of local radio talk shows started calling—from Boston, New York, West Virginia, Canada, Australia, New Zealand—asking if I would agree to be interviewed by telephone. It was heady stuff indeed. After being dismissed as a crank and a crook, I was suddenly being courted as an expert.

I still managed to make my pound rounds—no word yet on the greyhound—but my energies were elsewhere. My life became surreal. At four in the morning the phone would ring. I'd grab my blanket and stagger into the living room, a corner of which serves as my office, trying to remember who was calling. Oh, yes, that early morning commuter show in New York. Outside my window it was still the middle of the night; I tried to remember that in New York it was already seven o'clock and people were listening to the radio as they got up and went about their business.

"Just hang on, Sherlock," the announcer would say. "We're not quite ready for you yet."

So I'd shuffle to the kitchen, heat up some coffee, and try to wake up. From the receiver at my ear I could hear the professionally cheerful sounds of the radio show in progress: ". . . and so it looks like another beautiful day here in Manhattan, with clear skies forecast for the next twenty-four hours. We'll be back in a minute with a man who has a most unusual occupation. But first, this word."

Then the announcer would say, "OK, Sherlock, you'll be on in thirty seconds."

I'd gulp some coffee, glance out at the blackness, and try to imagine my words were about to be heard by God knows how many people three thousand miles away. Then I'd be on. "Good morning, Frank"—or whatever his name was—I'd say, and off I'd go into my spiel. I always wondered what those listeners would have thought if they'd known I was talking to them in my underwear from a pitch-black apartment with a sleepy sheepdog at my feet.

I have no idea where my fling with the media might have taken me had it not been for a man from Boston who called me late one evening at the end of that week. He'd heard me on the radio, he said, and needed my help.

"Glad to oblige," I replied confidently. "What can I do for you?"

"I want you to find my dog, Tippy," he said. "She's gone. I . . . I don't know how she—you see, she sits outside in the mornings, and when I went to get the mail, she was gone." He sounded like an old man.

"But you're in Boston, and I'm in California," I replied. "I'd be glad to give you some suggestions of things to do, but—"

"No, no," he interrupted. "It's you I want. I don't get out much, don't you see, and this neighborhood has changed so much, I don't know anyone any more. I want you to come. Now, I'm willing to pay whatever's fair, if that's what's bothering you. I'm not in the poorhouse yet, you know."

I was nonplussed. I couldn't let him fly me to Boston. I didn't know anything about that city, and besides, I had never actually tracked down a missing animal. To put it bluntly, the world's leading pet detective wasn't worth the price of a bus ticket to Boston, let alone air fare. But the man needed help. What could I tell him?

"Look," I said, with a sinking feeling, "I just can't get away right now. Anyway, I think you need someone who knows your city better than I do. But I've got a suggestion. Why don't you call a boy-scout troup in your area and ask if they'd take on the search for Tippy as a scout project? And maybe you could make a small donation as a token of your appreciation."

After some initial disappointment, he agreed that my idea might be best after all, and I think that when we hung up he was feeling more optimistic. I felt terrible. Sherlock Bones had gained a public reputation that John Keane couldn't live up to—yet. If I was going to bill myself as a tracer of missing pets, I had to learn some pet-detecting skills. Visiting pounds was just a beginning. I had to get some cases under my belt, find out more about how and why pets were lost or stolen, and develop some techniques for getting them back. I no longer wondered if I really wanted to make a commitment. The commitment had been made; now I had to back it up.

And the greyhound? She was eventually found, a week after she escaped, and although I was not the one who found her, my initial hunch as to her whereabouts proved accurate. She had indeed taken refuge in a cemetery, about two miles from the Coliseum. Someone spotted her stealing down to a McDonald's restaurant in the early hours of the morning to scavenge leftovers from the garbage cans. This person called the television station, which in turn notified the handler, and he found her up among the gravestones. It's always appealed to my sense of the absurd that the world's most expensive greyhound survived on her own by eating Big Macs. It just shows what the aristocracy will resort to when the chips are down.

Since my phone call from Tippy's owner in Boston, I think it's fair to say I've learned as much as anyone about the world of missing pets and how to recover them. Others who work with animals—vets, shelter employees, officials in animal-welfare organizations—get involved with aspects of pet-finding, but their primary responsibilities lie in the areas of health, animal control, lobbying, and/or fund-raising. To the best of my knowledge, no one else has made a full-time career of tracking down animals that have been lost or stolen. As a result of my on-the-job experience, I've learned techniques, things to look out for, and ways of dealing with people that can make a search for a pet as efficient and productive as possible. I've also learned what pet owners can do to keep their pets safe. Part of my reason for writing this book is to share all this information with pet owners:

- How to spread the word of your missing pet as quickly and effectively as possible
- The many different motivations behind petnapping, and how to deal with them
- The psychology of offering—and paying—rewards
- The potential of "positive imaging" for recovering a pet
- How to deal with public and private animal shelters

The cases I've worked on have opened my eyes to the many, many ways—bizarre and poignant, kind and cruel, funny and sad —the lives of owners and their pets are entwined. The stereotypes of the boy and his dog, the little old lady and her cat, and the family pooch basking in a circle of love do not begin to tell the whole story. I've had frantic calls from a priest who wanted his Doberman back, a pimp whose pit bull was stolen, and a traveling salesman whose Siamese cat escaped from his car while he was making an out-of-town call. People have paid me hundreds of dollars to fly to other cities in search of their pets; others have barely been able to afford an ad in the paper. I've had clients at both ends of the caring spectrum—from the man who admitted (with some surprise) that he was actually relieved at not having to feed and clean up after his lost dog, to the woman who offered a $10,000 reward and spent over a year in a full-time search for her missing mutt. The motivations of people who use my services have included love, desperation, guilt, status-seeking, vindictiveness, and a desire to pacify other family members.

What has been fascinating is how the loss of a pet becomes a moment of truth for the owners, during which they cannot avoid discovering, in very concrete terms, just how they feel about that pet—and, in the process, something about themselves as well. Declamations of undying love or protestations of cool detachment soon fall by the wayside, for in order to find a missing pet you have to *do* something. To understand what I mean, imagine that your pet is lost and ask yourself what you would do. Would you telephone one animal shelter to locate it? Several? Visit them in person? Every day? Place an ad in the paper? Several papers? Offer a reward? If so, how much? Stay home from work, or from a party, to answer the phone (or arrange to have someone else answer it)? Have posters printed and plaster them all over town? Change your travel plans to hunt down a pet lost during a vacation trip? Badger people you don't think are giving you straight answers? Keep going over a long period of time?

As the owners of missing pets know, there are no hard-and-fast rules telling you what to do or how to express your feelings. Society gives us acceptable rationalizations for almost any course of action (or inaction): "It's only a dog," "We really can't afford it," "My kids are crying their eyes out," or "He's just like a member of the family." It really boils down to a question of examining your own feelings and then acting on them. A large part of my work is helping people get clear about just how much effort they really want to put out to find their pets and then working with them to channel that effort into constructive activity.

Although I went through a period in which I disapproved of anyone who failed to exhaust every possibility of recovering a missing pet, I've long since mellowed. People's resources are not limitless. They do have other priorities. There frequently are good reasons for calling a halt before turning what I would consider to be the last stone. People will expend effort to find a missing pet in direct proportion to the importance to them of that animal. Love, after all, has its limits, although people don't always like to admit it. In fact, dealing with the guilt of letting go is perhaps my most valuable service. I lay no claim to solving every case; many animals simply vanish, and no amount of the cleverest detective work will get them back. What I do tell my clients, however, is that if I have given a case my best shot and still haven't found their pet, it can't be found. In the hundreds of cases I've worked on, I have yet to be proved wrong.

By the same token, however, many of my clients are looking for support for overpowering feelings of loss that come as a complete surprise to them. "I had no idea I loved her so much," they will tell me, or, "This is going to sound crazy, but I haven't been able to sleep since he got lost." It doesn't sound crazy to me at all. In today's world—where family life isn't so stable as it once was, where many jobs are impersonal, where people move around the country more, where young men and women are postponing marriage and children longer—people ask more of their pets than they used to, in the realm of what I can only call human interaction. The old sources of emotional sustenance aren't quite so reliable or readily available as they once were, and many people have replaced them, at least in part, with pets. Given this state of affairs, who is to say what constitutes a "sick" attachment to an animal? I'm reminded of the woman who called me three days after her dog disappeared. "It's really hitting me hard," she said. "At first I thought I must be crazy, but then I started thinking. I've had Caesar for eleven years, ever since I graduated from college and moved out to California. He's really my oldest friend. He's seen me through two jobs, several boyfriends, a marriage, and a divorce. When my husband and I split up, I must have cried nonstop for three months, but there was Caesar, constantly at my side. I used to wipe my eyes with his ears. I've always had friends, but Caesar is the only thread, the only constant. He goes back farther than anybody."

I've also learned that pets are more than providers of unconditional love and bulwarks against loneliness. I'm not referring just to expensive pedigreed animals that confer status, to guard dogs that offer protection, or to family pets purchased to teach children responsibility. I've worked on cases in which a pet's fragile health has served as a focus for emotional energy between a couple who had virtually no other common interests. I believe many pets serve as family scapegoats, bearing the brunt of the anger and hostility that family members are unable to express directly to each other. I'm convinced this process is the cause of many animals "getting lost." What happens in these cases, and especially with cats, is that they run away—if not in actual fact, then by opening themselves to situations in which other people take them in.

Say what you will about projecting our own feelings onto our pets and then ascribing these feelings to them, my experience has been that animals are incredibly attuned to their owners' emotional states, sometimes even more than the owners themselves. I know a woman who claims that whenever she's going through a period of anxiety and uncertainty, her cat will spend long hours sitting in a closet. "It's like she's meditating," she tells me. "Often she'll start to do it before I'm aware of what's going on myself." I took a dim view of these stories until I met a family therapist who told me she likes to arrange at least one session to include the family pet. "Pets are very sensitive to unexpressed feelings," she said, "and for that reason can be extremely helpful in opening up communication. More than once I've been with a family that seems blocked, and I will notice the dog paying particular attention to one person. Almost invariably that person is sitting on some feeling—pain, usually, or anger—and if I can get him or her to open up, we start to make progress."

Another eye-opener for me has been the uncanny fit between owners and their pets—not just in terms of physical appearance (a cliché that, like all clichés, is based on truth), but in terms of emotional process as well. I sometimes think we unconsciously choose the perfect pet with whom to finish off some part of our growing up, although it is not always apparent at the outset what that may be. I've learned this in my own relationship with Paco.

Sometimes, when I see other owners with their pets, I wish Paco were more demonstrative and affectionate. Although he would be happiest if I never left his side, he has always been a rather aloof dog, even as a puppy, and he is not given to constant displays of, and requests for, love. But if I'm honest with myself, I have to admit that deep down his attitude suits me fine. I don't think at this point in my life I would be comfortable with a dog that was always looking for a pat or a scratch or an extra nuzzle.

And while I'm on the subject of links between people and their animals, I might as well come clean about my belief in "positive imaging" as a means of recovering missing pets. With many clients I keep it under my hat, since it sounds like the very essence of California nuttiness, but I've seen it work too many times to dismiss it completely. Many people have a hunch about the whereabouts of a missing pet—like my hunch that the grey-hound was hiding in a park or cemetery—but don't trust their intuition enough to act on it. Now, I grant that many hunches are nothing more than educated guesses, but I submit that some have a compelling quality that exceeds a simple knowledge of a pet's habits or other matters of fact. I have found that if owners can clear their minds of worry and fear and simply imagine a happy reunion without trying to anticipate how or when it will happen, they increase the possibility of making that reunion take place. I've got no real stake in proving the theory; all I know is that I've seen it work many times.

Four years ago, if someone had predicted that I, an ex-marine, would one day be deeply involved in the world of missing pets (not to mention these fringe areas of owner-pet communication), I'd have told him to wipe off the old crystal ball and take another look. To this day I often wonder what the hell a grown man is doing chasing down lost dogs and cats. I tell myself I'm in business, out to turn a profit like any other business, but in fact I haven't made much money at it. There have been times when I haven't been able to pay my bills, and more than once I've been reduced to turning in empty bottles in order to buy enough gas to go out on a case. Being a pet detective presents endless opportunities to lose money, and despite my occasional pretensions of being a hardheaded businessman, I sometimes think I've taken them all. But I can't complain. After all, if I didn't love animals, I wouldn't be doing what I do. And besides, profit or no profit, it sure beats selling insurance.

3
No Time for
the Rules

CATHY WILLIAMS ARRIVED EARLY for our noontime appointment. I was on the phone with a man who was telling me more than I needed to know about a puppy he had found. With the receiver cradled against my ear I swept some papers off a chair and silently motioned for her to take a seat. She had brought some photographs of her dog, as I had suggested, and while I tried to wind up my conversation she hunched over them in the chair, her heavy blond hair obscuring what I had observed to be a very pretty face.

"Yes, well, I appreciate your calling," I told the man, "and I'll be happy to add the dog to my list, but I'm afraid I can't promise too much. Like I said, I'd try posters and an ad in the paper, if I were you." I could hear the impatience in my voice. This was one of my "hot potato" calls. The man's daughter had found the puppy, and he was desperate to get rid of it before she grew too attached to give it up. I had a clipboard of over a hundred found pets, and each time I got a case I'd scan the list for the new client's missing pet. A few times I'd been lucky, but it wasn't a very productive practice. Thus my impatience.

Besides, the sight of Cathy Williams's long golden legs curled up in the chair opposite my desk was a compelling distraction. Paco had the right idea. He had stuck his nose underneath her mane of hair, and the two of them had their heads together, gray mop to blond, as she scratched behind his ears.

53

"Sorry to keep you waiting," I said, finally managing to extricate myself from the call. "That was a guy who found a— Hey, are you all right?"

She looked up at me, brushing her hair back from her face, and I suddenly realized she had been crying. So that's why Paco had gone over to her. Usually when I'm with a client he lies at my feet.

"Yes. No. I don't know. Oh boy," she said, trying to smile. "This is really hard. I was sitting here looking at these pictures, and it suddenly hit me I might never see him again. I'm sorry, this really isn't my style, but it's been a hell of a week, it really has."

"Don't apologize. It's OK." I handed her a box of Kleenex and gave her a few moments to regain her composure. Even in her present condition, she was a beautiful young woman, the wholesome clear-eyed type who could have stepped out of an ad for an organic breakfast cereal, right down to her red-and-white checked shirt tied at the waist and a pair of trim hiking shorts. But now she was in trouble, and I wanted to help her.

"Why don't you tell me again what happened," I began, "and then we can get busy finding your dog. It's a Weimaraner, isn't it?"

"That's right," she replied. "His name is Harpo. He's just a great dog. You know that silvery-gray color they have, and those pale eyes? I fell in love the minute I saw him. He'd be a great show dog, except that he's much too big. I can't even lift him any more. The vet calls him my pet horse." She smiled at the thought. "I've had him for four years, and he's . . . well, it's true, he's like a member of the family. My *ex*-family, I should say. Oh, why did this happen now, of all times? Why didn't they take the damned truck and leave Harpo?"

Cathy's story, when she had calmed down enough to tell it to me, convinced me it had indeed been a hell of a week. She and her husband had recently split up. He'd gone sailing in Mexico; she'd managed to land a summer job as an instructor in a wilderness training camp in Montana that would allow her to have

Harpo. She'd closed up their apartment, put the furniture in storage, and was staying with friends across the street until she could sell the pickup truck her husband had left behind as payment for some money he owed her. She absolutely had to fly out of San Francisco on Sunday in order to make connections to the camp. Today was Friday, the truck still hadn't been sold, and yesterday someone had stolen Harpo from her friends' backyard.

It didn't sound very promising, but Cathy was in no shape to hear that. "We've still got two days," I said, "and besides, even if you have to leave without Harpo, I could always arrange to have him sent to you in Montana."

"No, that's the problem," she said. "This camp is really out of touch with civilization. That's part of the wilderness training. We don't even get any mail sent in. I knew it was too good to be true. It was just the perfect job. I'd get to keep Harpo and would be out of the city and meeting new people—all the things I need right now." Tears welled up in her eyes again.

"OK then, we'll just have to work a little faster," I replied, talking rapidly to keep her from crying again. "First thing, are you absolutely positive Harpo was stolen?"

"Absolutely. Well, I think so. The backyard's fenced in, and the only way in is through the house. I left him there when I went to the store. Normally I'd take him, but he'd been acting funny. He really misses my husband, and what with being in a new house, he's been sort of snappish with strangers. Anyway, when I got back he was gone. I'm sure someone spotted him and just grabbed him. Weimaraners are very expensive dogs, you know."

"I know, but—OK, I'll check that out later. Let's pick out a good photograph and get some posters made. It's too late for an ad in the paper, but I'll give you a list of shelters to check. I'll take care of putting up the posters. We'll find Harpo, you'll see."

"Just like that?" Her expression was incredulous. "I've got the crate all ready to ship him. If he could be with me on that plane to Montana, I'd be eternally grateful to you."

I sent Cathy off to the shelters and headed for the instant printer's. I wondered if I'd been a little too glib just to make her feel better. If we didn't find Harpo, she'd be that much more disappointed, but I'd learned with clients in her frame of mind that the first order of business was to get them out of their panic and into constructive action. If I really thought Harpo had been stolen, I might not have been so optimistic, but frankly I doubted it. Dogs act strangely during times of upheaval in their owners' lives. Some react by sticking close. Others take off. And I had yet to see a typical backyard fence that would hold a dog if he really wanted to get out.

I hung around until the posters were finished and then headed over to San Francisco's Mission district, where Cathy lived, to start putting them up. As I always do, I marked off an area with a twenty-block radius from the owners' house. Barring unusual circumstances, I've found that concentrating posters in this area yields the best results.

I also wanted to check out that fence, so I swung by Cathy's friends' house. Fortunately, Cathy was there to let me in. It took about a minute to see that the ground dipped slightly in the corner where the fence joined the house, creating an opening big enough for even a large dog to squeeze through. In fact, there seemed to be evidence of digging. Cathy was embarrassed at not having noticed the hole, but she felt better when I told her it was a good sign. Now we knew we weren't dealing with a well-planned petnapping. Of course, it was still possible Harpo had fallen into the hands of someone who recognized his value, but I figured Cathy's offer of a two-hundred-dollar reward would take care of that. Unless you're part of a petnapping ring, it's not easy to turn even the most expensive dog into quick cash.

Later that night I was back home in Oakland grabbing a quick bite when the phone rang. It was Flo. I realized she hadn't been on duty for a few days.

"Well, hello," I said. "I was wondering where you were. I thought maybe you got lucky at the races and took off for Rio. What's wrong with your voice?"

"How'd you guess?" she croaked. "Of course, it would have

been more fun if I didn't have laryngitis and a temperature of a hundred and two."

"Don't tell me you were sick, Flo. You never get sick. Sure you weren't goofing off? Great voice, by the way. Sounds like Marlene Dietrich."

"I should know better than to expect sympathy from you, Sherlock," she said. "Look, I still can't talk, but I wanted to tell you someone called about a dog. Name's Harpo. Is that one of yours?"

"Sure is," I replied, suddenly interested. "What did he say?"

"He said he had the dog."

"Fantastic! Why didn't you say so at first?"

"Well, he didn't leave his name or anything. In fact, he suddenly hung up right in the middle of our conversation."

"What did he sound like?"

"Just sort of average, you know." I realized Flo must really be sick. Usually she can pick out a person's life history after thirty seconds on the phone with him. "He had a hillbilly accent, you know what I mean?"

"Right. He'll probably call back. And you take care of yourself. Try a little honey and bourbon. I hear it does wonders for the voice—unless of course you like sounding like a foghorn in heat."

She hung up, apparently in no condition to appreciate my devastating wit.

I made a point of catching every call that evening, but the man with the hillbilly accent never phoned back.

The next day—Saturday—I forced myself to put up the rest of the posters, although my mind was still on that call. It's funny about posters. They have a cumulative effect that takes time to work. Occasionally someone will find a client's pet, see the poster, and call, but such instantaneous response is rare. If someone who has found a pet intends to return it, more often than not he'll call the shelters, run an ad in the paper, or (if the dog has tags) call the owner directly. I put up posters primarily to attract the attention of people who may remember seeing the dog or who later run across it. That's why I put up so many. Most owners think they're doing a lot if they put up ten or fifteen. I always put up at least six or seven hundred and in a concentrated area—on telephone poles, in stores, on just about any visible surface I can find.

Posters work like ads in magazines. The first time you see one, it may not register, but after you see five or six within a few minutes' time you begin to pay a little more attention. By the time you finally run across the one that makes you say, "Hey, wait a minute, I think I saw that dog"—or see the dog that makes you say, "Hey, wait a minute, I think I saw a poster . . ."—days can have passed.

We didn't have that kind of time to find Harpo. Cathy was due to fly out of town at one o'clock on Sunday—less than twenty-four hours away. That's why I was pinning my hopes on the guy with the hillbilly accent. It was a slim hope; most calls like that amount to nothing. Still, I kept checking with my service as I worked. Flo was off duty, but her replacement assured me no one had called in about Harpo. Why hadn't he called back? Why had he hung up on Flo so abruptly? By the end of the day I had put up the last poster. For the last two hours I'd been resisting calling Cathy and telling her about the call. I make a practice of not telling clients about half-baked leads, but I'd already stuck my neck out with my predictions of instant success. Sherlock, I thought, sooner or later you're going to have to face the truth with her, but not right now. I'll just call to see how she's doing.

"Hi," she said. "I'm afraid to ask if you—"

"Just reporting in," I interjected, trying to sound cheerful. "I've got all the posters up. Now we wait for the calls."

There was a long pause. "You're sweet, John, but it's not going to work, is it?"

"Oh, I wouldn't say that. I—"

"You know, twice today I almost called the camp director and canceled, but I just can't. I've got no job, no apartment. I can't even stay here. My friends are going off in two weeks and they've sublet their house. And even if you do find him, I can't afford to board him all summer."

"Well, if worse came to worst, I could always take him."

"That's really generous, but I've seen your apartment. And you've got a dog already. Besides, I want him with me. I really need him now. Does that sound crazy to you?"

"Not at all." I was afraid she might start crying again. "Look, Cathy, I probably shouldn't be telling you this, but I did get one call about Harpo yesterday."

"Yesterday? Why didn't you tell me? What did they say?"

I explained what had happened. "I held off telling you until he called back. But there's still time. Look, you go ahead and get packed. Don't worry about the truck; we'll deal with it later. And don't get discouraged. A lot can happen between now and tomorrow."

I'd almost managed to convince myself that we would find Harpo in time, but when eleven o'clock rolled around and no one had called, I was ready to throw in the towel. In fact, when the phone rang I thought it might be Cathy, so I let it ring three or four times while I rehearsed just how I would break the news.

"Sherlock Bones," I said.

"This here poster," a man's voice said, "is it on the level?"

"For a Weimaraner, you mean?"

"Big gray dog, name of Harpo. For sure you got that kinda money, two hundred dollars?" He spoke slowly, and there was a lot of country in his voice.

"Absolutely," I replied. "Do you have the dog?" I was certain this was the person who had called before. I tried to keep the excitement out of my voice. I didn't want to scare him off—or fall into a trap.

"That's right." He sounded nervous.

"Well, give me your address and I'll come right over." I wasn't being very cool.

"No way, mister, no way." There was a long pause. "Meet me tomorrow and we'll talk about it. And bring the money. In cash. I don't take no credit cards, you know what I mean?"

"All right," I agreed, "but it'll have to be tonight." I hated to sound so eager, but the time was too short to play around.

After some hesitation he agreed, on the condition that he name the place. It was a street behind the art museum in Golden Gate Park. "Stop when you come to the first turnoff," he said. "One o'clock. Don't be late, and don't bring no one."

He didn't give me the opportunity to ask why he'd chosen such an isolated area, but maybe that was just as well. The only reasons I could think of I didn't want to think of. Delivering two hundred dollars to a stranger in the middle of nowhere at one o'clock in the morning violated everything I told my clients about paying rewards, but I didn't have much choice. He'd said to come alone. Surely that didn't mean no dogs. I'd take Paco as protection. He wouldn't be much good, but maybe he could manage to look threatening. I was pondering that unlikely prospect when the fact suddenly hit me that I didn't have two hundred dollars and there was no place I could cash a check. Damn! I thought briefly of knocking off the local Seven-Eleven but, knowing my neighborhood, I figured someone had probably already cleaned them out by this time of night.

That left Cathy. I knew she didn't have much money. I'd agreed to pay the reward out of my own pocket and postpone my fee until she could sell the truck—another of my ironclad rules broken on this case. Besides, I didn't want to get her involved. This was part of my job, and if it turned out to be dangerous I didn't want her around. I knew if I called her she'd insist on coming. But I had no other choice.

"Hi," I said when she came to the phone. "Sorry if I woke you."

"Are you kidding? A bunch of us are sitting around trying to have a farewell party, but I can't get into a party mood. Why don't you tell me a joke?" The strain of the past few days was beginning to show.

She was ecstatic when I told her my news. "This is it!" she cried. "I just know he's got Harpo. He must!"

"There's just one problem, though," I said, "and that's the cash. I don't have it."

"Oh no," she groaned. "I've got some traveler's checks, but

not that much, and it's not cash. Now what are— Hold on, John. Can you hold on just a sec?"

She was gone for a few moments, and when she came back she was crying.

"Listen, Cathy," I said, "it's OK. We're too close not to think of something. Don't worry."

"No, no, you don't understand." She was suddenly laughing. "I've got it. My friends all chipped in, and I'm standing here with my hands full of money. Isn't it marvelous to have friends like that? I can't believe it."

Forty minutes later I'd stopped by Cathy's, stuffed the money in my shirt pocket, and with Paco in the seat beside me was barreling through the city to Golden Gate Park. As I'd figured, Cathy had wanted to come along, but I'd convinced her to stay at the party and wait for my call.

There'd been no time to plan a strategy for dealing with the man I was about to meet, but the fact of the matter was he held all the cards anyway. Without a doubt I was an easy target for extortion and worse. I had a vision of myself with a knife in my back, dumped under one of Golden Gate Park's more exotic giant ferns, the faithful Paco standing guard for days until my body was recovered. Maybe I should have brought Cathy after all. Maybe I should have invited the whole party to come along. Now, now, John, I told myself, knock off the melodrama. You're just picking up a dog. All the same, I took the time to pull over to the curb and take the wad of bills from my shirt pocket and stuff them in my shoe. They made an uncomfortably large lump under my foot, but I felt better. No sense playing fast and loose with Cathy's friends' money.

Golden Gate Park is a long narrow rectangle, about half a mile wide and maybe three miles long, that shoots from the Pacific Ocean toward the Haight-Ashbury part of San Francisco. By day a haven for nature-lovers, museum-goers, joggers, riders, golfers, and sunbathers, by night it is pretty much deserted, and the wide variety of the world's flora growing in its planned-to-look-unplanned terrain assumes a more sinister aspect. I swung off one of the residential streets that borders the park and in a matter of seconds was swallowed in near blackness. More quickly than I cared to, I located the turnoff the caller had mentioned and pulled in. I killed the lights, turned off the engine, and waited. Nothing. Paco must have sensed my tenseness, for he peered anxiously through the window and made quiet little woofing sounds.

"That's OK, Pac," I said, startled by the sound of my own voice in the silence. My watch said one fifteen. Where was this guy? Surely he hadn't left already. He sounded anxious on the phone, and my guess was he needed the money badly. But who could tell? I had gone against my better judgment at almost every turn of this case, and by this time I didn't know what to think.

Suddenly two quick raps on my side of the van lifted me out of my seat and sent Paco into a burst of serious barking. A face belonging to a kid of maybe nineteen or twenty had materialized at my window. He was wearing a dirty Stetson rolled up on the sides and a denim jacket that looked too big for his skinny frame. Paco was lunging across me at him. I started to roll down the window.

"Not too far," he said. "I don't want yer dog all over me."

"Oh, that's just Paco," I started to say and then shut up. Paco was doing a fair imitation of an attack dog, and I saw no reason to spoil it. Feeling hemmed in behind the wheel, I stepped down from the van but kept my hand on the partly open door, in case I had to let loose what suddenly bore all the outward appearances of a vicious beast.

"Well," he said nervously, "you got the cash?"

"That depends. You got the dog?"

"Lookee here, mister, I said to bring the cash." He was a little guy, with a bad complexion and a mean mouth. It was probably all because of an underprivileged childhood, but I couldn't work up much sympathy for him.

"First let's see the dog. It's my client's money. I've got a responsibility to her."

Without moving, he jerked a thumb over his shoulder. "Dog's back there." So far back in the shadows as to be almost invisible I spotted a beat-up car; it looked like a Hudson. I walked to it, the money in my shoe making me hobble, but couldn't see any sign of a dog.

I turned around. He was standing where I left him. "All right," I said as I walked back to him, "what's going on? There's no dog in that car."

"You'll get yer dog, mister, but you gotta give me the money first."

"Why should I?" This was no time for beating around the bush.

The kid put his hand into his pocket, and before I had time to worry about what he was going after he pulled out a grimy piece of paper and began to unfold it. "It says right here on this here poster," he said, his fingers tracing the words, *"Reward for information leading to the return of Harpo.* Now ain't that right?"

"You called Friday night and said you had the dog. That was you, wasn't it?"

"Maybe it was. So?"

"But you never actually had the dog, did you?"

The kid jerked at his collar. "Maybe I ain't got it now, but I sure 'n hell did when I called. And I know where it is. Ain't that 'information leading to the return' of this here dog?" His voice had a whiny insistency that was beginning to get to me.

"You're right," I said evenly, "if it's really Harpo. Now if it is, you'll get the reward as soon as we get the dog back."

"No deal, mister, no deal." He kicked the gravel with his boot. "I gotta have the money now. You get the message? No money, no deal." His whining had turned to anger, and I backed off a step or two. This guy was desperate, and I've learned to treat desperate people with a great deal of deference.

"Let's take it one step at a time," I said, hoping to calm him down. "First, how do I know it's Harpo you're talking about?"

Without responding he reached once again into his pocket and pulled out a dog collar. It was brown leather with hammered silver circles that matched the collar Harpo was wearing in some of the photographs I had seen. So he *was* talking about Harpo.

There was something ominous about an empty collar, though; it reminded me of a horse returning to the stable with an empty saddle.

"Is the dog all right?"

"Yeah, sure. Last time I seen him he was just dandy. I just kept his collar because—well, I just kept it, that's all. I'm gonna make me a watchband out of it." He began to shift his weight. "You gonna give me the money now?"

"What if I gave you part now and the rest when I get the dog?" It was a weak response and we both knew it. "OK, OK," I agreed, "I'll give you the whole two hundred, but I'll have to go to the van first."

"What fer?"

"For the money."

For the first time he smiled, a crooked grin that helped to make him look a little nicer. Not much, but a little. "Why?" he asked. "It's in yer shoe, ain't it?"

"What makes you say that?" I replied, trying to sound stern.

Now he was laughing. "I seen you limping, and I figured you probably hid it there. It's OK, I done that lots of times myself. You got the right idea, but the wrong kind of shoes, that's all. You need some western boots like mine. They got more room."

Feeling like the wrong end of a horse, I leaned against the van, removed the crumpled bills, and handed them over. He hunkered down on the ground to count them out, fashioned them into a smooth roll, and tucked them in his pocket.

"OK," I said, "let's talk about where Harpo is." He was much more relaxed. Now it was my turn to be nervous. This kid had me over a barrel.

"Honest to God, mister, I had him when I called Friday," he replied. "I came home from work, and there he was drinking out of a pail of water. He just followed me right into the kitchen and sat there waiting for chow. I damn near cleaned out the place trying to fill him up. He even ate pickles. Now that's hungry, in my book."

"Right," I agreed. "Now, if you could just tell me where—"

"Keep yer pants on, I'm gettin' to that." Now that he had his money he was becoming expansive. "See, every Friday I like to shoot a little pool, see what's going on, check things out, right? So I put the dog in the car and head down to the place I usually go, Jack's Pool Palace, down there off Mission somewheres. You know the one I mean?"

"No, but—"

"Well, anyway, I'm parking the car, and I see this poster on a telephone pole, and it looks like this here dog. See, this is the one. I tore it off."

"Yes, I know the poster. As a matter of fact, I'm the one—"

"Well, so I see the reward money, and I call the number, this here one, see?"

"Right. That's my number. It's my poster." This kid made a better talker than he did a listener.

"And I get this woman, and I'm tellin' her about the dog and all—hey, is she your wife?"

"No, she's—never mind. What happened? She told me you hung up right in the middle of the conversation."

"You bet I did. Spider walked in and seen me, that's why. You'd do the same."

"Why? Who's Spider?"

"Spider Johnson. He'd as soon cut you up as look at you. I'm tellin' you, he's mean. Wanna know how mean? He's been livin' with this woman for years, and he used to beat her up so bad she finally left. She's too scared to go to the cops, and he's still there all by himself. And it's *her* house. Why do you think I told you to meet me in this park? It's not 'cause I like trees, I can tell you that. If Spider knew I was talkin' to you, I don't even like to think about what he might do to me."

"OK, so he's mean. But what's he got to do with Harpo?"

"I'm comin' to that part," he said, looking down at the ground and scraping the gravel into little circles with the toe of his boot. "Well, I— See, I owe him some money, about fifty dollars. That's why I didn't want him to see me, right? Because I didn't have it. Well, but he seen me and says, 'Let's you and me go outside.' So we did, and he sees the dog in my car and takes a shine to it. 'Cept for that dog, I could be dead by now."

The light was beginning to dawn, and I did not like what I saw. "Wait a minute," I said slowly. "Are you telling me you gave Harpo to Spider?"

The kid looked at me defiantly. "Hell, yes. And I'd do it again. If you ever see Spider, you'll know I ain't kiddin'."

It sounded like that was exactly the prospect that now awaited me. "So I'm supposed to convince him to give me back the dog."

"Uh, mister," he cautioned, "if I was you I wouldn't waste no time talkin' to Spider. Not unless yer pretty good with a knife. Soon's he finds out you want it, he won't wanna give it to you."

We ended our meeting on that doleful prediction, and I headed out of the park. I wanted to get in touch with Cathy, but before I did that I decided to check out Spider's house. The kid hadn't known the exact address, but he'd described the house and given me the block it was on. I found it without much trouble and cruised by slowly. It was an old frame house with a front porch abutting the sidewalk and a long narrow driveway leading to a garage in back. The place was dark, and there was no dog in sight. Between the garage and the house I could make out what looked like a smallish yard surrounded by a wire fence of some kind. I considered walking back to check it out but decided against it. If Harpo were there, he'd probably start barking at me, and if he weren't, there wasn't much point in risking my neck. First I needed a plan.

By the time I called Cathy, it was almost three in the morning and I was fading fast. Despite her enthusiasm at the results of my rendezvous, she sounded exhausted, so we agreed to try to get some sleep and meet at her friends' house at eight thirty. I was on my way back to Oakland when it occurred to me that two trips across the bridge in five hours wasn't going to leave me much time for sleeping, so I pulled off on an industrial side street, locked the doors to the van, and tried to get some shut-eye. Before I drifted off, I gave my dreaming mechanism a message to dream up a plan for the next day. I've known this to work, but that particular night all I came up with was a series of sweat-soaked nightmares about flashing switchblades and long narrow driveways. With the dawn my nightmares ceased, and I drifted back into a more peaceful, deeper sleep—so deep, in fact, that it was almost nine o'clock when I finally woke up.

I raced for Cathy's house; there was no time for even a cup of coffee. And I still didn't have a plan. All I knew was Harpo's location—and even that wasn't definite—and the type of person into whose hands he had fallen. When I got to Cathy's house, the sight of her open-bed pickup truck gave me the inkling of an idea. It wasn't much, but I parked the van, left Paco with Cathy's friends, and told her to put her suitcases and Harpo's crate in the truck. With less than four hours to takeoff, I took the wheel and we headed for Spider's house, Cathy at my side, too keyed up to do much talking. I'd briefed her on Spider, but I think we were both too excited to think seriously about what might await us.

As we approached his block, I pointed out the house and slowed down as much as I dared. "Look in the back as I go by," I told her, "and see if Harpo is behind the fence in the yard. If he is, I've got an idea."

She craned her neck out the window, and as I passed his driveway she shouted, "There he is! I see him! It's Harpo!" She grabbed my arm. "John, why didn't you stop? He's right back there!"

"Easy does it," I said. "We'll get him, but we've got to get our signals straight first. Now. How good are you at driving this thing?"

"Damned good, if I do say so. I've taken this truck places you wouldn't—"

"OK, you drive, then, and I'll get in the back. Go around the block, and when we get to Spider's house, back into his driveway as fast as you can. It's fairly narrow. Do you think you can do it?"

"No problem. But why back in?"

"Because we may need to get out fast. Lock the doors and

keep the windows rolled up. When we get to the fence, I'll jump down and open the gate. You roll down the window just enough to call Harpo. Hopefully, he'll jump in the back, and—"

"Yeah, he used to ride there all the time."

"Good. And I'll jump in, and you floor it."

"But why don't you drive and let me open the gate? He'll recognize me, and—"

"Nothing doing. I want several layers of truck between you and Spider, if he's at home. I'd rather you weren't in on this at all, but we need Harpo's cooperation, and I don't think there's going to be time for me to make friends with him. If something happens, just get out fast and go for help. Don't do anything heroic."

We took our places, Cathy started the truck, and we rounded the block back to Spider's street. As his house came into view, my heart sank, for there on the porch was Spider himself, rocked back in a chair with his feet on the railing and a can of beer in his hand. I could easily see why that kid was so terrified: Spider Johnson was one big, mean-looking specimen. Even at a distance his strength was apparent. I knocked on the rear window of the cab, but Cathy had seen him, too, and she sped past his house. I ducked behind the crate in an attempt to make myself inconspicuous.

She pulled up at a gas station a couple of blocks away. "Now what?" she said, getting out of the cab.

"Now what?" I repeated. "Well, now we, uh . . ." I spotted a pay phone. "Hang on a minute. Just stay where you are. I want to make a call."

It was a long shot. The kid had told me the house wasn't Spider's, but maybe it would work. Johnson, Johnson. My fingers traced the addresses down the page of the telephone book. There was his address, with a number listed under Clarence Johnson. Clarence? No wonder you call yourself Spider, I thought. With a silent prayer that Flo was on duty, I called my answering service.

"Sherlock Bones." Thank God, it was Flo, taking the Sunday morning shift.

"Flo!" I exclaimed. "It's me!"

"Oh hi, Sherlock," she said with a voice still throaty from her illness. "I didn't know they had phones in church."

"Listen, Flo, if I get out of this in one piece, I'll spend a week in church, but right now I need a favor."

"I don't know, Sherlock. After your crack the other day. . . ."

"I'll send you three dozen long-stemmed roses. Look, this is serious." I gave her Spider's number. "After we hang up, wait three minutes and give that number a call. If there's any justice in the world, a man named Spider Johnson will answer. All you have to do is keep him on the line for—well, for as long as you can."

"Spider who?"

"Johnson. I can't explain now. Just keep him on the line for two minutes, and I'm yours for life."

"My dream come true. But what am I supposed to say?"

"How should I know? Just don't mention my name—or yours either. I'll explain everything later, if I'm still around. Now remember, give me three minutes before you call him."

I hung up and sprinted back to the truck. I had only a few moments to sketch out the plan to Cathy and get back to Spider's house before Flo made her call. As Cathy turned onto his street, he was still sitting there, beer in hand, but a few seconds later I saw him get up abruptly and go into the house.

"Go!" I shouted, banging on the cab, but Cathy had already taken off. She was right. She really knew how to drive that truck. With an expertise I never could have managed, she positioned the truck perfectly, twisted the wheel, and rammed it backward down the driveway right to the backyard fence. I jumped down from the truck and headed for the gate. By this time Harpo had started a fierce barking. Dear God, I prayed as I fumbled with the latch, please let me get this damned thing open.

The gate swung free, and Harpo leaped out. If I hadn't gotten myself wedged between the open gate and the fence, he might have gone for me, but at that moment Cathy yelled,

"Harpo! Harpo! Here boy! Quick, get in the truck!"

He leaped toward the truck at the sound of her voice. No sooner had he jumped on, with me scrambling right behind him, than I heard a roar at the back door of the house and saw Spider looming in the doorway. "Hey! What the hell's goin' on?" he shouted.

"Take off!" I yelled at Cathy. The truck leaped foward, catching me off balance. I struggled to heave myself all the way in, reaching frantically for something to hang on to. As the truck passed the back door Spider made a leap for it, grasped a side panel with two enormous hands, and ran alongside. For one terrible moment I thought he would vault in upon me, but when Cathy careened into the street, his hands slid off, and we left him sprawled in the gutter.

I didn't have to tell Cathy to keep going. I was vaguely aware of houses and stores blurring past as I flattened myself on the truck's floor. In the back corner stood Harpo, barking furiously at me. Sooner than I would have preferred, Cathy pulled the truck over to the curb, jumped out of the cab, and ran back to Harpo. They literally embraced—Harpo in the back of the truck with his front legs on Cathy's shoulders, Cathy on the ground with her arms around his neck, laughing and crying as he licked her face. His entire body was quivering, and his ferocious barks had turned into frantic whimpers.

"Harpo!" she said. "My God, I thought I'd never see you again! I thought you were gone for good. But you're back! You're really back! We found you! Oh, Harpo, you'll never know how much I missed you!"

I could have stayed there all day watching the two of them, but I looked at my watch and suddenly realized it was getting late. I took the wheel and we headed for the airport, Harpo doing his best to sit in Cathy's lap. It was wonderful to see. The two of them couldn't get enough of each other.

We wheeled up to the terminal. "This lady's on the one o'clock flight to Montana," I told the baggage attendant. "And she's got a dog. Do you think they can make it?"

KITCHENER PUBLIC LIBRARY

"Sure thing," he assured me. "Just give me the ticket, and we'll take care of everything."

Cathy led Harpo into his crate, gave him a long hug, and watched as he was trundled away, with her suitcases resting on the top of the crate. "Well, this is good-bye," she said, turning to me. "Wow, I haven't even thanked you. How can I ever thank you for what you've done?"

"No problem," I said. "All in a day's work." She started to say something, but instead threw her arms around my neck and kissed me. Before I could respond, she turned and ran toward the door. "Take care," she shouted. "And . . . thanks. You saved my life."

I stood staring after her for a long moment and then got back in the truck and drove back to Cathy's friends' house. I left the truck with them, since Cathy had arranged for them to sell it for her, picked up Paco, and headed back home. Despite our success, I felt empty inside. Probably a letdown after all the activity of the last forty-eight hours, I thought. Or did it have more to do with Cathy's departure? I realized that we couldn't even write to each other until the summer was over. By that time the experience that had brought us together would have lost its intensity, and whatever there might have been between us would be gone. I reached over and ruffled Paco's ears. "Come on, man's best friend, case closed. Let's go home and get some rest."

A nap, shower and shave, and a good meal did a lot to restore my equilibrium. I was lounging around the apartment that afternoon when I remembered Flo and gave her a call.

"Hey, Sherlock, what gives? One minute I'm having this nice conversation with Spider, and then I hear a lot of barking and the phone goes dead."

"I'll explain in a minute, after you tell me what you and Spider talked about."

"Oh, it was quite a nice conversation."

"It was?"

"Oh, yes," she replied, terribly pleased with herself. "You said to keep him on the line, so I told him I was starting a singles club and had heard that he might be interested in joining."

"A singles club, huh?" I was glad she couldn't see the expression on my face. "How'd that grab him?"

"He was quite interested. He said he liked the sound of my voice."

"I told you, you sound like Marlene Dietrich. You really ought to keep that going."

"What kind of person is this Mr. Johnson, Sherlock? Do you know him?" There was a coyness in her voice I hadn't heard before.

I explained the whole story as briefly as I could. When I finished there was a long silence on the other end of the line.

Finally Flo answered. "How could you, Sherlock? How could you do that to me?"

"Well, how did I know what you were going to say? Look at it this way, Flo. We couldn't have gotten Harpo without you."

She giggled. "It was fun, you know. But the next time you drag me in on a case, see if you can't dig up a nicer fellow."

4
A Moggy
for Michael

MRS. BENTWHISTLE WAS ONE OF THE PEOPLE that I
would have written off a few years ago as just another animal nut.
Every neighborhood seems to have one. Kindly or cantankerous,
garrulous or reclusive, sometimes wealthy but more often just
scraping along—they have in common a soft spot for animals
that, to the outside world at least, seems to have totally destroyed
their better judgment. I'm thinking of one woman I know who
got herself arrested for breaking and entering when she climbed
in the window of a neighbor's apartment to rescue a cat that had
been crying for thirty-six hours straight. And Mr. Simms, who
lived in a one-room apartment on meager Social Security payments but still managed to rescue one or two puppies a week from
the pound, have them checked over by a vet, and then place them
in homes that he carefully screened. Had people like these always
listened to their better judgment, a lot of pets wouldn't be around
today. To my way of thinking, some of these "nutty" men and
women are really the unsung heroes of the animal-welfare world
and, when it comes to Mrs. Bentwhistle, the human-welfare
world as well. I know that's what Mike Cunningham would say.

This case began one summer evening when I was doing my
laundry. It was about eight o'clock, and I was heading across the
street to check the dryer in the Laundromat when the phone
rang.

"Are you the man that looks for lost cats?" a small voice

asked. It sounded like a kid, maybe ten or twelve years old.

"That's right," I replied. "What can I do for you?"

"I want you to help me find Sam."

"Sam's your cat?"

"Yeah. He's one year old, and he's gray with black stripes."

"I see. He sounds like a nice cat."

"'My mom gave him to me. Do you know where he might be?"

"Well, that's a little hard to say," I said with a grin. "Tell me, what's your name?"

"Michael Cunningham. He's been gone four days. He went out after dinner, and now I can't find him."

"I see. Mike, could I talk to your mom for a minute?"

"My mom?" He hesitated. "She's . . . why do you want to talk to her?"

"Oh, that's just one of my policies," I replied.

I heard him put the phone down. I've learned in this business, whenever kids call me, to make sure I talk to their parents first and let them know what's going on, since they're usually the ones that control the family purse strings.

I could hear voices in the background, first Mike's and then a man's. It sounded like they were having an argument. In a minute the man came to the phone.

"I'm Mike's father," he said. "I'm sorry if he's bothered you."

"No bother," I replied, "I just wanted to make sure you knew what he was—"

"Look, I can't talk now. I'm already late for my other job. I told Mike not to call you." He sounded harassed.

"That's OK," I said. "I won't keep you. Maybe I could talk to your wife."

"My wife?" he said brusquely. "You can't talk to my wife. She's passed away. Look, I've got to get going. We already put an ad in the paper. I told Mike we couldn't afford anything else, but ever since he saw you on television that's all he's been talking about."

"I understand," I said. "Could I talk to Mike again? Maybe I could just give him a few little tips."

"You can talk to him all night if you want to," he replied impatiently, "but I've got to pick up my cab and get to work. Just make sure it doesn't cost me anything. That kid's pestering the daylights out of me over that damned cat. It's not normal, if you ask me."

"Well, kids get attached to their pets," I said. "Especially since his mom gave him Sam, he's probably—"

"That's just it," he replied. "When she died, he was a regular little soldier—no crying, nothing. I was real proud of him. It's been almost six months now, and he's been doing fine—until this business with the cat. It's just not normal, and I told him. Look, I've got to go. Maybe you can talk some sense into his head."

It sounded like Mike needed more than a few little tips. When he got back on the phone, I asked him where he lived. "That's good," I said. "It just so happens I'm going to be in that neighborhood tomorrow morning. Why don't I stop by and we can talk some more about Sam?"

"OK," he said eagerly. "And about what my dad said. . . . Well, I've got some money saved up, almost twelve dollars. Is that enough?"

In my career people have offered me hundreds and even thousands of dollars to find their missing pets, but no one had ever promised me everything he had. "Let's talk about that tomorrow," I told him. "I'll see you about ten o'clock."

Michael and his father lived in the bottom half of a house in a mixed-bag neighborhood in the western part of San Francisco. Some of the houses had been restored to their former Victorian grandeur; others, like the Cunninghams', showed the neglect that comes with tenants who have better things to do than put time and money into maintaining other people's property.

Mike answered the door. He was a small, dark-haired kid, maybe ten years old, with pale skin and big brown eyes. He had the look of an altar boy. The inside of the house was neat enough, but it smelled dusty, as if it hadn't had a good cleaning in months.

It wasn't hard to put the picture together: mother recently dead, father working at two jobs, and Mike on his own most of the time. Sam had been given to him by his mother. No wonder the kid was so anxious to get him back, even to the point of driving his father crazy, whatever that meant. His father hadn't really sounded like a bad guy over the phone, just frantic from trying to keep his head above water and provide a home for his son. He was probably still too emotionally fragile himself to deal with Mike's feelings about Sam. Fortunately, I'd had a good month, because I could see this was a case I was going to have to take, money or no money.

"OK, Mike," I said. "I've checked my schedule and it looks like I'm going to have some time to help you find Sam."

"Oh boy," he replied, eyes lighting up. "Do you think we'll find him today?"

"Not so fast, my friend," I said. "First we've got some work to do." I took out a blank poster from my briefcase. In response to my question, Mike told me Sam hadn't been wearing a collar, but he did have a distinguishing feature—a white spot under his chest, between his two front legs.

"It looks just like an egg," he said.

"Then that's what we'll put on the poster. See?" He watched with wide-eyed fascination as I printed the words. I explained about putting up posters and checking the animal shelters. "And then we wait and see what turns up," I said, walking to the door. "I'll let you know as soon as I hear anything."

I could tell he was disappointed. Like a lot of kids, he was sure Sherlock Bones had magical powers. "But how long before we get him back?" he asked.

"Well, it might take some time," I said. "And I can't make any promises. You can understand that, can't you?"

"I guess so," he said hesitantly.

He looked so forlorn standing in the doorway I said, "Hey, Mike, I tell you what. Would you like to come with me today? Maybe you could be my assistant, and then I could give you a reduced rate."

He jumped at the chance, and we spent the rest of the day together. By six o'clock we had visited the animal shelters—with no luck—and begun the task of putting up posters in his neighborhood. I enjoyed having him with me. Mike was a very intense ten-year-old who was being pushed by circumstances to grow up faster than he was ready to. Losing first his mother and now his pet was more than most boys his age had to go through. Perhaps that's why he kept his feelings to himself. Had he let them out, they might have overwhelmed him. I knew he cared. For a boy to call me up against his father's wishes and then spend the entire day in what was not very exciting work meant he cared a lot. I wished there were some way I could help him open up, but the most I could do was show him that I took his feelings seriously. It's tough enough, after all, to lose someone close to you without also being told it's not normal to feel bad.

By six o'clock we had grabbed a quick bite to eat and were back in front of his house. A couple of times during the afternoon I'd tried to steer the conversation around to his mother, but he had avoided it. The most he told me was that she had gotten sick and spent a lot of time in hospitals. Before she had gone in for the last time she had given him a kitten and told him to take good care of it. "I'll bet you miss your mom, don't you?" I asked as we sat together in the van.

"Yeah," he said quickly, looking out the window. "Dad's car is here. I gotta go now. See you." Before I could say anything else he raced for the house.

Now that was pretty ham-handed, I thought to myself as I headed back to Oakland. Better leave therapy to the therapists and concentrate on getting Sam back. That would be the best therapy possible, anyway.

I hoped Mike didn't have yet another loss in store for him, but I wasn't very optimistic. Cats are much harder to find than dogs. They tend to hide out and avoid people, and therefore you don't get many good leads—lots of false alarms, but not much solid information. Often cats will revert to a semi-wild state, living on garbage and scraps they scavenge at the edges of settled areas

—if they live, that is. Many are hit by cars, and many others perish in boxes, closets, sheds, and garages they find their way into and then can't get out of, often because someone unwittingly locks them in. No one had answered the ad in the paper. The most optimistic conclusion I could draw was that Sam had been found by someone who wasn't eager to give him back.

When I got home there were several messages from my service about cats people thought might be Sam. One woman said she had spotted a cat matching Sam's description about five blocks from the Cunninghams' house. Someone else reported seeing a cat in the same vicinity—probably the same cat, I thought, but not necessarily Sam. There were the usual calls from people who see the poster, don't read any further than "lost cat," and call in to report any stray animal they happen to see, whether it matches the description or not.

The next day I checked out the leads and finished putting up the posters. I'd left Mike at home, since I didn't want to get his hopes up with all the wild-goose chases I anticipated. Shortly after noon I was putting up a poster in the window of a smallish supermarket when I noticed it had an honest-to-goodness meat counter—the old-fashioned kind with a butcher who waits on customers instead of standing behind a glass panel wrapping squares of ground beef in plastic. When I was a kid, our butcher knew the name of every pet in our neighborhood, so I took a little ticket from the machine and waited for my number to come up.

"Excuse me," I said when it was my turn, "have you heard of anyone finding a cat recently? Gray with black stripes, white spot on its chest?"

"A cat?" the butcher repeated. He was a heavy guy with gray hair parted in the middle and an apron tied so high it was almost under his arms. "No. No cat. I hear more about dogs, you know. People come in for dog bones. Can't recall anything about a cat. You lose one?"

I handed him a poster and explained who I was.

He read it and laughed. "Sorry, Sherlock, can't help you. But if I hear of anything, I'll—say, have you talked to the cat lady?"

"The cat lady?"

"Well, that's what we call her. Old English gal, comes in once a week and loads up on fish scraps and bones. Says she boils them down for her cats. She's real nice, but I don't think she's playing with a full deck, if you know what I mean."

"Do you by any chance know her name?"

"No, but she'll be in later this week. I can give her one of your posters, if you like. She must live around here. She's always complaining about having trouble walking to the store. Seems to me she's got a limp."

"I guess it's worth a poster," I said, handing him one. "Thanks for the tip."

"I should tell you one more thing, though," he cautioned. "Lots of old people come in here asking for food for their pets, but they're really buying it for themselves. It's all they can afford, you see, but they're too proud to admit it."

"You mean she might not have any cats?"

"Well, let me put it this way. With the amount she buys, either she eats like a horse or she's got a houseful of cats. And I mean a houseful."

Sometime that afternoon I was driving along a street when a couple of cats caught my eye halfway down a street off to my left. Thinking one of them might be Sam, I turned off to get a closer look. Even without getting out of my van I could see the markings were all wrong. But then I spotted another cat, and another, and another, lounging in various graceful feline poses in the front yard and up the front steps. Could I have been lucky enough to have found the cat lady's house?

There was only one way to find out, so I parked the van, walked up the front steps, and rang the doorbell. No one answered. I walked back down the steps and looked up to see if anyone was home. It was a ramshackle old house with at least two stories, of a color that had probably once been white but now was a mottled gray. Thick vines had overtaken most of the first floor and appeared to bear much of the responsibility for keeping the house upright.

I was just about ready to give up when the door opened a crack, and from behind the safety chain stretched across the narrow opening a voice called out in a strong English accent, "Yes, ducks, what is it?"

"Excuse me, ma'am," I said, dashing back up the steps, "I'm—"

"Speak up, luv. Can't hear ya."

I handed her one of my cards, which she scrutinized closely. "Bones?" she said. "You've got it wrong, dear. It's Holmes. Sherlock Holmes."

"No, ma'am," I shouted. "That's my business name. I help people find missing pets."

"Do ya, now?" she said amiably. "My, that's unusual, ain't it?"

"Yes, ma'am," I shouted, feeling my frustration level rise, "I suppose it is. The reason I'm here is—"

"Well," she pronounced, as if I hadn't spoken, "don't stand on the doorstep. Come on in and have a cuppa tea." With that she started to close the door in order to unfasten the chain. Then she stopped and, fixing me with a beady eye, said, "Here now, ya wouldn't be the law, would ya?"

"No, ma'am, I'm not."

She took another squint at me and, apparently reassured, opened the door. "Well come on along, then," she said. "I just put the kettle on the cooker." She turned and walked toward the back of the house. I noticed she had a definite limp. "And mind me moggies," she warned.

I had no sooner stepped into the house than unassailable olfactory evidence of cat hit my nose. Then I saw. On the stairs, on the table, on the floor, on the chairs, going about their business in the corners, scampering out of my way, walking stiff-legged, crouching watchfully, languidly lounging—there were cats everywhere. The butcher was right. She literally had a houseful. No wonder she had been afraid I was the law. In the city of San Francisco you are allowed to have four small animals, and although this ordinance is not enforced unless neighbors complain or unsanitary conditions appear to exist, this woman clearly had good reason to be wary. Given the number of cats, the house didn't smell as bad as it might have, but there was no getting around the fact that she was way over the legal limit.

She led me into the kitchen, a large room in the back of the house designed in the days when kitchens were for servants who kept out of sight and not for mothers who run busy households and cook at the same time. Against one wall was a stove, with a kettle and an enormous pot cooking away. On the other side of the room was a long counter with glass cabinets that reached up to the high ceiling. In the center stood a large wooden table and two chairs. Every available surface was covered with bottles, cans, old magazines—and more cats. The overall effect was one of an incredibly cluttered but cozy lair.

"Have a seat, luv," she said. "I'm Mrs. Bentwhistle, and I'm goin' to make us a nice cuppa."

"My," I said, unable to avoid commenting on the obvious, "you certainly have a lot of cats."

"You like me moggies, do ya?" she said with a bright smile.

"Moggies?"

"That's right, moggies. Me mum come from Lancashire, and that's what she called 'em, and so do I. Now where's me tin of tea?" I watched as she rummaged through the jars and cans on the table. She was a short, wide woman somewhere in her late sixties, I judged. Over a faded housedress with an uneven hem she wore a man's cardigan sweater that she tugged across her ample bosom from time to time. On her feet were old house slippers and white socks. Her gray hair was caught in the back with a couple of combs in loose approximation of a hairdo she had probably affected when she was much younger and had never bothered to change. Bright pink lipstick and rouge, enthusiastically if errati-cally applied, kept her from fitting my image of a grandmother. In fact, despite her appearance, there was something decidedly youthful about Mrs. Bentwhistle.

"There you are," she said to the tin of tea she had been looking for, and began the ceremony. First she warmed the teapot with hot water from the kettle, which she then threw out into the sink. With a metal scoop she carefully measured out the tea— "One, two, and one for the pot"—and added more boiling water from the kettle. She gave the pot a good stir with a spoon, set the lid on, and put it aside. "There, let that stew for a bit," she said to herself. She took two mugs from the cupboard and without asking put milk and sugar in both, poured in the tea, and handed me mine. "Now that's a proper cuppa English tea," she pronounced as she settled herself into the chair.

The liquid inside the mug looked black. I took a sip and almost gagged. It was both sweet and strong, and I was sure the proverbial spoon would easily have stood upright in the pungent brew.

"How do ya like it, then?" she asked brightly.

"Oh," I replied weakly. "It's . . . tasty. Very unusual."

"Nothin' like it," she agreed, taking a good swallow. Fortified by her brew, she fixed her attention on me for the first time since I had gotten there. "Now then," she said, "what can we do for ya, luv? It's lost pets ya find, is that it?"

"That's right. Right now I'm looking for a cat who belongs to a young boy."

"Is that so? And what kinda moggy would that be?"

"A gray with black stripes and—"

"Gaw!" she exclaimed, "I got millions of 'em."

"This one had an egg-shaped white spot on his chest. He was lost about four days ago. I thought perhaps you might have seen him."

"Let me think," she said, narrowing her eyes. "A striped moggy . . . I did pick up a coupla moggies a time ago. Weren't no striped one, though. Gaw! You shoulda seen 'em, poor little devils. Thin and dirty and fulla fleas, they was. You could tell they was strays. I don't know why people have these moggies when they don't care for 'em proper. It's not bloomin' right, it's not."

"But none that might be the one I'm looking for?"

"No . . . Wait a minute, wait a minute, I did pick up a striped moggy, but I don't mind exactly when. I think he took off up the stairs when I brung him home. Why don't ya go up and have yourself a look?"

I started to rise.

"Here," she said sternly, "you'll not move from that chair till you finish your tea. The moggies'll wait."

"Well," I replied, looking at my watch, "I really don't have too much time."

"Suit yourself," she said, heaving herself up and shuffling to the stove. "It's almost feedin' time anyway." She lifted the lid on the enormous pot and a terrible aroma escaped. "Food for me moggies," she said. "Bones and fish heads and lovely potatoes. I feed 'em well, I do. Well, go on now. I ain't comin' with you, ducks, because of me bum leg. Mind the steps now, and don't hold on the banister. It's none too sturdy, not any more it ain't."

I carved a path through the cats and carefully picked my way up the stairs, where I found what appeared to be a totally different feline population. I started after the ones that looked like Sam, picked them up and turned them over to find the egg-shaped spot. It took a long time; I had no way to separate out the ones I'd already inspected. Besides, some were less willing to be handled than others. What I needed, I decided, was a pair of gloves to protect my hands.

I was on my way downstairs to find some when the noise began—a dull clanging sound that grew louder and louder. It was Mrs. Bentwhistle banging on a pot with what sounded like a metal spoon.

"Here, you moggies, come on, grub's up," she yelled.

At the first sound the cats upstairs moved en masse for the first floor, running and diving around my feet on their way to their food. The stairs were alive with furry bodies. I hugged the wall and picked my way down, trying to remember which were the treacherous steps. One false move, and I was afraid I might fall through to the basement.

When I got to the kitchen, Mrs. Bentwhistle was ladling the foul-smelling brew into two large sheet-metal troughs, and the cats were frantically lapping it up. Within five minutes the food was gone and so were the cats, retired to parts unknown to clean up and take an after-dinner snooze.

"There," she said with satisfaction, "that's over for another day."

"I didn't know cats ate so fast," I said.

"Oh, my yes, ducks. Around here they've got to, haven't they? Did ya find the one ya were lookin' for, then?"

"I'm afraid I didn't," I said. I explained about Mike, and his mother's giving him Sam right before she died. "He was very brave," I said, "at least his father thinks so. I think he was a little too brave."

"Oh, it's a shame, a crying shame," Mrs. Bentwhistle said sympathetically. "And he's only ten, did you say?" She shook her head sadly. "Here, why don't ya come back tomorrow and have another look? Sam might turn up by then. I get new ones every day. They come in the windows, ya know. I call 'em me moggies, but they could be anybody's. Come tomorrow then, and I'll fix ya a cuppa that tea ya took such a fancy to, and a lovely cucumber sandwich besides."

"You've got a deal," I said. "Is there anything I can pick up for you?"

"Not a bloomin' thing, luv," she said. " 'Course, if you'd like to make a small contribution for me moggies' food, I wouldn't turn it down."

I took out my wallet and gave her a five-dollar bill.

"Oh, isn't that grand of ya, lad," she said. "Now I can buy the moggies a treat." She folded the money, stuffed it down the front of her dress, and gave a little wiggle. "There now," she said with a wink, "safe as the old Bank of England, ain't it?"

By the time I got to Mrs. Bentwhistle's the next day, I was almost looking forward to a cup of her tea. I had gotten many more reports on Sam, but none had proved out, and I was fast becoming frustrated and discouraged. This time I'd brought an old pair of gloves, but after half an hour I'd checked every gray-and-black-striped "moggy" I could get my hands on and still hadn't found Sam. Once again I joined Mrs. Bentwhistle at the table and watched as she went through the ritual of the tea.

"Tell me, Mrs. Bentwhistle," I said, "have you always had so many cats?"

"Oh no, ducks." She laughed. "Me Ernie wouldn't have put up with 'em, not at all. 'Course, he's been gone now almost ten years, rest his soul. Oh no, Ernie with all me moggies? But I just can't see havin' 'em all killed, though. That's what they do, ya know, just blow 'em up, so there's nothin' to be done but take 'em in, is there? Here now, eat your cucumber sandwich I just made, all lovely and refreshing. Keeps your bowels in an uproar, it will. That's what me mum said, and it's true."

The sandwich was delicious, and even though I knew I should be getting back to work, I found myself lingering at Mrs. Bentwhistle's kitchen table. The more I got to know her, the better I liked her. Behind her eccentric facade was a warm, rather shy woman whose existence was now bound up in her "moggies" but who had once led a very different life. She and her husband had come to this country toward the end of World War II from the bombed-out part of East London where they had made their home.

"Them was terrible days, terrible," she said solemnly. "We had nothin' but the bloody clothes on our backs. Thank the Lord me cousin was here to sponsor us, like, and get Ernie a job with the old Cunard Lines. They're gone now, too." She sighed, lost in momentary reverie. "Still, I can't complain. We had a good life here, Ernie and me, a good life. Do miss the pubs, though, miss the pubs, and the beer's not the same as back home. Gives you the gas, it does. And too bleedin' cold. Still, now I've got me moggies to look after. Life goes on, ain't that right? And poor Mikey. It's a shame, ain't it, all these moggies, and none of 'em Sam? What're ya gonna do?"

"I guess I'll get back to work," I said, and with her permission called in for messages. One message hit me in the pit of my stomach. Someone had seen the body of a cat matching Sam's description right down to the egg-shaped spot on his chest. It was lying in some bushes not far from Mike's house, where it was just beginning to decompose. The person calling in had said the cat looked as if it had been hit by a car. Some sixth sense told me this was Sam.

I hung up and told Mrs. Bentwhistle I was afraid I had come to the end of my search. "I've got to check, of course, to be sure," I said. "If it's Sam, I don't know what Mike will do. He's got it in his head he's supposed to be brave, but I know he's not ready for this."

"Oh, the poor lad," she said, shaking her head sadly. "It just don't seem right. Well, off you go, then, and do what you must."

I moved toward the door.

"Here," she said suddenly, "wait just a minute." She disappeared back down the hall and emerged with a shoe box. "If it's Mikey's moggy, you'll need somethin' to bury it in proper-like."

I found the cat in the bushes just where I had been told to look, and its markings matched Sam's exactly. Using my pair of gloves, I gingerly placed the body in the shoe box, doing my best to make it look as natural as possible. With a heavy heart I drove to Mike's house, hoping his father would be there to help me break the news.

Mike answered the door. "Hi," he said eagerly. "Did you find Sam?"

"Hi, Mike," I replied carefully. "Is your father home?"

"No, not till dinnertime."

"Oh," I said, trying to sound casual. "Well, maybe I'll come back then."

"Why?" His face had assumed a set expression, and I suddenly had the distinct impression he knew why I had come.

"Well, I wanted to . . . look, Mike, I'm afraid I have some bad news for you." Mike just stared at me. "It's Sam. I think he may have been hit by a car. He's dead, Mike."

"Where is he?" he asked. His expression hadn't changed, but the blood had drained from his face.

"Out in the van," I replied.

Before I could stop him he ran down the steps. He was opening the door when I grabbed him.

"He doesn't look too good, Mike. Are you sure you want to see him? Are you sure you wouldn't rather have me bury him for you?"

"No," he said with a firm voice, "I want to see him."

I took the shoe box and lifted up a corner of the lid, just enough so he could see the body inside. He looked in, grabbed the box, and started for the house.

"Wait a minute," I shouted, catching up with him and taking hold of his arm. "Why don't we bury Sam together? This is a bad time to be by yourself, don't you think?" He stood in front of me, saying nothing. "Why don't you get the shovel," I said, gently removing the box from his hands, "and we'll bury him right here by the front steps."

Mike said nothing as we went about laying Sam to rest. I was worried. He had been too quiet, too controlled. I didn't want to leave him by himself until his father came home, and even then I didn't know how sympathetic his father would be. What Mike needed now I didn't think either his father or I could provide. Then I thought of something.

"Tell you what, Mike," I said, "there's an awful nice lady not far from here. I was telling her about you and Sam. She's got quite a few cats of her own. How's about we pay her a visit?"

"I don't know," he said evasively. "I should wait for my dad."

"Come on," I insisted. "It won't take long. You don't want to be all alone now, do you?"

"Yeah, OK," he replied passively, and without another word he walked to the van and slid into the passenger seat. It was a heavy, silent ride. I didn't know what to say. Idle chitchat was out of the question, yet anything else seemed too explosive. Nor did I know exactly why I was taking him to Mrs. Bentwhistle's, unless it was to buy some time. She'd been open with me, but I knew she was a reclusive woman, and I couldn't predict how she would react to Mike, or he to her.

"Mrs. Bentwhistle," I said quickly when she answered the

door, "I hope it's all right. I brought Mike with me. We just buried Sam."

"Come in, come in," she said in the same absentminded tone she'd used when I'd first visited her. "I've got me kettle on the cooker. You're just in time for a lovely cuppa tea."

I watched Mike's face carefully as he took in Mrs. Bentwhistle's cats, searching for some reaction. If he had any, he hid it well. While she went about preparing the tea, I tried to signal to her silently that Mike was in pretty bad shape, but she continued to bustle around, and I couldn't tell if she had caught my message or not.

"Now you just sit in that chair, Mikey," she said, "and I'll get the tea, and we'll have a lovely chat."

As soon as he sat down, a small black cat jumped up on his lap, and he stroked it mechanically. I stood off to one side next to the door and wondered what was going to happen.

"Now then," she said affably, passing out the tea and settling into her chair, "you lost your moggy, is that it?"

"That's what Mrs. Bentwhistle calls cats, Mike," I explained.

"Yes," he said in a frighteningly matter-of-fact tone. "He was hit by a car."

"Ain't that a shame, just a shame." She sighed, sipping her tea and shaking her head. "Somethin' ya love done in like that. It's not fair, is it? Not fair at all." Mike wasn't saying anything, but Mrs. Bentwhistle appeared not to notice. " 'Course, it's all part of life, ain't it? Drink your tea, lad, there's nothin' like a cuppa tea when you're feelin' down in the dumps."

Mike took a sip, betraying no reaction except for a quick glance in my direction.

"And to think your mum gave Sam to you, God rest her soul. And now they're both—ya know, lad, it reminds me of me own mum."

Mike looked up from the cat.

"Oh yes, I had a mum, too, and right before she died she gave me a set of dishes. Beautiful blue dishes, they was, me pride and joy, and I kept 'em in the front room where everyone could see 'em. Well, wouldn't you know, one afternoon while we was out, one of Hitler's bleedin' buzz bombs up and smashed half the house. But all I cared about was them dishes. I just felt so bad, because me mum give 'em to me."

Mike had stopped stroking the cat.

" 'Course it wasn't me fault," she continued, "but I still felt bad. It's a bit like you and Sam, ain't it, your mum givin' him to you and all, and now he's been done in. Weren't your fault neither, now were it? Your mum knows that, wherever she is, just like me mum does. Ain't that right, Sherlock?"

"That's right, Mike," I said. At some point, I'd stopped worrying about what would happen. Like Mike, I was totally caught up in Mrs. Bentwhistle's story. This old woman, who the butcher said wasn't playing with a full deck, knew exactly what she was doing.

"Yes, and your mum still loves you, just like me mum loves me," she said softly. "Well, that's enough about me. Can't hang your hat on the past, as ya might say. It's you what's in a pickle now, ain't that right?"

"I'm OK," he said stiffly.

"Well, of course you are, lad," she agreed. "But I was just lookin' at the moggy on your lap. Thinks you're real special-like, he does. Now, I was just thinkin'." She paused for a moment, looked at me, and then said, "How would you like to have him? 'Course he's not the same as your Sam, but he's a nice moggy."

Mike didn't say anything.

"Come on now, lad," she insisted. "Do you want him, then?"

Mike shook his head vehemently. "I don't want him," he said, his voice breaking. "I want Sam!"

The black cat jumped off his lap, and Mike bolted for the door. I moved to intercept him, but he eluded my grasp and ran down the hall toward the back of the house. I started after him, but Mrs. Bentwhistle stopped me.

"Leave him be," she said. "He can't go nowhere. There's

just the pantry, and the back door's nailed shut."

"I guess it's a little too soon for him to think about getting another cat," I said. I could hear Mike sobbing. I was surprised by the insistence of her offer; she had seemed so tuned in to his feelings.

"'Course it is," she replied firmly, "but he's got to get it out somehow, ain't that right? It's just not natural to be so stiff-like, not when your moggy's been done in, not when it's such a special moggy. Just listen to him. He's crying his heart out."

"I know," I said. "Shouldn't we do something?"

"All in good time," she said. "He needs a good cry, he does, and he won't cry if we're there, now will he? You just sit here and drink your tea, and in a bit I'll go see how he is. Lads has got to be on their ownsome when they cry. Oh yes, it's not just moggies I know about. I know a thing or two about lads as well."

Before I could respond, Mrs. Bentwhistle got up, passed her hand over her face as if to close off a subject she hadn't meant to bring up, and with her cup of tea limped down the back hall. In a few moments Mike's sobs had subsided, and all I could hear was Mrs. Bentwhistle's low voice.

After what seemed a long time they reappeared, Mike red-eyed and spent, Mrs. Bentwhistle with her arm around his shoulder.

"Here now," she said briskly. "Who's for another cuppa? Sherlock, you ain't touched a drop. Must be all the carrying on."

I saw Mike glance at me and almost smile. "You know what?" he said. "Mrs. Bentwhistle told me I can come over and help her feed the cats whenever I want to."

"Here now," she said, not unkindly, "can't have you underfoot all the time. Still, I could use a lad to help with the moggies. An assistant, as you might say."

"I think that's a fine idea," I said. I wondered what it was Mrs. Bentwhistle had said to Mike in the pantry. Whatever it was, it had totally transformed him from an unhappy, bottled-up person into a regular little boy who no longer seemed to be carrying a too-heavy burden on his young shoulders. In fact, now it was Mrs. Bentwhistle who seemed shy and rather uncomfortable.

"Sherlock," Mike said, "did you know Mrs. Bentwhistle had a little boy once? He got killed in the war."

"Hush now," she interrupted quickly. "Sherlock don't want to hear about that. You go along now, Sherlock. Mikey and me's got to feed the moggies. He can get himself home."

I excused myself as quickly as I could. It was clear that, whatever the nature of the bond that had sprung up so quickly between them, there was no room at the moment for a third person. I drove home with my head full of awe at the unseen forces that had taken the tragedy of a boy's dead pet and used it to bring two lonely people together at a time when each needed the other. Who could have predicted that an eccentric, reclusive "cat lady" would be the one to break through a young boy's grief-impacted facade of bravery, or that he would strike a long-buried maternal chord within her?

In the next few weeks I forced myself to stay away and give them the privacy they needed to get acquainted with each other —and with the fragile parts of themselves they had revealed that afternoon in the pantry. I thought about them frequently, though, and wondered how they were getting on. One afternoon when I thought enough time had passed, I gave Mrs. Bentwhistle a call.

"How's everything?" I asked.

"Couldn't be better, luv," she replied cheerily. "Mikey's a lovely lad, just lovely. He helps with the moggies and goin' to the store. Don't know what I did without him. Oh, and he took that little black moggy home with him." She laughed. "He said it was just for a bit, but he don't fool me, not at all. He's a stubborn one, he is."

"Mike stubborn?" I said. "He never seemed stubborn to me."

"Oh yes!" she exclaimed. "He won't drink me tea! Me good English tea! Did ya ever hear the like? But don't you worry, he'll come round. We'll make a proper lad of him yet, just you see."

5
Notes from a
Pet Detective's Journal
(I)

IT COULD ONLY HAPPEN in Berkeley. Yesterday was designated "Dog Day" by the city's health department. They swept the streets to impound strays. It was a large-scale effort, complete with a mobile unit announcing the sale of dog licenses, information on leash laws, and animal health services. Result: five collarless strays impounded and nine citations to owners with leashless or unlicensed dogs. Thanks to an article in the paper, Berkeley's army of dogs laid low for the day, either at home or on the university lawns, where they seem to know they are safe from the city dogcatcher's net. One woman called in to protest "this repressive political move." It's all well and good to support pet liberation, but the situation really isn't funny. The streets of Berkeley are overrun with dogs, especially in the summer. Many are pets of university students who simply abandon them when they go home for summer vacation.

Yesterday's case takes the cake. I stop by this house in Berkeley to talk to a woman who wants me to help find her male basset hound. She sounded very British on the phone, and the house was right in character—charming stone cottage, windows with lots of little panes, and roses climbing the chimney. She and her husband are in their early fifties and fit my image of the upper-class British horsey set. He's wearing a ratty but well-cut tweed jacket, and she's got on a sweater and skirt and some very sensible shoes. We're having sherry in their living room, which is full of antiques and expensive-looking Persian rugs, and I'm asking if their dog—whose name is Boris—has any distinguishing features.

"Why, no," the woman says, "none that I can think of, can you, dear?"

Her husband hems and haws and finally says, "Well, now that you mention it, I believe he does. He has . . . well, he has a rather large member. Quite extraordinary, actually."

"Member?" his wife says. "Penis, do you mean?"

"Um," responds the husband, giving her this funny look.

"Do you really think so?" she says. "I never thought it was all that remarkable."

For once, I have the sense to keep my mouth shut. Thank God, she called this morning to say Boris wandered back home, so I'm saved from having to find a delicate way of wording a poster to mention Boris's generous endowment. As a matter of fact, bassets frequently do give that impression, because their legs are so short.

Heard a story from a vet that's hard to believe, but he swears it's true. A woman brought in her dog to be castrated. A week later another woman brought the same dog in, told him someone had had it castrated, and asked him to check to see if the operation was properly performed. He was afraid to tell her he did the job, but he checked the dog over, took the stitches out, and sent them both home. The next day the first woman came back with the dog, said that he must have chewed his stitches out, and asked the vet to examine him. He told her the whole story about the other woman. It turns out that the women live in the same neighborhood in houses that back up to each other. Each woman thought she was the dog's sole owner. One let the dog run during the day and locked it in at night, while the other kept it in during the day and let it roam at night. Apparently this arrangement had been going on for years, with neither woman knowing about the other.

I've heard similar stories about cats but never about dogs. Once a woman called me to say she had lost her cat. Three days later she called again, outraged. Her cat had come home, all right, but with a note fastened to its collar that read *Please stop feeding my cat.*

Passed a woman on the street today walking an enormously fat dog with skinny little legs and a blimplike torso. She was pretty hefty herself. Usually I wouldn't comment, but I couldn't resist telling her that hers was the fattest dog I had ever seen.

"Oh, I know," she said shamefacedly. "Isn't it just terrible? The vet has her on a diet, but you know what? I think she steals the cat food."

Lady, I felt like saying, unless you're feeding twenty cats, that dog is not getting fat on cat food alone. Maybe the dog has a sucker list of easy touches in the neighborhood, but my guess is both of them are dyed-in-the-wool refrigerator raiders. I'll bet her owner feeds her tidbits all day long, diet or no diet. It's unhealthy. Misguided love, that's what it is.

The wages of sin may be morning-after doggy breath in your face. A client called me first thing this morning. He'd left his door open for some very late visitors the night before, and Eric, his Doberman, had gotten out. Eric was attack-trained, so the guy was plenty worried, but, being a retired cop, he knew better than to ask the police for help. We decided on a reward of $150 and worked up a poster, and I sent him to a place that would print them while he waited. I told him to put them up around the bars in his neighborhood, since at that hour of the night that's where the action is.

This afternoon he called to say he got his dog back. "I was putting up posters," he said, "and passing them out to kids, as you suggested. This one kid takes a look at the poster and tells me his dad has the dog. So I follow him home, and there's his father. Now, it's about two in the afternoon, but the shades are all drawn and the guy looks like death warmed over—bloodshot eyes, sweating, pale, the whole bit. Seems he hit a few bars last night. And there's Eric, definitely looking anxious. So I thank the guy and start writing out a check for the reward. 'Never mind that,' he says. 'Just take your damn dog, will you? I'm in no shape to deal with a dog today. I didn't get home till four this morning, fell into bed, and the next thing I know it's light, there's hot, smelly breath in my face, and an enormous dog's staring at me about five inches away. He hasn't let me out of his sight all day. Every time I make a fast move he snarls at me.' He had no idea how he got Eric. He thinks maybe the dog got in his car at some point, but he doesn't really remember. I couldn't make him take the reward."

I really missed Paco last night. I took him to the vet to be wormed in the morning, then I got busy, and when I noticed the time it was too late to pick him up. So he had to spend the night at the vet's, and I had to spend the night alone here. When you live by yourself, you really notice a pet's absence. The place seemed empty without him.

Today I finally made friends with the cockatoo in the pet store. Every time I go there, I see this beautiful white cockatoo with a yellow crest, and for some reason it's become a challenge to make it like me. After several visits, it allowed me to scratch its head—birds really like that—but it would never let me hold it. I'd stick out my hand, but it wouldn't get on. Well, today it did, stared me right in the eye, and dropped a messy token of its affection directly on one of my newly polished shoes. Then it kissed me, a sweet little peck right on the lips. I'm not sure it was worth it.

6

Foiling a
"Good" Samaritan

IT WAS ONLY TUESDAY, but this was already shaping up as my week for attracting society's fringe element. It had started Monday morning.

"Mr. Bones," a voice on the phone said. "This is Malcolm Musgrave, and I have the feeling we're going to become very close business associates."

I'd never heard of the man, but I was definitely in the mood for some business, so I said, "Delighted to hear it. What did you have in mind?"

"As it happens," he replied, "I dabble in creative investments, and I have an idea I think can make us both a lot of money. With my business sense and your animal connections, in fact, it can't miss."

It didn't sound too promising but, with a quick glance at the stack of unpaid bills on my desk, I sighed and said, "I'm all ears."

"Very good," he said. "How shall I begin? Well, you know how these young male dogs get from time to time."

"Not exactly."

"Well, you know, they get excited. They grab onto your leg with their front paws and do this little dance with their rear end. Surely you know what I mean."

"Ah, yes," I replied, wondering a little at his coyness. "You're talking about the old mating urge."

"Exactly," he said. "Exactly so. The old mating urge. Very well put."

"I'm afraid I'm still not following you."

"Well," he continued, "you know how embarrassing that can be, especially to ladies. And frustrating to the dogs. So many people are having their female dogs spayed these days. Just imagine how you would feel with no female dogs around who were, how shall we say, interested."

"Oh, absolutely," I agreed. "I would feel terrible." He had so far said nothing to make me get my hopes up, but I couldn't resist stringing him along. "So, Malcolm," I said, since the nature of our conversation seemed to justify first names. "What's your plan?"

"My plan," he said proudly, "is to start a chain of places where owners can take these frustrated animals to meet lady dogs and satisfy their urges. For a decent fee, of course." The man seemed to be serious.

"Let me see if I understand you correctly," I replied, hardly able to contain myself. "You want to set up cathouses for dogs, is that right?"

Malcolm was not amused. "I'm perfectly serious," he replied testily. "I've checked it all out. They've developed chemicals for females that put them in the mood, so to speak. It's all perfectly harmless—even enjoyable, I dare say."

That was Monday morning. In the afternoon a lady called who wanted me to find her cat. I was in the process of taking down a description when she interrupted to say how happy she was to have me on the case, since she had missed her cat for so long.

"Exactly how long?" I asked, pencil poised.

"Let's see. It must be almost seven years now," she answered brightly. "But I always leave her window open and a dish of cat food out in case she comes back while I'm gone and wants something to eat."

It took me almost half an hour to disabuse the woman of the notion that I, or anyone else, would ever be able to find an animal missing for so long. I felt sorry for her, but the only suggestion I had to make was that she get another cat from among all the strays at an animal shelter. She decided that was a good idea, but I bet she never did anything about it.

When ten o'clock rolled around, I decided to call it a day and trust that tomorrow would be better. It had to be. Business had been slow lately and bills were piling up. I was in a deep sleep when the phone rang. It startled me into action and, without thinking about my answering service, I dashed into the living room and picked it up.

"Sherlock Bones," I mumbled.

"Bow wow!" a voice barked. "Rufff, rufff, rufff. Grrrr."

"What?"

"Meeoow. Pffft. Rufff, rufff, rufff." I could hear people laughing in the background and then the phone went dead.

Very funny, I thought, as I fell back into bed. The perfect end to a perfect day.

The next morning promised little improvement. Yesterday's thunderstorm had continued through the night, and now a light drizzle was falling. Water had soaked through the cracks in my apartment ceiling and had caused the paint to pull away in large flaps. They now hung down at rakish angles, as if on hinges, and were doing nothing to lift my spirits. Nor was the fact that I had run out of coffee. The quickest, easiest caffeine fix was the neighborhood Seven-Eleven so, donning a raincoat over my pajamas, I shuffled into my slippers and out the door—my eccentric attire totally puzzling Paco. Don't think for a minute that a dog doesn't know the correct outfit for every occasion.

I had bought a plastic cup of coffee and a paper and was picking my way back through the drizzle when the man who owned the local barbershop greeted me from his doorway.

"Good morning," he said.

I mumbled something noncommittal and continued down the block, clutching the collar of my raincoat.

"Just a minute," he yelled after me. "Can I have a word with you about the dogs?"

Aha, I thought, retracing my steps, here's a little business, maybe. I had never talked to the man before. Although I passed his shop twenty-five times a week, it was almost never open. I always wondered how he managed to make a living.

"I've been meaning to talk to you," he began, one foot up on a barber chair. He was an older man, slightly balding, with wire-rim glasses and piercing gray eyes. His face wore the look of someone who knows something you don't. "You're the pet guy, right? Just down the block?"

"That's right," I said.

"So. Have they raised your rent?"

"No," I answered, and for want of a better response added, "have they raised yours?"

"No, but they'd like to. I've got a lease, though, so they can't."

"That's good." I nodded. My coffee was getting cold, and I wanted to know why he had called me in. "What can I do for you?"

"They're commies, you know."

Oh no, I thought, another one. And so close to home. My hopes for any business from him fading, I took the bait. "Who are *they?*"

"The big oil companies," he said. "They own the whole block, you know. They're trying to squeeze out the small business-man." His voice had assumed a conspiratorial tone. He was almost whispering. "I thought you must know about them because of the dogs."

"The dogs?" This guy had it all figured out.

"That's right. Haven't you seen all the dogs around here?"

"Yes, but I can't see what they've got to do with raising my rent."

"That's funny," he said, moving in closer. "I was sure you would. It's the transmitters. I thought you'd know about them, since you work with animals."

My better judgment notwithstanding, I couldn't resist asking him what he was talking about.

Before answering he glanced over his shoulder. "They put them under the dogs' skin," he whispered. "At first they attached them to their collars, but people took them, so now they put them under the skin. They use them as spies to get the goods on us. You've got to do something about it. You work with animals. They wouldn't suspect anything."

Why me, Lord, I thought, why me? Promising him I'd do what I could, I backed out of his shop and headed for home.

"Say!" I heard him shout after me, "Aren't those pajamas you're wearing?"

"That's right," I yelled back. Wondering if that put me in league with the oil companies, I made it back home, exchanged my raincoat for a bathrobe, toweled off my hair, and settled down to lukewarm coffee.

Animals can bring out all sorts of hidden facets in people, and in my business I suppose I run into more than my fair share of cranks and crazies. Most of them are harmless enough. Many —like the lady and her long-lost cat—are quite pathetic, and some are just plain funny. Every once in a while, though, among the gently rolling loose screws, I come across people who can be malicious or dangerous, or both. Who can fathom their motives? Many feel powerless and take out their frustrations on creatures even more powerless than they. Others, I think, suffer from inner conflicts and obsessions that a particular situation involving an animal can trigger, setting them off on their own little holy war of vindication. It's all in the name of what's right, as far as they are concerned, but innocent pets and their owners often end up the victims of this misguided righteousness. These people are frequently difficult to deal with since, at first, they may seem perfectly rational—model citizens, even. It's only when you talk to them further that you realize they mean trouble.

I was going through the lost-and-found pet ads in the paper when Flo called.

"Good morning, Sherlock. Look here, don't you believe in calling in for your messages?"

"I've gotten all my calls," I countered defensively.

"Oh, yes? Then where were you last night at eleven?"

"Out with Linda Ronstadt." I didn't remember sleeping through a call, but it was possible.

"Linda who?"

"Never mind," I said. "What's up?"

"Oh, the singer lady. Sherlock, you devil, you." She probably believed me. "Well, anyway, some guy called who lost his dog yesterday, and he's got to go to a funeral in Chicago today and needs help. Isn't that just terrible? I knew you'd want to get on it right away."

She gave me his number, out in the Richmond district of San Francisco. I decided I'd feel more businesslike if I got dressed before I called him, so after a quick shower and shave I returned his call. The man was beside himself. His sister's son had been killed in an auto accident. She was falling apart and he was about to take the noon flight to Chicago to be with her. In the midst of all his final preparations last evening, his dog had escaped from his backyard. It was a ten-month-old Rhodesian ridgeback. A neighbor had spotted him tearing down the street. The man thought the thunder might have spooked him.

"He's just a pup," the man said, "but really a swell dog. I named him Oley, after Olympia beer. My girl friend and I have already taken him camping with us several times. He just loves it. Under any other circumstances I'd stay and hunt for him, but I just can't do it now. My vet recommended you, so I thought I'd phone on the chance you'd have the time to help me."

At last, I thought, a real case. Assuring him that, busy as I was, I could squeeze him in, I took all the necessary information, including the home and business numbers of his girl friend in case I found Oley before he got home. Ordinarily I like to be paid something in advance, but in this case that didn't seem feasible. There was something in the guy's voice, though, that made me trust him. Anyway, I didn't have much choice. Pickings were slim, and this was the only sensible prospect on the horizon.

Rhodesian ridgebacks are interesting dogs. They originated in South Africa, the result of crossbreeding between European hounds and mastiffs and half-wild African hunting dogs. They are large animals, with a glossy light-brown coat and a distinctive ridge of hair growing the wrong way up their spine which they inherited from their African ancestor. Except for this ridge, they look rather like a cross between a hound and a golden retriever. Although they are becoming more popular in this country, they are still far from common, and I felt that Oley would be a fairly easy dog to spot.

By the next morning I was busily at work putting up posters featuring a drawing of a ridgeback I had had copied from one of my dog books. Late in the afternoon I returned to my office, and the phone started to ring as I walked in.

"Hello, I'm calling about the dog you're looking for in the Richmond area." It was a woman's voice. She sounded fairly young, probably in her late twenties.

"Oh, yes," I answered. "Did you see the dog?"

"I'm sure I saw him yesterday, but he wouldn't come to me."

"Where was that?"

She mentioned a medium-sized supermarket I remembered seeing, although I hadn't checked it out yet.

"Are you sure it was a ridgeback?" I asked.

"Oh, yes," she said. "I didn't get a really good look, but I did notice that funny strip of hair. I thought at first there was something wrong with the dog."

I thanked her for calling and asked her to let me know if she saw him again.

"Sure," she said. "Oh, by the way, if I do see him again, it might be a help if I knew his name."

"It's Oley," I replied.

When I first started putting up posters, I always omitted the pet's name, on the theory that a potential petnapper would have greater control over an animal if he knew its name. But I was already beginning to wonder if it made much difference. In fact, knowing a frightened pet's name might help a concerned citizen gain its confidence and get it back to its owner.

Making a mental note to stop by that supermarket the next day, I called in for my messages. Flo was on duty.

"Listen, Sherlock, something funny happened just after lunch. A girl called in and wanted to talk to you about the ridgerunner."

"You mean the ridgeback."

"Whatever. You know, the funeral guy's dog. Don't give me a hard time."

"What's so funny about that?" I asked. "I could use a lead or two."

"I don't know. She sounded nervous, and she wouldn't leave her number. She wanted to know the dog's name, but I remembered what you told me, Sherlock, and I didn't give it to her."

"Well, if she calls again, try to get her number. Use your fatal charm."

I wondered if this was the same woman I had talked to. I saw no reason to mention it to Flo or to tell her I had given out Oley's name. I had had a hard enough time getting her not to give names out. Flo likes clear-cut, hard-and-fast rules, and I didn't want to confuse her with any possible changes until they were definite. I wished I had talked to Flo first, though, before I had talked to the young woman—assuming, of course, it was the same person. After all her years of dealing with faceless voices, Flo's an expert in picking up the meaning behind the message.

The next morning, about nine thirty, the phone rang. I recognized the voice of the young woman. "I'm calling about Oley," she began.

"Right," I said. "Did you ever see him again?"

She didn't answer me directly. "He was very dirty, you know, and very thin."

I explained that since he was just a puppy and hadn't yet grown into his bone structure, he probably would look thin. And as for being dirty, with the rain we'd been having that wouldn't be at all unusual. It was the same woman that Flo had talked to, I felt certain. Funny. This made her third call.

"I also wanted to ask you," she continued, not acknowledging my answer, "why he ran away from home."

I wanted to ask her what she was getting at, but decided it

would be best to deal with her questions first. "He didn't exactly," I said. "His owner thinks the thunder the other night scared him and he crawled under the backyard fence."

"The backyard?" she asked, her voice rising. "You mean he was left out in the rain?" Her voice had a hard edge. I started to explain about the funeral but stopped. Why was she asking me all these questions?

"Maybe you could tell me if you've seen Oley again," I said as evenly as I could.

"Not exactly."

"Not exactly? What does that mean?" I couldn't keep the anger and impatience from my voice. Nothing I could say seemed to be enough to satisfy her. She was asking questions but had no interest in the answers. "Do you have Oley now?" I asked.

"Why isn't the owner looking for Oley?"

I get it, lady. You think Oley's owner doesn't care about him. I explained about the funeral. "Look," I said, trying to be patient, "do you think he'd hire me to find his dog and offer a fifty-dollar reward if he didn't care about him?"

"I knew Oley's owner would be a man."

Uh-oh, I thought, with the same sinking feeling that had hit me two days before when the barber told me about the "commies." This could be a whole new ball game. "Does that make a difference?" I asked.

"I don't know," she replied. "All I know is that Oley doesn't want to run away from me."

So you do have him. "OK," I tempered. "Why don't you give me your address, and I'll drop around and we can talk about this further? Then I can give you the reward."

"I don't think that's a very good idea."

Careful, John, I thought, don't get her angry. She'll hang up, and you'll never find her again. "OK, tell you what," I said. "Why don't you give me your phone number and I'll have this guy's girl friend call you, and you can ask her if Oley is well taken care of."

"What makes you think I want to talk to some guy's girl friend? Besides, I don't give out my number."

"How about if I give you her number? Or arrange for you to call Chicago?" I didn't know what to say. Who could tell what emotional minefield I was walking on?

"I'll think about it. I've got to go now. We're not supposed to make personal calls at work."

Think about it?! What was there to think about? She had my client's dog and for some unknown reason was not about to give it back. But then why had she kept calling me? I wished we were face to face so I could get a better idea of what was going on in her head—and not have to worry about getting cut off. A telephone is the damnedest instrument. It can connect you with people halfway around the world, but if they choose to hang up, there is nothing you can do to stop them.

I decided to try another approach. "It sounds to me like you're really attached to Oley already," I said. "He must be a nice dog. His owner certainly thinks so."

"Forget it," she replied. "That stuff won't work."

"You're going to keep Oley, aren't you?" I asked quietly.

Her silence was my answer. Things were beginning to fall into place.

"And the whole reason for calling is to get me to justify your stealing my client's dog, isn't that it?" I was using harsh words, but I was angry. Besides, if she had enough moral qualms to call three times, there was an outside chance she might respond to some stern language. Realizing this was probably my last opportunity to reach her, I said, "If you're looking for a moral nail to hang your evil cloak on, you're not going to get it from me. What you're doing is wrong. You're breaking the law. Who are you to sit in judgment on someone else anyway? You don't even know the man. And what difference does it make if it's a man or a woman?"

"I don't know what you're talking about," she said sullenly. "Besides, there's nothing you can do about it."

That tore it. "Oh yes there is!" I shouted. "If you don't return my client's dog, I promise if it's the last thing I do I'll track you down and have you prosecuted for dognapping. I'll make a hobby out of finding you, and I really enjoy my hobbies. Do you understand what I'm saying?"

She hung up.

I was so furious I stood up and kicked the wastepaper basket across the room with a vicious clang that sent Paco scurrying out of range into the kitchen. She had really gotten to me, right where I live. How dare she set herself up as God and determine what is right and what is wrong? How dare she be so high-handed as to play out her personal problems with someone else's pet? By God, I thought, I *will* find her, if I have to walk every street in San Francisco to do it! If it took three years, I'd track her down!

I stormed around the room, and the more I stormed the more angry I became—angry and frustrated. I slammed my fist in my palm. She was right, dammit, there wasn't anything I could do. By overplaying my hand, I'd let her get away. I'd totally blown my professional detachment, and now I would pay for it. Forcing myself to cool off, I sat down and turned on the radio.

Paco heard the music and, thinking the coast might be clear, stuck his head out from the kitchen. I called him over and tried to make amends. Poor dog, my temper tantrums always make him think he did something wrong. No, Pac, I'm the one that goofed, I thought as I scratched his ears. He put his head in my lap and gave me one of his "now what?" looks. Now what, indeed? Unless I could come up with something brilliant, I'd have to throw in the towel. I hated having to disappoint Oley's owner, especially after everything he was going through, but I didn't see another choice.

Then I thought of something. If this was the same woman that had called before, she had found Oley at a supermarket. Hadn't she told me which one? Yes, she had, and I remembered just where it was, at the edge of the Richmond district not far from Oley's home. Maybe someone had seen her take the dog, or perhaps she had asked around about Oley before she took him in. Not much to go on, but it was worth a try, so with Paco in the van I tore off toward the Bay Bridge and San Francisco.

Anger can be a marvelously galvanizing emotion. By the

time I reached the bridge I had psyched myself into a state of mental alertness and total confidence. Since she had chosen to throw down the gauntlet, I was going to give the battle everything I had. This was the case in which Sherlock Bones would live up to his namesake's reputation or know the reason why.

I handed my money to the toll-taker.

"Out for a drive with your pillow, I see," he said, glancing at Paco.

But I had no time for trading witticisms, and with a perfunctory smile I put the van in gear and headed onto the bridge. Midway across the bridge, traffic came to a complete stop—there must have been an accident up ahead—but I barely gave it a second thought. That's when I knew I was riding high, because normally I suffer from stop-on-a-bridge-phobia. Have you ever noticed how a bridge moves up and down beneath you? I think it has something to do with the expansion factor. Whatever its engineering function, you can only feel it when you're stopped, and it usually throws me into a controlled panic. Thank God traffic doesn't back up often, or I'd never get across the bay, not without a boat.

I reached the supermarket about noon. It was set at a right angle to the road and opened onto a fairly large parking lot. Along the back of the lot there was a collection of smaller shops. I noticed a beauty parlor, a restaurant, and a seedy-looking real-estate office, but the woman had mentioned the supermarket so I started there. Inside were four or five checkout counters, each one with a long line. Not being the patient type, I approached a checker who was waiting while his customer wrote out a check. He was a young kid, about nineteen, with long blond hair and thick glasses. I pegged him as a student working his way through college. Had he seen this dog, I asked, showing him a poster, or had anyone asked about it? He shook his head and finished putting the customer's grocery bags in her cart.

She was somewhere in her late thirties, with a slightly pinched face and a tightly curled, rather severe hairdo a little like the Queen of England's. She was wearing a bright-yellow fuzzy sweater that seemed slightly at odds with the overall prim and proper impression she created. I watched her as she finished writing and made a complete entry in her checkbook. Her handwriting, I remember thinking, was just like my third-grade teacher's, a perfect example of the Palmer method.

"You know," she said, as she carefully closed her purse, "when my sister was over last night, she told me that her roommate had picked up a dog. I think she said it was a golden lab. Funny dog, though. There was something strange about the hair on its back." She moved to the grocery cart and began rearranging the bags that the checker had just arranged. "And wouldn't you know, she never even asked my sister if it was all right to—"

"Hey!" I shouted, interrupting her. Something strange about the hair on its back? It's Oley, I thought. What a stroke of luck! Without the slightest trace of doubt, I said, "Lady, that's the dog I'm talking about! Look at this poster! Isn't that him?"

She took a step back and clutched her purse a little more tightly. Her shopping cart was between us. "I wouldn't know," she replied. "I haven't actually seen the animal. I can't remember what she said. It could have been female."

"Look," I said, realizing I had upset her, "maybe she was mistaken. Maybe you heard her wrong. Why don't you give me your sister's phone number and I'll check it out."

She frosted over like a winter pumpkin. "Oh, I couldn't do that," she replied, pushing her cart toward the door. "I'll tell her about you, and perhaps she'll call you. I can't go around giving my sister's number to strangers, now can I?"

"I understand," I said, wishing she would stop for a minute. "But this is a special case. See, the dog's owner is in Chicago for a funeral, and he hired me to find his dog. I have reason to believe that the dog you mentioned may be his, and—"

"Now I've told you what I can do," she said sharply. "And that's all."

"I wish you'd reconsider," I said. "This is a special . . ."

It was futile. She was heading for the door as fast as she could without actually appearing to hurry. What could I do? Tackle her? I couldn't rely on the fact that her sister would call me. I'd tried that routine once today already. People always tell me they'll call, and they never do. I could see her making her way across the parking lot. I know, I thought, I'll follow her home and get her address.

My van was on the far side of the parking lot. I could see her loading her groceries into her car, a dark-green Volkswagen with a white convertible top. Doesn't seem like the convertible type, I thought, as I tried to avoid drawing attention to myself. Once in my van, I put the key in the ignition and turned it. Nothing. I knew instantly what had happened. I have a capricious starter, and whenever I forget that we're all at the mercy of fickle fate, it reminds me by not working. This was one of those times.

"Damn!" I shouted, and I pounded the steering wheel with both fists. I could see her car pulling out of its space and moving toward the exit. I jumped out of the van to give it a push, and then I thought of her license plate. "Dummy!" I screamed, and kicked the door of the van. That's what I should have gone after in the first place! I kicked the door again. Paco, this time with no place to run, flattened himself on the back seat and prepared for the worst.

But for the gathering crowd of noontime shoppers, I might still be in that parking lot, heaping abuse on my sorry excuse for transportation. Instead, I gave a mighty, adrenaline-fueled heave to get the van rolling, clambered in, popped the clutch, and heard the engine turn over. I careened into the street and tore after her. The only problem was I hadn't seen which way she turned, but I was too angry to let that stop me, so off I drove in mad pursuit, tilting around corners in a frenzied search for a green Volkswagen with a white convertible top.

After forty minutes of this lunacy, I had worked off my anger enough to realize that my Keystone-cops routine was a waste of time and gasoline. I headed back to the supermarket and checked the other shops I had seen, starting with the beauty parlor, traditionally a great underground source of everything unfit to print, but no one knew anything. Ditto the other establishments. I was slumped in the restaurant over a fast-food version of a hamburger, pondering on why I had ever thought I could solve this case, or any other, for that matter. Better I should go back to making my pound rounds and leave the harder stuff to the big boys.

There was a tap on my shoulder. It was the checker from the supermarket. "Hi," he said. "I see you've found our local gourmet's delight. Any luck finding your dog?"

"Not much," I answered. "Anyway, it's not mine. It belongs to one of my clients."

"You a lawyer?"

"No, as a matter of fact I'm a pet detective. Sherlock Bones." I handed him one of my cards. I wasn't impressing myself; maybe I could impress this kid.

"No kidding. What a great idea! I lost my dog once when I was a kid," he said, "but she came back by herself after three days."

He was full of questions about my business and about Oley. He was a nice boy, quick on the uptake and eager to let me know he wasn't your typical teenager. I could picture him as a seventh grader, concocting wild experiments with his chemistry set while the rest of his friends were playing baseball.

"By the way, that lady called the store," he said. "The one you were talking to."

"She did?" Maybe she had changed her mind. "What did she say?"

"I don't know exactly. She talked to the manager. He said she was all upset about being accosted. You know, like a single woman can't even go out of her house these days. I've seen her a few times before. She's a little weird, always giving me the fish-eye. I guess she thinks I'm padding her bill or something."

We sat quietly for a few moments, shaking our heads over weird women. I didn't know about him, but I seemed to have run into quite a few weird people of both sexes recently.

He looked up and started to say something, then changed his mind.

"What?" I prompted.

"Oh, nothing," he said. "You've probably already thought of it, but—well, I was just trying to remember. Didn't she pay by check?"

"Yeah," I said absently. "She did."

His face assumed the hesitant expression of one who was searching for some polite way of stating the obvious. "Well, wouldn't her check have her name and address on it?"

Oh boy, I thought, some detective I am. Scrambling to redeem myself in his eyes, I said, "Probably, but not necessarily. By the way, do you know where her check is?"

"Yeah, but it won't help you now. I turned in my drawer to the manager before I went to lunch. It's in his office now."

"Oh," I replied, trying not to appear too disappointed. "It's probably impossible to get to, isn't it?"

"Yeah, we're not supposed to go in there. And I don't think the manager would be too keen on letting you see it."

"That's for sure," I said. "Anyway, you must get lots of checks. How could we tell which one was hers?"

"That's true," he sighed. I sensed his disappointment in me. I was the expert, the one who was supposed to provide the answers, not the questions. "Of course, maybe he hasn't gotten around to going through my drawer yet. They'd still be in a bundle." He paused for a minute. "There were a lot of checks, though."

"Hold on!" I interjected. A slight whirring in my memory bank drew my attention back to the woman's appearance. What was it—her hairdo, the purse, the fuzzy sweater? Click. "It was yellow, a yellow check, the same color as the sweater she had on. That should narrow it down, shouldn't it?"

His faith totally restored, the boy's eyes lit up. Since he only had to look for the yellow checks, he said, he was sure he could slip into the manager's booth and get the information I wanted. I didn't want to be responsible for getting him in trouble, but he insisted on giving it a try. Feeling a little like Batman talking to Robin, I gave in.

"Give me an hour or so," he said, "and then come in and

stand around the dairy case, on the other side of the store from the manager's booth. I can't promise, but if you can spare the time from your other cases it might be worth waiting."

Oh kid, I thought, if you only knew. But why spoil youth's illusions?

We parted company outside the restaurant, and I went back to the van to let Paco run around and to gather what was left of my wits. This whole exercise, it occurred to me, could be a wild-goose chase. The woman had said there was something strange about the dog's hair. Who knows? Maybe it had mange. The fact that she thought it was female didn't bother me much, since she didn't seem too sure. But even assuming the dog was Oley, I was still at several removes from him. The woman in the yellow sweater had said it was her sister's roommate who had found a dog, so first I had to find the woman in yellow, then her sister, and then her sister's roommate. The links were tenuous. It was clear the woman in yellow was not about to give me any information. Simply showing my face would probably guarantee me a run-in with the police. No, I had to be a little more devious—and a lot more unemotional—if I wanted to trace the chain of people back to Oley. Up to now I had taken the challenge too personally, and as a result I was flying off in all directions at once. I had had a couple of fantastic breaks, and had already managed to blow one of them. I couldn't afford another slipup. "Don't work hard," they used to tell me in the insurance business, "work smart." From now on, that's what I would have to do.

An hour later I was standing in front of the dairy case, keeping my eyes peeled for anyone looking like a manager. I had read the list of ingredients on all the brands of cottage cheese and sour cream and was working my way into the cheeses when my young partner in covert data retrieval emerged from the back room.

"Sorry I'm late," he explained. "They've got me uncrating oranges."

"That's OK," I said. "How'd it go?"

"No sweat," he replied with a grin. "When I got back the manager was collaring a couple of guys who got light-fingered in the liquor department. While he was waiting for the cops, I snuck in the booth. The checks were right where I'd left them. Here's a list of the yellow ones."

I started to look at it but my friend, by now feeling very much a part of the team, warned sternly, "Better do that outside. Let's not push our luck."

"Right," I agreed solemnly. I pocketed the piece of paper and thanked him warmly.

"Hey," he replied self-consciously, embarrassed at my effusiveness, "it was fun. Beats uncrating oranges any day. I'd better go now. Good luck."

Thanking him again, I walked nonchalantly out of the store and then beat it to my van. There were five names on the list. Two were joint husband-and-wife accounts; the other three had women's names. Remembering her remark about single women, I zeroed in on them. According to my map, they were all in the neighborhood, so once again I sallied forth, but this time I had an itinerary.

I got lucky at the last address. It was a modest single-story Spanish bungalow, cream stucco with brown trim and set so close to the sidewalk that there was just enough room for four or five fastidiously pruned shrubs against the front wall. And right at the curb was the green Volkswagen convertible.

So Emma Cameron, according to my list, was the woman in the yellow sweater. But now what? As far as Emma Cameron was concerned, I was just one step short of being a mad rapist, and she wasn't about to tell me anything. My only hope seemed to be that her sister would visit her and lead me back to her house, her roommate, and Oley. It was a long shot, but I couldn't think of anything else to do. OK, John, I thought, it's stakeout time. I checked my watch—three o'clock. Assuming that the sister, like the roommate, worked somewhere, I decided I could wait until at least five o'clock before beginning my vigil. That gave me time to get a sandwich for me and some dog food for Paco.

But first I took down Emma Cameron's license number and, just to double-check, called it into my data-finding outfit. These are amazing information-gathering organizations I had recently discovered to be enormously useful in my line of work. Once you've established yourself as a customer, you can call in requests for all kinds of information about people, from their credit ratings to driving records. There was a time when I might have objected to this service as an invasion of privacy, but since the information they track down is open to the public I haven't hesitated to use them. Besides, they know just where the information is located and can find it fast. What I wanted from them was the name of the owner of the VW. They said they would check the Department of Motor Vehicles records and leave the name with my answering service.

Just before I returned to the house, I called in. Flo answered.

"Say, Sherlock," she said, "some guy said to tell you the car belongs to Emma Cameron. Does that make any sense to you?"

"Yeah, thanks. I wish it had been her sister's, though."

"What? Is this the ridgerunner case you're working on?"

"What else?" I responded. "Listen, I can't talk now. I might not be back till late tonight."

"Oh, another date with Linda what's-her-name?"

"You got it," I said. "Talk to you later."

By five thirty I was back in front of Emma Cameron's house, everything just as I had left it. Her car was still there, the curtains were still pulled over the big arched window in front, and I could see no signs of life. My guess that she led a quiet life proved a little too accurate, at least that night. I stayed until ten o'clock, but when the light behind the curtains clicked off and nothing had happened, I decided to call it quits.

The next day I returned at five o'clock and parked down the street under some trees I hoped would protect the van from the streetlight. Her car was in the same place, and the curtains were still drawn. About seven the light went on. Once again I waited.

Being on a stakeout is a strange experience—tedious, yet calling for constant vigilance. You've got to fight the temptation to drift off, but at the same time you can't do anything that might call attention to your presence. And of course, as in this case, you've got to sit there with the possibility that the whole exercise could be a waste of time.

As I waited, I turned over in my mind the assumptions I had made that brought me to this street: that her sister would visit her, that she would only visit in the evening, and, most critical, that the dog in question was Oley. Any one of them could have been wrong, and as the minutes dragged on I began to convince myself that all of them were. It's during times like these, when I'm full of doubt and feeling very much alone, that I'm grateful for Paco's unconditional love and trust. There's something about just his presence that calms me down. "Hang loose," he seems to say, "you're doing the best you can. We'll solve this case yet."

I was jolted out of my reverie by a slamming car door. It was just after eight thirty. I looked down the street and saw a woman get out of her car, reach in the back seat for a basket of laundry, and head in my direction. Come on, I prayed, turn in at Emma's house. As if she had read my mind, that's exactly what she did, using her own key to open the front door.

That's the sister, I thought triumphantly. She's the one I've been waiting for. Forcing myself to hold still until I was sure she wasn't coming right back out, I hurried to her car. It was a dark-blue two-door Cougar. I hastily wrote down the license number and went back to the van. She had to be the sister. Who else would have a key? Who else would bring her dirty laundry over?

In my confidence, I refused to consider any other possibilities, and the next hour and a half flew by. At ten o'clock she emerged from the house, laundry neatly stacked in the basket, and got in her car. I followed as closely as I dared. She was my crucial link and I was determined not to lose her.

In less than five minutes she slowed down, wheeled into a driveway, and parked behind another car. It was another single-family house, but shabbier than Emma's, set farther back from the street and with a veranda a few feet off the ground that ran the width of the house. I parked around the corner, gave her time to get inside, and then walked back. The other car was an older model Chevrolet. I noted the license number and headed back to the van.

I felt sure Oley was just on the other side of that veranda, and I was strongly tempted to storm the place and retrieve him, but I checked myself. Bullheadedness had gotten me in trouble already. Besides, before coming on like gangbusters I had to make absolutely certain I had the right person.

First thing the next morning I phoned in both license numbers to my data-retrieval company and within a matter of hours had hit pay dirt. The blue Cougar was registered to a Virginia Cameron, and the other car was owned by a Barbara Atwell. So it was Barbara Atwell who had taken Oley and thumbed her nose at me. I had found my nemesis.

Now it was just a question of how to get him back. It is one thing to locate a missing pet, I've discovered, and another to retrieve him safely. You can believe me when I tell you I thought long and hard about a plan. Getting someone to back down from a strong stand is a delicate process. You've got to apply enough force, or the threat of force, to convince them they have no other choice, yet at the same time offer them some means of saving face. If they feel completely boxed in, they can resort to desperate, self-destructive measures in which everyone ends up a loser. All in all, it can turn into a negotiation requiring the skills of a Henry Kissinger.

I spent the early afternoon reviewing my situation. The first idea I discarded was a person-to-person meeting with Barbara Atwell. If Oley's owner had been in town, I might have suggested we visit her together, but on my own I didn't think it would work. Her remark about knowing Oley's owner was a man disturbed me. Furthermore, I had read her out pretty thoroughly over the phone. For her to knuckle under right in front of me seemed unlikely. Going to her house also raised the possibility that she would call the police. I knew I would eventually be able to explain myself to them, but it would take time and might end up involving Oley's owner. (Incidentally, I never even considered going to the police myself. They take a dim view of tying themselves up with missing-pet cases, and besides, I didn't have much hard evidence. It all boiled down to my word against hers.) Another possibility was dumping the whole case in the owner's girl friend's lap and letting her take over, but that clearly would have been an abdication of my responsibility. No, I had to find some way to do this myself.

By two thirty I had formulated a plan. I checked both the phone book and directory assistance. As I suspected, there was no listing for either Barbara Atwell or her roommate, so I called my contact in the phone company, an organization fortunate enough to be one of my many previous employers. I asked him for their unlisted number and also to check their original application for telephone service, on which I knew customers had to supply certain information about themselves in order to establish their financial reliability. In an hour he called back with the information I needed.

Next I phoned Oley's owner's girl friend at work, told her who I was, and asked her if she owned a car.

"Sure," she said, "a white Mustang, nineteen sixty-five. Why?"

"I'd rather not tell you now," I replied, and asked if she could arrange to come home right after work. "Someone will be calling you."

She said she could, and then asked, "What's this all about? Have you found Oley?"

I told her I'd go into the details later and said good-bye.

I did nothing else until five o'clock, when I took my notes and headed back across the Bay Bridge to the street where Barbara Atwell lived. It was full of cars, but I managed to find a parking place a few doors down from her house. At six thirty her car pulled into the driveway. She got out and walked inside, and I got my first look at a woman who until that moment had been only a voice.

She was small of stature, about twenty-five, as I had guessed, with longish brown hair, glasses, a raincoat, umbrella, sensible shoes, and a canvas bag that could have served either as a purse or a briefcase. She was a totally average-looking person, with nothing to distinguish her from thousands of other women who crowd the lunchtime sidewalks in the business districts of every city in the country.

I felt a tingling at the back of my neck upon finally seeing the person who was standing between Oley and his owner. I realized I had built her up into some kind of ogre, and now I couldn't attach the feelings her voice had aroused in me to the nondescript woman who had just entered the house across the street. It was as if they were two different people, yet I knew they were both Barbara Atwell. My God, I thought, how many people like her I've passed on the street without a second glance! How many of them harbor inner lives like hers? And how many ever act on them?

Seeing her had taken the wind out of my sails. I felt suddenly creepy and a little dirty at what I had already done and was about to do. For a moment I considered taking another tack. Surely I could sit down with this perfectly ordinary woman and straighten things out. But then I thought of her strident, unhearing, twisted righteousness and realized the risk was too great. I would have to proceed with my plan.

I waited fifteen minutes and then drove to a gas station I had spotted three blocks away. Taking a few deep breaths, I entered a phone booth, took one last look at my notes, and dialed.

"Hello."

"Hello, Barbara," I said evenly.

"Who is this?" she asked.

"This is Sherlock Bones. Remember me?"

There was an eternity of silence at the other end of the phone.

"Remember I told you I'd find you?" This should have been my moment of vindication, but it didn't feel that way. Knowing I had to get it all out before she hung up, I didn't wait for her response. "I'm asking you for one last time to return Oley to his owner."

"Listen," she said finally, "I don't have to put up with this. You have no right to—"

"Let's not talk about rights," I interrupted. "Let's talk about choices. Your choice is either to call my client's girl friend in the next five minutes and have her come and pick up Oley, or I'll have the police and animal-control people on your doorstep so fast it will make your head swim."

"You can't frighten me," she said. "The police wouldn't listen to you. You can't do anything. Oley's my dog now, get it?"

"Don't be so sure," I responded. I had given her every opportunity. She was forcing me to roll up my big guns. "I've been doing quite a bit of work on this case," I said, "and have learned quite a bit about you."

I then proceeded to tell her where she worked, how long she had been employed, and the name of her immediate supervisor. Then I went on to describe her house in considerable detail, and for good measure I added the name of her roommate, her sister, and her sister's address. That was all I said. I didn't threaten her further. I was banking on the fear implicit in the realization that a total stranger knows so much about you, and on her deciding that anyone who had gathered so much information really meant business.

She didn't respond, but she had stopped her belligerence— and she hadn't hung up. That was a good sign.

"Oh, and there's one more thing I should tell you," I added. "The woman you're going to call knows nothing about any of this. As far as she's concerned, you're a good samaritan who found Oley and wanted to make sure he came from a good home." I gave her the girl friend's number twice, repeating it so she could write it down.

There was a pause and then the phone went dead.

Feeling shaky in the knees, I got back in the van and drove to her street. Since she was aware of what I was doing, I parked much farther from her house, closer to the end of the block. Now that it was all over, all I could do was wait and let the enormity of the calculated risk I had taken sink in. I honestly doubted that she would do anything to harm Oley, but as to whether she would make that phone call, I wasn't sure. I figured she would need time to absorb what I had said, but when an hour and a half had passed, I got worried. That's the trouble with the big bluff, I said to myself, if it doesn't work you've got to give up—or get nasty. Just how nasty was I prepared to get?

At that moment a white Mustang passed my van slowly, stopped in front of Barbara Atwell's house, and pulled in the driveway. A woman walked up the stairs to the front door, stood for a few moments on the veranda, and then went inside. Almost immediately she came out again, leading a big dog who was biting his leash and jumping all over her. She got him in the car, backed out of the driveway, and in a few seconds sped past me. There was just enough time for me to see a smiling woman with blond hair—and a very happy dog, standing on the back seat.

I sat quietly for a few moments until the realization that the case was closed hit me with a hollow thud. Oley was back home, or close to it, I had pulled off my plan, but just down the street there was Barbara Atwell, dealing with the events of the last two hours. What was going on in her mind? I knew better than to hope she had learned a lesson. Probably she was already beginning to bend the experience to fit whatever view of the world had impelled her on the path she had taken. I suddenly felt an overpowering urge to get out of there and go home.

Oley's owner returned from Chicago the next week and gave me a call to thank me for my help. "It was so great to come home to Oley," he said. "You don't know how glad I was to see him with my girl friend at the airport. She'd called me to say he was home, but I didn't believe it until I actually laid eyes on him myself. But what was that business when she went to get him all about?"

I never told him the real story. Instead, I dismissed it all as a whim of the woman who picked up his dog, saying that she wasn't interested in the reward and didn't want to be contacted again. I suppose I left the impression that she was a little strange, but that was fine with me. I saw no reason to upset him or to precipitate an angry confrontation with Barbara Atwell. It wasn't that I felt sorry for her—although I did, a little—but I knew nothing would be resolved in that way. With people like Barbara Atwell, nothing ever is.

7
Betsy,
the Missing
Basset Hound

THERE WAS A TIME when I assumed basset hounds couldn't run very far or very fast. With those stumpy little legs, that fat body, those long dangly ears? Waddle, maybe. Run? No way. I realize that any decent book on dogs would have told me that basset hounds were originally bred to hunt in the kind of dense underbrush that hampers bigger dogs, and that hunting would logically call for occasional spurts of running. But I've never been much for learning from books. I always seem to have to find things out the hard way. If, as in this case, it took an all-out assault on my body—well, experience may be the best teacher, but she takes her toll, she does.

When the woman called, the last thing I was ready for was a cross-country chase. For the last couple of days I'd been coming down with a cold. I could feel it tickling around the edges, making little forays into my body as it decided whether to lodge in my head or my chest. If I'd been eight years old I could have stayed home from school and gotten some sympathy and hot chocolate from my mother. Also, it was two days after Christmas, that anticlimactic period that feels like a holiday but really isn't. All things considered, I'd have preferred snuggling beneath my counterpane, but I had to be grown-up and face the world. I couldn't afford any downtime.

Her opening line notwithstanding, she sounded like a nice person.

122

"Sherlock Bones? You mean there really is such a person? I thought my girl friend was kidding me, a crazy name like that."

"No, your girl friend was right," I said. "Of course, my real name's John Keane." Where Sherlock ended and John began sometimes got a little fuzzy in my mind, but that was my problem, not hers. "What can I do for you?"

"Find Betsy, I hope. I feel so dumb asking, but I can't take time off from work, and my kids are miserable. She's been gone over a week now, and I'm at my wits' end."

"I can imagine," I said, hearing the telltale rumblings of bronchial congestion in my voice. "Losing your dog right before Christmas is rough. What kind of dog is it?"

"A basset hound, really the sweetest dog. We all just love her. Oh, you don't know the half of it. See, my husband and I recently separated, and the kids and I moved into this house about two weeks ago. They don't know anyone in the neighborhood yet, so Betsy is especially missed. The whole move and everything has been so hard on them, and now this. It just doesn't seem fair to them, does it?"

She didn't fool me for a minute. Parents are funny sometimes about pets. They buy them for their kids, then complain mightily about having to take care of them, but often end up becoming much more attached to the animal than their kids are. And in this case, the fact of the separation made Betsy's loss doubly poignant, another severed link with the familiar past that was bound to be felt by the mother at least as much her children.

Wouldn't you know, I thought, that I would get a case like this just when my body was giving me a clear message that it was time to lie down? There didn't seem to be much choice, though. My body would just have to hold out as best it could while I did what I could to put their lives back on a more even keel.

Reminding myself to check my arsenal of cold medicines, I asked about the circumstances of Betsy's disappearance. One suspicion that had cropped up as soon as she said she was separated was that her husband might be involved in some way. You hear a lot about divorced parents getting at each other through the children; pets can sometimes serve the same function. In this case, however, that didn't seem to be true. Betsy had dug her way under the backyard fence one afternoon and had simply vanished. None of the neighbors had seen her, neither where they lived now nor where they had moved from. She hadn't turned up at any of the pounds or shelters. In other words, the trail was cold. It seemed my fate to get only the cases with no leads.

For some reason, however—maybe it was the lingering spirit of Christmas—I had a hunch Betsy wouldn't be so hard to find. There aren't that many basset hounds running loose on the streets. If she could steer clear of petnappers and avoid getting hit by a car, I thought we stood a good chance of finding her. Perhaps I shouldn't have been so optimistic, but I simply couldn't imagine anyone being able to resist helping out a creature with such a loving and trusting disposition and such great sad, brown eyes. As I saw it, all I had to worry about was my impending cold.

So I had some posters printed up with a drawing of a basset hound and FIFTY DOLLARS REWARD in big black letters, and the next day I started canvassing the neighborhood where Betsy had been lost. I marked off an area on the map with a radius of twenty blocks from their house and included a mix of stores, shopping centers, gas stations, and small office buildings. I had hoped when I woke that my cold might have decided to subside, but if anything it was more solidly entrenched than ever, so I dosed myself with a little of everything from my medicine cabinet, bundled up in a heavy sweater and raincoat, and tried to pretend I wasn't really sick.

It was a perfect December morning—warm in the sun, chilly in the shade, with a brisk breeze off the bay. Posters at my side, Paco in the back seat, I set off to plaster the area—up and down streets, in and out of my van, passing out posters to mailmen, asking merchants if I could tape copies to their windows. It was slow going. Sometimes I'd stand in line at a cash register for what felt like hours, only to be told that they didn't allow posters. By this time I was feeling dizzy and light-headed. I couldn't breathe through my nose, my tongue felt two sizes too big for my mouth, and my internal thermostat was haywire. I'd be chilled to the bone one minute, and dripping with sweat the next. I must look like a junkie overdue for a fix, I thought. So much for my professional image.

About noon I checked the stack of posters and figured I had two more hours of work before I could legitimately collapse. Time was beginning to blur. It seemed as if I had been climbing in and out of my van forever. Was it my imagination or were the steps getting steeper? Just one more poster, John, I told myself, just one more. I had a sudden flashback to my days at boot camp when every day I would have to sweat out some sadistic drill instructor's exercise to make a marine out of me, except that in this case there was only myself to blame. If this is what doing your own thing entails, I said to myself, I'll take insurance. That's how sick I felt.

I was swinging back in the general direction of home when I spotted a group of people on the sidewalk, congregated in front of some sort of natural-food and juice-bar establishment. There were a couple of benches on the sidewalk, where a motley collection of what looked like leftover flower children were whiling away the afternoon, so laid back they could have walked on their elbows. They didn't give me a tumble when I got out of the van and put my poster on a bulletin board that was already overloaded with faded slips of paper probably dating from the sixties. As I heaved myself back in the van for the last time, I happened to see a couple of boys walking down a side street. They couldn't have been more than eleven or twelve years old. What the hell, I thought, let's get this over with. I turned down the street and pulled up next to them.

"Hey, fellows," I shouted through the window. "Got a minute?"

They eyed me suspiciously. "What for?" one of them said, as they kept walking. They looked like pretty savvy kids to me, too street-wise to get involved with a deranged-looking man driving around in a beat-up van. Even Paco's friendly face wasn't cutting any ice with them.

"I'm looking for a dog," I said, "and I thought you might

have seen it. See, here's a poster with her picture on it."

"We haven't seen no dog," the other kid said. They were walking backward now and looked like they might bolt at any minute.

"Well, if you do, I'd appreciate a call. There's a fifty-dollar reward for whoever finds her."

I had said the magic word. They stopped walking and looked at each other.

One said, "Fifty dollars? Hey, let's see that poster."

"Her name is Betsy, and she's a basset hound," I said, handing them the poster. "She belongs to two kids about your age. They just moved to a new house and they don't know any other kids in the neighborhood yet, and they really miss their dog. Either of you guys got a dog? You'd probably feel pretty bad if you lost yours, especially right before Christmas, wouldn't you?" I could hear myself babbling, but they weren't paying any attention. They were whispering between themselves.

Finally, the first one said, "Is that the truth, mister? Whoever finds this dog gets fifty bucks?"

"That's right," I said. "Do you know where she is?"

"Nope, we ain't seen her. But for fifty dollars we're gonna *find* that dog!"

"Maybe you could get some of your friends to help."

"You kidding? No way, man. We're gonna get that money ourselves. Hey, is that your dog on the poster, the one with the hat?"

"That's right," I said. "He's Paco, and I'm Sherlock Bones. There's my number right on the poster. Just give Sherlock Bones a call if you find Betsy."

"OK, Mr. Bones," they said, and the two ran off down the street to earn their money. Feeling no such determination, I called it a day and headed home. All I wanted to do was die.

When I got back to the apartment I headed directly for the bedroom, shedding clothes on the way. I should be doing something for my condition, I thought weakly. Lots of liquids, wasn't it, or vitamin C—or perhaps a plot at the cemetery of my choice?

Did you feed a cold and starve a fever, or was it the other way around? It didn't matter. The bed drew me to its bosom like a nail to a magnet.

Is there anything more pleasurable than the feel of cool sheets against a fevered body? Not when you're sick enough, there isn't. I had just slid under the covers, laid my head on the pillow, and was sinking into a beautiful oblivion when the phone rang. I heard it through my fever as a distant buzz from another planet. Let Flo get it, dear old Flo. It kept ringing. The hell with it, I thought, let it ring, I'm too sick to get up. No one could blame me for not answering. No one except Paco, that is. When the phone rings he runs right to it, and if I don't follow immediately he comes and gets me. If only he could talk and take shorthand, he'd make a hell of a secretary. He was dancing from the living room to the bedroom, up on the bed, licking my face, woofing furiously. Even from a bed of pain, there's no ignoring an agitated dog sitting on your face. Good old Pac, I thought ruefully, you won't let me get away with anything.

Grabbing the covers as a temporary bathrobe, I trailed my way into the living room, fended off Paco, and answered the phone.

"Hello?"

"Hey, man, what took you so long?"

I didn't recognize the man's voice, and the truth was too complicated for my enfeebled brain to relate. "Just walked in the door," I said. "What can I do for you?"

He seemed a little vague. "Is there a—uh, Sherlock Bones around?"

"That's me."

"It's him," I could hear him saying. Whoever he was talking to erupted in hysterical laughter. "Far out, man, far out. Hey, what's your trip, Sherlock?"

I spread germs around the Bay Area, I felt like saying. It was possible I was becoming delirious. "I find people's missing pets."

"Oh, wow," he said. "That's great karma, you know?"

There was a long pause. I felt myself drifting off. Was this conversation happening or was it all a product of my overheated brain? With an effort, I pulled myself back from the edge of blackness and managed to ask, "Is there anything I can do for you?"

"I don't know, man," he cackled. "What did you have in mind?"

I hadn't roused myself to trade wisecracks with a total stranger. "Look, buddy," I said, "just exactly what's going on?"

"OK, OK, man," he said. "Don't get heavy on me. Mellow out, huh? Some kid asked me to call you."

"Yes?"

"Yeah, he said he and his buddy found the dog you're looking for. Hey, like a missing pet, right?" Struck by the brilliance of his deduction, he dissolved once more into laughter. Whatever he was on must have been good stuff.

"Was it a basset hound?" I was suddenly interested.

"Hey, man, I don't, like, relate to labels, you know? We're all part of the universal energy, can you get behind that?"

I was in no shape for a discussion of what I could get behind, so, wondering if he related to addresses, I asked him where he was. As I suspected, he was calling from the natural-food and juice-bar place. Judging from his conversation, dialing my number had probably been his last brush with rational activity before he started drifting toward the ceiling. The chance of getting any more specific information from him now seemed, in a manner of speaking, to have gone up in smoke. I told him to stay where he was and wait for me.

"No problem," he assured me. "Hey, man, the kid said to tell you the dog bites."

"Bites?" I repeated stupidly.

"Yeah, you know, teeth. Dig it? I mean, that's a real doggie trip, right? Outasight."

Leaving him convulsed in the laughter of self-appreciation, I hung up and started thinking about whether I was capable even of getting dressed. Way down there on the floor I could see a trail of clothes. My first challenge, obviously, was to bend over and pick them up. Gingerly I aimed for a sock, retrieved it, snagged my shirt with my toes, and, after what seemed like several weeks, got everything back on. My head was bursting, my body pouring off sweat. I could see this was going to be a character-building experience. I grabbed a collar and leash and a half-empty box of dog biscuits and told Paco to hold the fort. If this dog was a biter, I didn't want Paco along.

As I drove to the rendezvous with my spaced-out informant, I struggled to put the pieces together. I had the feeling that the two boys who claimed to have found Betsy were the ones I had last talked to, but it was too soon for them to have come up with anything—unless, of course, they had had the dog all along and were simply waiting for the best offer. But that didn't seem to fit either. They had been too suspicious of me. Besides, if they had had Betsy they would never have let me get away—not those two mercenary types. Also, Betsy didn't sound like the kind of dog that bit people. Maybe the whole thing was a hoax hatched during a slow afternoon at the juice bar. I couldn't figure it out—but then, I wasn't functioning at my tip-top.

My fears were not allayed when I drove to our meeting place. No one there seemed to know anything about a missing dog or Sherlock Bones. Cursing myself for being a sucker, I got back in the van and, since I was so close, turned down the street where I had met the two boys. Sure enough, there they were a little farther down the block. One was crouched next to some shrub-bery in front of a large apartment building, and the other was scanning the street.

"He's here!" he shouted when he saw me pull up. "Hey, Mr. Bones, we found your dog. She ran into these bushes, but she keeps biting at us when we try to get near."

Mindful of my throbbing head, I slowly bent over and peered in. There certainly was a basset hound in there—and, by all appearances, a terrified basset hound. My heart always goes out to animals in these circumstances. Desperately frightened, not knowing what or who to trust, they seem torn between reaching out for help and holding the world at bay. She had her back to the wall, her head down, and she was making little growling noises from a half-open mouth. I spotted the lump on her right hip that her owner had mentioned, so I knew this was Betsy. Poor little dog, I thought, you've had a hard time, I'll bet. No wonder you're frightened. This isn't much like life at home, is it?

"Well, guys," I said, feeling vastly relieved, "looks like you've found her. This is Betsy, all right."

"Oh, boy," one of them shouted. "Now we get the reward, huh?"

"Right," I said, "just as soon as I get her out of there." Figuring she must be starved, I reached into my box for a dog biscuit.

"Don't do that, Mr. Bones," one of the boys said. "She'll bite your hand off."

"That's all right," I replied confidently. "You've just got to take it slow. She's frightened, that's all." That was enough. I had no sooner offered her the biscuit when she nipped my finger. I drew back, and she took the chance to bolt along the wall about fifteen feet to the corner of the building and then into the street.

Without stopping to think that footraces are not the best remedy for a cold, I took off after her, one hand clutching the box of dog biscuits, the other with the flailing leash and collar. "Here, Betsy," I crooned, "here, girl, it's all right, here's a dog biscuit for you."

Betsy was having none of it. She raced for the opposite curb, and I tore after her, my two young friends right at my heels. Whatever our reasons, none of us was about to let her get away. Betsy, however, had other plans. As soon as she saw us coming for her, she zigzagged back across the street to the other curb, then turned and gave us a wild look. If I hadn't known she was so desperate, I'd have sworn she was playing with us. The street wasn't normally a busy one, but the evening rush-hour traffic was building up, and I was aware of the sounds of sudden brakings and honking horns. Well, they'll have to take care of themselves, I thought. I've got no time to observe traffic rules.

Back we went after her, whereupon she, of course, repeated

her earlier move and ran to where we started on the other curb.

"Head her off! Head her off!" I shouted at the two kids, who had been trailing me trailing Betsy. I was grateful not to have time to consider the spectacle we were making—traffic stopped in both directions, two hysterical kids, and a sweating, wheezing, overweight guy with a flappy raincoat, a box of biscuits, and a flyaway leash.

"No way!" one of them said. "Then you'll catch her and we won't get the reward!"

"You'll get it, you'll get it, I promise you! Let's just catch the damned dog!"

They ran into the middle of the street in anticipation of Betsy's next move, but she outfoxed us. Seeing the way clear back to the apartment, she made a beeline for the bushes where the chase began, but at the last second turned and ran around the side of the building.

"You go around the other side!" I yelled. "I'll run after her!" And we took off.

From somewhere in the neighborhood a group of five or six other boys had materialized. "Hey!" I heard one of them shout. "There's the dog on the poster!"

This was turning into a community affair, and it occurred to me I might have to divide that fifty dollars several ways. I'll think about that later, I said to myself, and hoping against hope that Betsy would run into some kind of cul-de-sac, I set out in pursuit. I swear the side of that apartment building was five miles long. I could feel my heart pound. Come on, legs, I thought, just keep moving. I knew I was going to pay for this. Why hadn't I kept up my jogging? Why hadn't I lost that extra weight? Why wasn't I home in bed? And where were those damned kids? We should have met up by now.

Then I saw why we hadn't. The apartment building wasn't freestanding but was attached to other buildings I hadn't seen from the street. It must have been a housing project, one big building attached to another with an array of walkways, lobbies, plantings, and courtyards that created a giant low-cost labyrinth.

And ahead was Betsy, always just far enough out of reach to keep me running. Good God, I thought, as the bands of steel tightened across my heaving chest, is it all going to end like this? What an ignominious way to die, laid low with a coronary brought on by chasing a basset hound! Still, something made me continue —not a sense of duty or sympathy for Betsy or even a will to win; I was like a chicken with its head cut off, and there was no stopping.

At the moment when I really don't think my legs would have carried me another step, I rounded a corner and saw Betsy less than eight feet away, sitting on a concrete slab in front of some low bushes. Out of the corner of my eye I saw the pack of kids running toward us.

"Hey!" one shouted. "That's where we found her, right in those bushes!"

Motioning them frantically to stay back and be quiet—I had no air left for talking—I took a good look at her. But let's be honest. First I just stood there, panting and wheezing. She panted right back. It was a great moment in the annals of the low-speed chase: two stylish stouts regrouping their forces for the final heat.

Once I had caught my breath, I could see that we had ended the hostilities and were about to enter into negotiations. Her tongue was hanging so far out of her mouth it looked longer than her ears, if that's possible, and her little body was heaving like a furry brown-and-white bellows. Poor Betsy. I may have had the flu, but Betsy had been out on her own for over a week and looked as if she were about to cave in. The eyes of a basset hound normally droop, but hers had an extra sag or two that I was sure came from sadness and desperation. She had clearly exhausted every trick from her book on survival tactics. Behind her I could see a hole in some shrubbery. The boys said they had found her here. She had probably sought it out as a temporary lair, a place of refuge in a frightening and unfamiliar world.

The trick was to get her without being bitten, although I didn't think she was up to it. Talking softly, I walked up to her and slipped the chain collar over her head. It was as simple as that.

The change in her was instantaneous and astonishing—from a beaten-down, hunted animal to a friendly, calm pet. She got up, swished her tail once, and looked at me expectantly. It was one of those moments when I could read an animal's mind with absolute clarity. Well, thank goodness, I knew she was thinking, it's about time somebody got this circus under control. Now that we've all come to our senses, let's get on with it. And make it snappy!

Feeling a little like a pied piper too winded to blow on his pipe, I led Betsy and the boys back to the van. Betsy was swinging along, her stubby little legs carrying her in that distinctive rolling basset trot, both perky and sedate, that until a few minutes ago had been all I thought the breed was capable of. Ears aflap, her eyes looking in every direction, she seemed to be up for anything. The boys were running and laughing, delighted with having been a part of an exciting and profitable adventure. As for me, I was struggling simply to sustain forward motion. My breath had returned, and my heart was no longer about to go into seizure, but my knees were doing a funny little dance, and I had to keep reminding them to stick to business. I never knew that walking could require such intense concentration. If I'd been chewing gum, I'd have been in real trouble.

Before I left—Betsy, incidentally, had to be hoisted into the van, so it's possible she wasn't quite as perky as she looked—I took the names of the two boys (who turned out to be brothers) and gave my solemn promise I would be back the next day with their reward. My worries about having to divide the money eight ways proved groundless. In that absolute moral code that operates in the world of children, they all decided the money belonged to the two brothers.

I stopped at the first pay phone I could find and called Betsy's owner. When no one answered at home, I tried her work number.

"Hello," I said. "This is Sherlock. Just thought I'd call to see if you heard anything about Betsy. Isn't it about time to call it a day?"

"Oh, hi," she said. "Yeah, probably, but the kids went to visit their father today, and I'm putting off going home to an empty house. No, I haven't heard anything, but—"

"Well, I've got a belated Christmas present, and I thought I'd drop it off at your office. Would that be all right?"

"Uh, sure, I guess so," she replied. I could tell her heart wasn't in it. "Why a Christmas present?"

"Oh, it's just something I picked up I thought might make you feel better. Actually, it looks like a basset hound to me."

"A basset hound?" she cried. "What are you saying? You mean you found our dog?"

"I don't know, but whenever I call her Betsy she wags her tail. She's got a lump on her right hip, and she sure can run."

"Oh, I can't believe it! You *did* find her! Oh, my God! I was just sitting here thinking I'd never see her again, and—I can't believe it!" I could hear her crying. "I'm sorry. You'll have to excuse me. This is ridiculous, but—it's only a dog, I know, but I've missed her so much. I thought—I know this sounds silly, but when she got lost it seemed almost like it was some kind of punishment, like if Frank and I hadn't split up Betsy wouldn't have left. Isn't that stupid? I can't tell you how relieved I am. How is she? How did you find her?"

"She seems fine. Two boys spotted her in some bushes and—"

"Oh, never mind," she interrupted. "You can tell me when you get here. Just come as fast as you can. This is going to be my all-time best Christmas present."

Her office was less than ten minutes away. When I arrived, Betsy, who had spent the trip devouring the contents of the dog-biscuit box, slid out of the van and toddled up the steps of the office.

Her owner was waiting inside the door, and when she saw Betsy her anxious expression dissolved into a big, trembly smile and tears of joy. She sat down, and Betsy rolled over on her back, licking her mistress's face and surrendering completely to a big hug and tummy rub. She had gone as limp as a rag doll, openly reveling in all the affection she was getting. No wonder people form such strong bonds with their pets, I thought. How many humans are capable of handling that kind of unadulterated closeness?

When the reunion was over, Betsy trundled off to explore the office as if nothing had happened. She had clearly finished with one adventure and was ready for the next. Her owner, however, was not nearly so resilient, and we sat for a half hour or so while she absorbed the events of the day and got used to the fact that Betsy was once again a member of the family. Then I took my leave. Now that the adrenaline had stopped flowing, I could feel just how weak I was. If I didn't get home soon, I might find myself sleeping on the floor of the van.

The next day, I was surprised to wake up feeling much better. After all the punishment I had subjected my body to, I was sure it would retaliate, but aside from some aches and shakes in my legs, I felt almost normal. It was as if all my running around had speeded up the process of whatever germs had seized me and made their impact stronger but briefer. In any event, I felt fine when I dropped in on the two boys after school to deliver their reward. Having had dealings with those two sharpies, I was sure they would put out a contract on me if I wasn't there right on the dot.

"Well, here's your money, guys," I said. "You certainly earned it. Do you know how you're going to spend it?"

"Yeah," said the younger. "I'm going to get a bike."

"Dummy," his brother retorted. "You can't buy a bike with twenty-five dollars. I'm going to put mine in a bank."

"Good for you," I said. "Well, I've got to be going now. If you see any more of my posters, keep your eyes peeled. Who knows, you might find another missing pet and make some more money."

I was walking back to the van when the younger boy ran up to me and said, "Hey, Mr. Bones, you didn't say what happened."

"What happened?" I asked. "What do you mean, what happened?"

He looked embarrassed. "You know, when you brought the dog back and all."

"Oh, sorry," I said, suddenly catching on. "Well, the lady was so happy she cried. She hugged Betsy, and Betsy rolled over and kissed her face."

His face had that absolutely rapt expression of a boy totally engrossed in a fairy tale. "And what about the kids?" he prompted. "What did they do?"

"The kids weren't there. See, their mom and dad are separated, and they're visiting their father right now."

"Oh. They are?" He gave me a look of disappointment that immediately turned to blankness, once again the tough kid, too tough to admit feeling cheated out of a happy ending to his story. "Come on, Tommy," he shouted back to his brother, "let's go play basketball."

And they ran off, leaving me to ponder tough kids, loving animals, and the imperfect world we live in.

8
Raggs,
the Family Dog

In order to last in my business, you need an internal alarm system that goes off when things aren't adding up—and you've got to learn to pay attention when it first goes off. Otherwise, you can invest so much time in proving one theory that your ego blocks out anything that doesn't support it. That's what happened to me with Alice and Frank Russell. In retrospect, I can see something was fishy about them almost from the very beginning. When Mrs. Russell first called me, though, there was nothing in what she said to arouse my suspicions. In fact, I remember being impressed with her businesslike manner. So many clients tell me more than I need to know about their missing pets that I found Mrs. Russell's to-the-point approach refreshing.

"This is Alice Russell," she began, in a professional, well-modulated voice. "Our dog, Raggs, was stolen from the car two days ago while my husband was shopping. I think we may need your help. Could you tell me how you work and what you charge?"

I explained briefly my two types of service—for which I then charged $100 a day plus expenses for my full time, and $35 for a one-shot consultation.

"I think we'd best engage you full time," she said decisively. "Let's say for three days, starting immediately. Today's Friday, and I'd like to get started before the weekend. Is that convenient for you?"

"I think that can be arranged," I replied. "Shall we set up

an appointment, or would you prefer I meet with your husband?"

"No, I think I can give you all the information you need. Frank's not well, and I don't want him disturbed. We'll have to do it by phone, though. I simply can't get away from the office today."

"OK," I said, "in that case, you'd better tell me what happened."

"As I said, on Tuesday Frank drove me to work so that he could have the car for the shopping. He shops at those stores on Ocean Avenue, near Nineteenth. You know the ones I mean?"

"I think so, yes." She was referring to a string of shops several blocks long, with occasional parking lots in back and in between buildings. Many of the stores had entrances from the parking lots as well as from the sidewalk.

"Well, he left Raggs in the car with the doors locked and was gone for about forty minutes. When he came out, Raggs had disappeared."

"And were the windows open?" I'd had clients tell me their dogs had been stolen before, when in fact they'd simply squeezed out through an open window.

"Yes, but not enough for Raggs to escape. Frank's very particular about that. And, oh yes, the doors were all locked when he got back."

That's unusual, I thought. It often happens that kids will let a dog out of a car, even reaching in to unlock a door, but I didn't think they would bother to relock it. "Tell me, Mrs. Russell, what kind of dog is Raggs?"

"He's a white cockapoo about a foot high, five years old, with a long tail and shaggy fur. I assume you know what they look like."

I did indeed. Supposedly part cocker spaniel and part poodle, cockapoos are so prevalent as almost to constitute a breed of their own. They come in various sizes, colors, and shapes, but they all look like rag-mop, doggie-in-the-window pets. Even as adults they manage to retain a puppylike appeal. But they aren't usually candidates for the professional dognapper interested in making a quick sale. My mind turned over possibilities. Maybe someone was after a little ransom money.

"What kind of car was your husband driving?" I asked.

"A Mercedes," she replied. "Dark blue. Why?"

"Just wondering. Has anyone contacted you about the dog?"

"No, no one," she said. "If anyone had, Frank would have been there to take the call. Frank is really quite attached to Raggs. Raggs is actually his dog. After all, they spend all day together while I'm at work. He asked everyone at the store if they'd seen Raggs, but no one had. That's why I'm sure he was stolen."

"I see. Mrs. Russell, is there anyone you can think of who might have a reason to take Raggs? A neighbor, perhaps, or someone at work? Where do you work, by the way?"

"At a savings and loan. No, I can't think of anyone. Of course, we do turn quite a few people down for loans, but I can't remember any recently who seemed upset enough to do something like that. Besides, how would they know my car or, for that matter, where it was on Tuesday afternoon?"

Oh lady, I thought, you don't know the lengths people will go to if they're angry and frustrated enough. I didn't want to worry her with that possibility, though, until I knew more about the case.

I suggested that she offer a higher-than-average reward in order to flush out anyone who might be holding Raggs for ransom, and we agreed on three hundred dollars. I told her I'd put up posters in three places: around the stores, in their neighborhood (which was less than a mile away), and near the savings and loan where she worked, even though it was several miles from where Raggs had disappeared. I also told her I'd need a photograph for the poster.

"Do you have any clear black-and-white photographs?" I asked.

"Yes," she replied hesitantly, "but they're at home with Frank."

"Well, why don't I drop by and pick them up? Perhaps he could have a check for me as well, and I could get right to the printer's."

"No, no," she said quickly, "I don't want him disturbed. He's . . . but you're right, we do want to get started quickly. All right, I'll call him and tell him to put the photographs and the check in an envelope and leave it outside the door. That way you can pick it up without bothering him. It's his back, you see, and he occasionally needs complete bed rest."

"I'm sorry to hear that," I replied.

"He'll never be completely over it," she said. "They think it's from an injury he got in the army. Frank was in the army for years. It flares up just enough to keep him from working. Thank God he's got his disability payments."

I promised I'd do my best not to disturb him, hung up, and, after making a couple of calls to rearrange my schedule, drove into San Francisco to the address she had given me. It was in the Sunset district, a neighborhood of mostly one-story Spanish-style bungalows—streets and streets of evenly spaced pastel houses, immaculate postage-stamp lawns, and shrubbery manicured to the point of appearing plastic. Despite the fact that the Sunset is solidly middle-class, it has always seemed slightly unreal to me, as if it might once have been a set for an avant-garde film made in the 1930s. Perhaps it's because you seldom see anyone on the streets and the windows all seem to have curtains drawn to prevent passersby from looking in.

I had no trouble finding the Russells' house. Even among its well-tended neighbors, it stood out as the recipient of hours and hours—and hours—of fussy care. In fact, it was well on its way to becoming one of those places people slow down to stare at on Sunday afternoon drives. Every surface had been painted, decorated, planted, or fenced off. There was a birdbath in the front yard, tiny white fences around each flower bed, two flowerpots on each front step, and tiles outlining the door. White stones marked off the corners of the lawn next to the sidewalk and formed a border along the bright-yellow cement walk that led up to equally yellow front steps. The aluminum screen door boasted an elaborate palm-tree motif. Someone with too much time on his hands, I thought, had raised puttering to a full-time job, and I bet I knew who it was.

The envelope was just inside the screen door. Mindful of not disturbing Mr. Russell, I took it and went back to the van to examine its contents. I put the check in my shirt pocket and took a look at the pictures. Raggs was one cute dog, all right: bright eyes, partially covered by an unkempt mop of hair, and an inquisitive tilt to his head that was accentuated by one floppy ear and one that stood straight up. I checked my watch and saw I'd have just enough time to get to the printer's and have him run off a thousand posters before six o'clock. That meant I could get an early start Saturday.

The next morning I began at the stores, affixing posters to utility poles and shopwindows. No one I talked to remembered seeing Raggs, but they promised to keep their eyes open. I was sure they would, for even from his picture Raggs radiated the kind of doggy appeal that would be hard to resist.

About ten o'clock I stopped what I was doing, got back in my van, and made the rounds of veterinary hospitals in the area. I knew most of them closed at noon and I wanted to drop off posters while they were still open, even though I didn't think vets would be much help in this case. People who find pets, especially if they appear injured or in poor health, will sometimes take them to a vet for care. The problem, though, is that the vet only knows what he is told. If someone presents a pet as his own, the vet has no way of knowing otherwise. Even if they should harbor some suspicions, most vets are reluctant to blow the whistle on someone who is, after all, one of their patients. In this case, the possibility that whoever had taken Raggs would consult a vet seemed pretty slim, but still worth an hour of my time. I was therefore surprised when, at the third vet's office I visited, I got a reaction.

"Oh, I know that dog," the receptionist said. She was a young girl with long brown hair and granny glasses.

"You do?" I asked. "Do you know where he is?"

"Well, I haven't seen him recently," she replied, "but he comes in here a lot. What happened, did he run away?"

"No, he disappeared from his owner's car while it was parked over on Ocean. Mrs. Russell thinks he was stolen." I was disappointed. For a moment I thought I had a lead, but I had obviously stumbled upon the Russells' vet.

"*Mrs.* Russell?" she said. "I didn't know there *was* a Mrs. Russell. Raggs always comes in with Mr. Russell."

"You say he comes in a lot. Is there something wrong with Raggs? Is he on medication?" This added a new dimension to the case. If Raggs had a problem requiring regular medication, he was in trouble now. I wondered why Mrs. Russell hadn't said anything about this.

"No. No one thing," she said. "You'd really have to talk to Dr. Shively, though. We can't discuss patients. He's booked up through the rest of the morning. Would you like to wait around and see if he's got a free minute?"

"No, that's all right," I replied. "I'll call him later, maybe on Monday." I still had several hundred posters to get up. As long as Raggs didn't need daily medication, I could talk to Dr. Shively later.

By the end of the day I had completely covered both the stores and the Russells' neighborhood with approximately seven hundred posters. There was no sign of life at the Russells' house, but the rest of the neighborhood seemed deserted as well. About six o'clock I headed back to Oakland, having decided to poster the area around Mrs. Russell's office the next day. I wanted to get home and see what leads had come in. I felt sure that the three-hundred-dollar reward would hook anyone after ransom. At least they would know the Russells were serious enough about getting their dog back to put up hundreds of posters and offer a substantial reward.

I was surprised, and a little disturbed, to find no one had called. That was unusual. Ordinarily, there would have been several callers who thought they might have spotted the dog. Of course, the fact that the poster bore a clear photograph of Raggs would sharply cut down on the number of false leads. Also, maybe whoever had taken Raggs was playing a waiting game, counting on the Russells' growing anxiety to extort a larger payment. I wished I knew more about who this person might be. Was he or she simply after cash, or was there a darker motive—some kind of twisted retaliation, perhaps, or revenge?

By ten o'clock the next morning I had still received no calls. The only thing I could think of was that the person we were looking for had something to do with Mrs. Russell's work. It was a thin possibility, but that was the only area I had yet to poster. I was getting ready to leave when the phone rang.

"Sherlock Bones."

"Good morning, Mr. Keane, this is Mrs. Russell," a frosty voice said. "Where are those posters you promised to put up? I thought we agreed time was of the essence."

"Right," I said guiltily. "You mean around your office. I was just on my way out the door to do that."

"Oh, you mean you haven't put up any there, either?" There was a sharp edge to her voice I hadn't heard before. Alice Russell was apparently accustomed to instant obedience.

"Either?" I replied. "Didn't you see the ones I put up yesterday in your neighborhood and around the stores? There must be almost seven hundred."

"I most certainly did not," she snapped. "I spent the day at my sister's, thinking you'd be putting up posters, as I paid you to do. I got home last night at ten thirty, and there wasn't one poster in sight. I drove to the shopping center, and there weren't any there, either. And now you tell me you haven't been to my office yet. Just exactly what *have* you been doing with the three hundred dollars I paid you?"

"Mrs. Russell," I said, torn between anger at her accusation and puzzlement at what was going on, "I can assure you I put up seven hundred posters yesterday. Now, it's true I haven't gotten to your office yet, but as I said, I was just on my way there when you called. I don't know what's going on, but someone is taking those posters down."

"Taking them down?" she repeated sarcastically. "Frankly, Mr. Keane, I find it hard to believe that anyone would go to the trouble of taking down seven hundred posters."

"I agree it doesn't make much sense," I replied, my mind searching for some reason. "Clearly it's someone who doesn't want anyone looking for Raggs. Think again. Is there anyone who might want to get at you or your husband through your dog? Someone you may have unconsciously offended? Someone with a grudge against you?"

"I told you before," she said angrily, "there is no one. In fact, I don't like your insinuations. My husband and I do not go around offending people."

"I didn't mean to imply that you did," I countered. "But there are some people who—"

"Look," she said, "I don't intend to get into an argument with you. I paid you good money to find our dog, and I expect you to do what was agreed to. Now, I'll give you one more day, but if I don't see any posters, I intend to take steps. Don't think I'm the kind of person you can push around."

I hung up, after promising to investigate the matter, still more puzzled than angry. Part of me was tempted to mail the Russells' check back, since I still hadn't cashed it, and tell them to get lost, but I was too intrigued to give up. This was a new twist. I'd run across people who hadn't wanted to give up a dog they'd found, but why go to all the trouble of taking down the posters? For a moment it occurred to me that some city employee had removed them. Strictly speaking, it's not legal to put posters on telephone or utility poles, but with the exception of some zealous bureaucrats in a few small towns, no one had ever given me a hard time. A poster about a missing pet, after all, wasn't the same as a commercial ad for a rock concert or a stop-smoking seminar. Besides, she had said they were all gone, and that would include all those I had taped to store windows.

Grabbing the remaining three hundred posters, I climbed in the van and headed for Ocean Avenue. Sure enough, almost all the posters I'd put up the morning before were gone from stores and poles alike. I was furious. If whoever was doing this thought I was going to give up, he or she had another think coming. Spurred by anger, I took part of my stack and repostered. I'd have to wait until tomorrow, Monday, to get some more from the printer's to do a complete job, but at least I was giving notice that I was still in the game.

Next I went to the Russells' neighborhood, where the same situation presented itself. This is strange, I thought, as I put up more posters, very strange. I considered stopping in to talk to Mrs. Russell, but I didn't want to see her until I had something concrete to report. I had no intention of giving her the satisfaction of thinking she had been right and that I was scurrying around only because she had caught me trying to cheat her. I saved a few posters for the area around Mrs. Russell's office, even though it seemed clear that the action on this case was elsewhere. After I finished there, I headed for the stores. Good, I thought, the posters were still up. By this time it was a little after five o'clock. I swung by the Russell's street. They were still up there, too. Well, maybe it was just a fluke. Maybe some kids had made a game of taking them all down.

I noticed a car parked in front of their house. It was a dark-blue Mercedes, and a man was wiping off the hood. The ailing Mr. Russell? I hesitated. I needed to talk to him. He was, after all, the last person to see Raggs, and so far I had only heard his story as filtered through his wife. On the other hand, I had no desire to get into another argument with her at this point. Keeping my eyes peeled, I drew closer in my van. Mrs. Russell was nowhere in sight, so I pulled up next to the man and stopped.

"Mr. Russell?" I asked. "I'm Sherlock Bones."

For a moment he didn't look up from his work. Then, straightening slowly, he turned to me with a guarded look, and said, "Oh, yes. John Keane, isn't that right?"

"That's right," I replied. Frank Russell was a tall man in his early sixties, slightly overweight and with a somewhat slack, puffy face that seemed at odds with a military-style crew cut shaved so short his scalp shone through above his ears. He was wearing gray slacks with a razor-sharp crease and narrow cuffs that stopped well above his highly polished black shoes to display two bands of white sock. An olive-green sport coat and open-collared shirt that revealed an inch or so of T-shirt underneath completed the look of a military man who even in civilian clothes seemed to be wearing a uniform.

I wanted to ask him if he had seen anyone taking down the posters, but I decided to avoid that touchy subject for the moment. Instead, I asked him the circumstances of Raggs's disappearance and got essentially the same story his wife had told me.

"And you're sure Raggs couldn't have gotten out through a window?" I asked.

"Oh no, absolutely not," he replied. "Well, there was some busybody dame in the parking lot that told me I wasn't giving the dog enough air. You know how women are with animals. There's always one around to tell you you're not doing it right. So I lowered one window a little more, but I can tell you that dog wouldn't jump out. No sir, not with me around."

"Why is that?"

"Well," he said, as if the reason should be self-evident, "because that dog minds me. He knows there'll be hell to pay if he doesn't, that's why. He can't get away with that stuff any more, and he knows it."

"I see. Mr. Russell, can you think of anyone who would want to take Raggs? Someone with a grudge against you or your wife, maybe, or someone who wanted the dog?" I could feel little pieces of this case begin to shift inside my head.

"No way," he said, with a harsh laugh. "Oh, he's cute enough, I'll give the little bastard that much. But just try cleaning up after him all day long and you'd sing a different tune. He messes up the yard, throws his food all over the kitchen, and pees on the rug whenever I come near him. What that dog needs is discipline, and there aren't many people willing to discipline today. Look at the kids on the street. Hooligans, that's what they are. They run wild. Let me tell you, if I had a kid, he'd toe the line or I'd know the reason why."

Another little piece in my head shifted. "Mr. Russell," I asked carefully, "would you say Raggs is primarily your dog or your wife's?"

He looked at me suspiciously. "Why do you want to know?"

"Well, it's just that she's the one that called me. Then I got the impression from her that he's more your dog. And now from what you say—well, frankly, I'm wondering why you're paying me all this money to find him."

Mr. Russell bent down to wipe an imaginary spot off an already spotless hubcap. His back, I noticed, didn't seem to be bothering him at all. "That's because you don't know my wife," he said finally, tilting his head to catch any traces of dust on the fender's mirror finish.

"I'm afraid I'm not following you. Could you be a little more explicit?" I had the feeling I was about to become more involved in the Russells' private life than I cared to.

"OK," he said, turning to face me. "Here's the story. I figured she didn't tell you. She got Raggs about a year ago, from someone at the office who didn't want the dog, and just drops him in my lap one day, bang, out of the blue. Tells me I need something to keep my mind occupied. Well, that's easy for her to say. She's gone all day, comes home and gives the dog a couple of pats, and that's it. I'm the one who has to clean up after him. Her idea of cleaning the rug is one wipe with a damp sponge. Well, let me tell you, that's no good. You've got to use a brush and disinfectant and apply a little good old-fashioned elbow grease. If you're going to do it, do it right. Get my drift?"

"I suppose so," I replied. Poor Raggs, I thought, an absentee mother and an uptight disciplinarian father.

"But," he said, "Alice's just like every other woman. She always has the last word, so we've got Raggs. So I don't know. You tell me—whose dog *is* he?" With that, he went back to polishing his car, our conversation apparently concluded.

I drove off down the street. Frank Russell had left a very sour taste in my mouth. In fact, the entire case was turning into a can of worms I wished I had never opened. Whose dog *was* Raggs, anyway? The more I thought about it, the more he seemed to be nobody's, really, not a pet in the true sense of the word. For Alice Russell he was a solution—or maybe a punishment—for her husband's idleness that she intended to inflict on him at whatever cost to the dog. I had been the recipient of some of her high-handedness over the phone. She was a woman who always had to be right. No wonder she hadn't wanted me to meet her husband. She must have known he would contradict her story. As for Frank Russell, Raggs was just another symbol of his wife's domination, against which he felt powerless to take any direct action. And so there was Raggs, bearing the brunt of Frank's resentment toward his wife, and all in the name of good old discipline. It was a bad scene. I was glad I hadn't cashed their check yet. Clearly I had some thinking to do.

I must have been about five blocks away when I realized I hadn't asked if Frank had seen anyone taking down the posters. I was considering whether to go back when one of those little pieces that had been jarred loose in my head suddenly fell into place. Of course. I knew who had taken down the posters. It was Frank Russell himself! I should have suspected as much when his wife was so adamant that I not meet him. She didn't want him turning me off the case. She wanted Raggs back home with her husband, making his life miserable—although she might not put it that way, even to herself. Poor Frank, he probably thought he had seen the last of Raggs, and now his wife had brought in Sherlock Bones to get him back.

When I rounded the corner of their street, I could see Frank, having progressed from polishing the car to sweeping the front walk. I knew he would never admit to what he was doing—he was too indirect for that—so I decided to park at the end of the street and just watch. He knew I had put more posters up; he could see them on streetlights up and down the block. Sooner or later he'd start taking them down.

Once it grew dark, Frank went inside and turned on the lights; three hours later at ten o'clock they went off. I hung around for another half hour, thinking he might sneak out, but when he didn't, I decided to call it a day.

More or less as a reflex action, I drove by the stores on Ocean Avenue on my way home. At the first intersection I checked a utility pole. There was no poster. I thought I had put one there today, but maybe I hadn't, since I hadn't had enough to poster everything. The next pole was bare as well, though, and the next, and the next. I drove around to the parking lots in back. The posters were all gone there, too.

What the hell was going on? There was no way Frank Russell could have taken down those posters. They had been up minutes before I had talked to him and, except for the brief time between our conversation and my stakeout, I'd had his house under surveillance every minute. My brain had turned into a kaleidoscope. Every time I shook all those little pieces, a totally different picture popped up. Something was wrong, but what? Did I need more information, or was I misreading data I already had? I sat in the van and struggled to put together a new hypothesis that accounted for all the facts, something that would suggest a plan, but my mind had gone blank. I had been so sure Frank was the person I was after, and now I was back at square one. Numb with disappointment, frustration, and sudden fatigue, I put the van in gear and headed back to the Russells' neighborhood. I had no clear idea of why I was going there, except that I wanted to check the posters I had put up earlier.

By this time it was after eleven o'clock, and the streets were deserted. The streetlights cast a cold light on the rows of sterile houses; except for a few wisps of fog, they looked more than ever like a movie set. Two blocks from the Russells' house I noticed a car with one door open parked next to a streetlight. As I approached, the door slammed shut and the car roared off. Too late, it occurred to me the driver might be the person I was looking for. I took off after it, but it was already one corner ahead of me, and I lost it. Easy, John, I said to myself, you're getting spooked. It's no good charging off half cocked unless you know what you're after.

I pulled up in front of the Russells' house and stopped. Like the other houses on the block, it was dark. I sat there for a long time, wondering what to do next. This is silly, I thought. What did I have in mind, waking them up and telling them I had falsely suspected Frank of taking down the posters, and then apologizing? Besides, I didn't feel much like apologizing. He still struck me as a pretty weird guy, and I didn't like his wife much either. This was ridiculous. What I needed was a good night's sleep. Maybe by morning things would sort themselves out in my brain, and I wouldn't feel quite so paranoid.

The next morning I was still confused, but sleep had restored my determination to get to the bottom of this case. Those posters hadn't just blown away; someone out there was trying to get the better of me, and I intended to find out who. I stopped by the printer's to order another thousand posters, and while they were in the works I drove over to Alice Russell's office. There were a few matters I wanted to get straight with her before I cashed her check. As I parked the van, it seemed to me that some of the posters I had put up the day before had been removed, but I was so suspicious at this point I couldn't be sure. At least there were enough to show Mrs. Russell I had been working.

The savings and loan was a totally nondescript office, neither down-at-the-heels nor especially fancy. I asked the first employee I saw for Mrs. Russell.

"Mrs. Russell?" she said. "She's back there," pointing to a gray-haired woman sitting at an imposing desk against the back wall. "Oh, no," she added quickly, as I started to swing open the gate in the railing. "She wants us to announce people first. Give me your name and I'll tell her you're here. Was she expecting you?"

"I'm sure she wasn't," I replied, "but I think she'll see me."

I watched impatiently as she tottered off on her platform shoes to announce my arrival, heavy legs exposed by a miniskirt someone should have told her was no longer in style. I saw her approach Mrs. Russell timidly, gesture in my direction, pause, and then totter back.

"Mrs. Russell will see you now," she said with an irritating air of self-importance.

Fighting off the feeling that I was an overextended customer challenged to demonstrate a good credit rating, I passed through the gate she held open for me and approached Mrs. Russell's desk. One look at her and I knew what her husband was up against. Nothing happened in her world that she did not control. I was sure not a penny in this office went unaccounted for under her steely gaze. She had a hard face, which black-rimmed glasses and a severe skinned-back hairdo did nothing to soften, and a stern expression, which no doubt my presence had something to do with. I introduced myself and took a seat next to her desk.

"So you're Sherlock Bones," she said, elbows on the desk and a thin gold pencil in her fingers. "I was glad to see a few posters this morning. I trust there will be more."

"I'm just about to pick them up from the printer's," I replied, ignoring her innuendo, "but I thought I'd drop by first. There are some things about this case I'm having trouble with."

"Yes?" Her expression was impenetrable as she coolly took my measure. She did not look happy with what she saw.

"Yes, well, I understand from your husband that you gave Raggs to him a year ago."

"That's correct," she said curtly. "One of my employees— she's not here today—owned the dog, but her building changed hands, and the new owner didn't like dogs. I saw no reason to go into that with you."

She certainly wasn't making this conversation very easy.

"What I was getting at," I continued, "was that your husband doesn't seem all that attached to Raggs. In fact, I got the impression he finds Raggs a bit of a chore."

"My husband told me you spoke to him yesterday," she said. "And I had expressly told you he was not to be bothered. He's not a well man, as I said. You had no business going behind my back."

"I'm afraid I don't see it that way," I replied, my hackles rising. "You hired me to find Raggs, and as far as I'm concerned I was just doing my job. Now, your husband tells me that you're gone during the day and he's left to care for the dog, and he seems to resent the—"

"I don't think we need to get into that," she cut in abruptly.

Carefully laying her pencil down on a pile of papers, she paused for a moment, and then said, "I've been thinking about my decision to hire you. I'm afraid it isn't working out."

"Well, it's just that I'm confused. I understood from you that Raggs was your husband's dog, and then I learn from him that . . . Perhaps there's something I don't understand, but I can't help wondering why you hired me. Now if we could just—"

"I said that's enough! I did not hire you to pry into my private affairs!" She caught herself beginning to shout, looked around quickly, and lowered her voice. "First you come to me with some wild, unbelievable story about the posters getting pulled down, and now you make insinuations that I do not like at all. Not at all. I think we'll call a halt to this little fiasco right now."

It was either throttle her or get the hell out of the office. "Perhaps that's best," I said, reaching into my wallet. "Fortunately, I haven't cashed your check. Here, take it back, and we'll just pretend none of this ever happened."

She glanced at the check and tore it neatly in two. "Fine," she said. "And the cost of printing the posters? I hope you don't plan on sending me a bill."

"Don't worry," I assured her, "I wouldn't dream of it." You may not want me to know the truth about your home life, I felt like adding, but don't think I've finished with this case yet, lady, because I haven't.

I left her office with my professional cool still intact and headed back to the printer's, but inside I was steaming. The Russells were a perfect match. If ever two people deserved each other, it was that pair. Mr. Russell and his military discipline—I'd met men like him in boot camp, the kind who take out their sadistic impulses on helpless recruits under the guise of building character. My anger at him boiled up a memory from my past I hadn't thought about in years. I was going through boot camp. On this particular day I had fallen from a rope I had been told to climb and had landed boot-high in a muddy creek. Wanting to change my boots, I asked the drill instructor if I could return to the barracks. That was bad enough, I suppose, but my fatal mistake was beginning my request with "Would you mind" instead of the required "Private Keane requests permission to . . ."

"A ewe is a female sheep, private," the drill instructor had said. "Report to my quarters after the evening meal."

By the time I got there I was almost paralyzed with fear, as he knew I would be.

"You've got a choice, private," he barked. "I can give you two hours of calisthenics or one punch. Take your pick."

I'd seen what he called calisthenics. "Sir, I'll take the punch, sir," I stammered, and with that he aimed a fist at my mouth that knocked me to the floor, lips bleeding profusely. "Sir," I said, struggling to my feet, "thank you, sir."

I should have run away, but of course I couldn't. None of us could. It wasn't allowed. After all, what's an abuser without something to abuse?

"I'm so glad you came," the receptionist said. "If you hadn't come in, I was going to call you. I showed Dr. Shively your poster." She led me into one of the examining rooms, where I was soon joined by Dr. Shively, a youngish, slightly balding guy with the friendly manner that seems to go with the profession of veterinary medicine.

"Dr. Shively," I said, "can you tell when a dog's been abused?"

"Sometimes," he said cautiously, "in gross instances. Usually, though, it's hard to detect with any real certainty. You need a pattern of injuries over a period of time to be sure—a series of broken bones, bruises, and certain kinds of internal injuries that result from being kicked or struck with hard objects. You'd be surprised, though. Some people freely admit beating their animals."

"What about Raggs?" I blurted. I'd finally found the figures I was looking for. Now I was adding them up.

"I'd prefer to keep this discussion hypothetical, if you don't mind," he said as he looked through a folder. "But take a white dog like Raggs. It would be easy to spot bruises on his sides and abdominal area where he'd been kicked. We sometimes see that when owners bring in their pets for shots or general checkups. Also, when you run your hands over a dog's body you find tender spots, and the dog will wince when you manipulate them."

"What about frequent urination," I asked, "when a dog is approached by a particular person?"

"In puppies that's often just excitement," he replied. "In older dogs it's much more unusual. Generally then it's a sign of submission."

"Or fear?"

"Or fear, right." He looked at me impassively.

It's funny. When the pieces finally fall into place, it feels as if they've been there all the time. "Dr. Shively," I said, "do you—"

"Look," he interrupted, "I think I know what you're getting at, but you'll have to appreciate my position. Legally, you're going way out on a limb when you try to prove animal abuse in all but the most severe cases. Let me just say, though, that if you were to tell me that Raggs has been abused, I wouldn't give you an argument."

"Thank you," I replied. "That's what I wanted to hear. Just one more question, and I'll let you go. Have you ever heard of a dog running away?"

"Unfortunately, no," he answered, "not in the circumstances we're talking about. Sometimes I wish they would, but as you know, dogs are incredibly loyal, too loyal for their own good."

I left his office buoyed up by a whole new game plan, the first I had felt comfortable with since I started this case. Dr. Shively had given me the final reassurance I needed for what I now intended to do—locate Raggs, make sure he had a good home, and, if not, find one for him. No matter what it cost me, he wasn't going to spend one more day with Frank Russell. That meant I had to make contact with the phantom poster thief before the Russells did. I had thought of the thief as an adversary. Now he or she seemed almost an ally. Since I'd already picked up my second order of posters, I decided to return to the shopping center and slap up a few more in store windows. They would be more difficult to sneak down than those on phone poles. If I thought it would have worked, I'd have added a personal message: "You can come out now, the coast is clear."

I had put up maybe twenty-five posters and was retracing my steps to the van when the owner of a liquor store saw me and said, "Congratulations! That was quick work!"

"Congratulations?" I asked. "What do you mean?"

"Finding the dog so fast! The owner was just in here, taking down the poster, and he told me all about it."

"Quick!" I yelled. "What did he look like? He wasn't an old guy, was he?"

"No, a young kid—beard, black hair, red jacket. You probably passed him. He just left."

Without pausing to reply, I turned and ran back up the street. I saw him coming out of a florist's shop with a poster in his hand. He took one look at me and stopped dead.

"Hey," I called, "can I talk to you for a minute?"

He took a few steps backward, then turned and started to run.

I grabbed the tail of his jacket. "Hold on!" I shouted.

He started to struggle free, and then just gave up. "Oh, jeez," he said, "oh, jeez. What a mess."

"You know who I am?" I asked. He looked about nineteen or twenty and, despite a fierce black beard, plenty scared.

"Yeah, I know you," he replied. "You're the guy that's been putting up all these damn posters. OK, OK, you win. I'm sorry, really, I'm sorry. Christ, I never thought you would put up so many. I should never have started this."

"You're right about that," I agreed. I still had the corner of his jacket in my fist, but he didn't look like he was going anywhere. "Can we talk?"

"Yeah, sure, let's talk. Oh, God, what a mess, what a stupid mess." He ran his hands through his hair.

"Where would you like to start?" I asked quietly.

"I don't suppose you'd believe Raggs was my dog, would you?"

"Start somewhere else," I responded dubiously.

"Yeah, but . . . OK. Well, last week I was here buying some beer, and I saw Raggs in this Mercedes. It was a pure coincidence, you've got to believe me."

"Coincidence?"

"Yeah, I hadn't seen him in over a year. I mean, I knew where he was, but I stayed away. I didn't want to see him any more."

"What do you mean, *any more?* You mean, you used to have him?"

"I told you, he used to be my dog," he replied. "So when I saw him, I went over and said hello. That was my first mistake. I hoped he'd recognize me, but I also hoped he wouldn't, you know what I mean? Like it would be easier if he didn't remember me."

"Yeah, maybe. So then what happened?"

"Well, he was so glad to see me he just went crazy, so I said what the hell, I'll take him out and play with him a little. I just reached in, unlocked the door, and took him out. You gotta remember, I never thought I'd see him again."

"And you just kept him." I was believing his story, coincidence or no coincidence.

"No!" he shouted. "I played with him, but then I put him back and locked the car again. I didn't feel so hot about doing it, but I did. I mean, he wasn't mine any more, right? Anyway, I got back in my car and was driving off when I see him running after me. He must have squeezed through a window somehow. Honest to God, I never touched those windows. He just squeezed through and started after me, jumping up against the car and barking. So I stopped and opened the door and he jumped in, right in my lap. I couldn't get him off. He was out of his gourd, he was so happy to see me."

"So *then* you kept him." If only I'd known all this three days ago.

"I hadn't planned to," he said earnestly. "I wasn't really thinking of anything. I just wanted to see him and take him home. He didn't look too good, you know. He seemed sort of puny and run-down. I thought I'd feed him and . . . hell, I don't know. I guess I just wanted him back, that's all."

The kid looked like he was heading for the electric chair. "If he meant so much to you," I asked gently, "why did you get rid of him in the first place?"

"It wasn't my idea!" he said. "It was my mom. See, she never liked him much, and when the new landlord took over, that was just the excuse she was looking for to get rid of him. So she gave him to her boss where she works. I admit I felt like stealing him, but I didn't want to get my mom in trouble at work. Her boss is a woman, and I guess she's a real bear. And Raggs would just have to go back again anyway, so I cooled it. I figured it was better all the way around."

"But didn't your mother see him when you took him home?"

"No. See, I don't live there any more. We had a big fight, and I moved in with some guys, and I don't see her. We don't get along too well."

"I see," I replied. "So you were really happy to see your dog."

"I knew he wasn't really my dog any more," he said quickly. "But yeah, I really was. I'd really missed him. At first I thought I'd keep him overnight and then take him back, but I couldn't decide exactly how to do that, and the longer I kept him the harder it got. So I figured I'd just cool it and after a while everything would blow over and I'd have Raggs. But then these posters started appearing and I panicked. I even saw you putting them up."

"Did you see me one night?" I asked, knowing what he would say.

"Yeah, near where Raggs lived. I recognized your van. I thought you'd catch me. I almost wish you had. I was getting crazy."

"I'll bet. What did you think the Russells would do? Didn't you think they'd try to get him back?"

"Yeah, but I never thought they'd hire a detective! So all of a sudden I feel like a criminal stealing someone else's dog. I had to get those posters down. I figured if no one saw them, then maybe it would die down. I don't know. I wasn't really thinking, I guess. And then you kept putting them back up, and I was running around taking them down, day and night. It was ridiculous, but once I started I couldn't stop." He stopped talking for a moment. "It's actually a relief, having it all over. So. I guess you want Raggs back, huh? His owners probably miss him a lot. They must, to have hired you."

"That's something we've got to talk about," I said. So this was the person I thought might have taken Raggs because of some grudge he held against the Russells. What would he do now if he knew the life Raggs had led? I didn't dare risk that. "First, though, let's take the rest of the posters down."

"Huh?" He looked dumbfounded. "Are you kidding?"

"And then you're going to take me to see Raggs, and we'll decide what to do."

There was really no decision to make, but to be absolutely sure, I wanted to see the dog. When we had finished, he got in his car and I followed him the mile or two to his house. I knew he wouldn't try any funny business. He was obviously not the sort of kid who was comfortable breaking the rules. When he pulled into his driveway, I heard a furious barking commence from inside the house. He opened the front door, and a small white cockapoo tore out and jumped into his arms. I'd seen his face on a thousand posters. It was Raggs, all right.

"Isn't he a great dog?" the kid said. "Ever since I got him back he hates for me to leave him, but I didn't want to take a chance, so I've kept him inside." He was sitting on the front steps; Raggs had gotten into his lap and rolled over on his back, squirming frantically between the urge to lick his master's face and the desire to have his belly rubbed. His master gave in for a few moments and then looked at me and slowly got to his feet. "So here he is," he said. "You've seen him. Now what?" He stood on the steps, his eyes fixed on me, trying to ignore the little dog jumping up on him.

"Now what?" I said. "Now I'm going to leave you and Raggs and take off."

He couldn't believe what I was saying. "But what about the people who hired you? They must have paid you a lot of money."

"As it so happens, they didn't pay me a penny," I replied. "But that doesn't matter."

He hesitated, torn between curiosity and not wanting to risk his sudden good fortune. "Then why?" he asked finally.

"Let's make a deal," I said. "You just take my word for it that it's OK for you to keep Raggs, and I'll pretend I never saw your dog. I'll write this off as one of my unsolved cases. What do you say to that?"

"I say it's great. But . . ."

"But what?"

"Nothing, I guess. Just thanks. Thanks a lot."

"Don't mention it," I replied with a smile. "This is one case I can truly say I'm glad I didn't solve."

9
A Canine
Con Artist

ALTHOUGH MACDUFF is one of the missing pets I never found, I always think of him with pleasure. I have no doubt that, wherever he is, he's having a good time—because if he weren't, he'd light out.

MacDuff is a Doberman who always goes where the action is, the dog who knows how to get exactly what he wants. I suspect he stayed with Sandy as long as he did—five years altogether, if you include the six months he spent with a cocktail waitress in Sausalito—because Sandy is just as free a spirit as Mac is.

Sandy's a graphics designer with her own studio who knows how to have a good time and included Mac whenever she could. She recognized his uniqueness and respected his individuality. "Mac's very much his own dog," she said. "He's a smart dog, and you've got to treat smart dogs well. They need to know the whole story. Dumb dogs are a lot easier to deal with."

When Sandy called me, it wasn't the first time Mac had taken off.

"The first time I was frantic," she said. "I went to the SPCA three times a week, and every night on the way home from work I'd zigzag through different neighborhoods to see if I could find him. The reason he left is a perfect example of what I mean about dealing with smart dogs. See, he's got this overnight bag for his dishes and food that I always take whenever Mac goes on trips with us. Well, this particular trip we couldn't take him, so we'd made arrangements for a friend to come over Saturday to feed and walk him. As soon as Mac saw I wasn't packing his bag along with mine, he just disappeared. When he didn't come home, I figured that he'd gone bar-hopping and someone had decided to keep him. Mac is in his element in bars. Now, I know a lot of dogs like to hang around groups of people, but Mac has it down to a science. Instead of just milling around wagging his tail, like most dogs do, Mac finds a receptive soul and focuses all his attention on him. He suddenly goes into his devoted-dog routine—sitting at this person's feet, looking up into his eyes, following him everywhere. Who could resist it? People are always taking him home. Once I got a call from a girl he had latched onto who asked me if she could keep him. I told her I wanted him back, but she seemed so upset I suggested she might want to stop by and visit with him from time to time. She decided that would be too painful. That's what I mean about Mac turning on the charm. She had only kept him for one night.

"That's what happened this time. Six months after Mac left, my attorney and his partner were sitting in a bar on Jackson Street talking about dogs, and a waitress told them they should see this other waitress's dog—a Doberman who did these weird tricks like stand on his head. Well, that's one of Mac's famous stunts. He puts the flat part of his head right down on the ground and just sort of growls until people laugh at him. The more my attorney heard, the more he was sure this dog was Mac, so he talked to the other waitress. He learned that her boyfriend had picked up the dog in a bar six months earlier and had given him to her when he was transferred to Ohio.

"I called her up and went out to see her. It was a very emotional scene. She lived in Tiburon with her little girl and really didn't want to give Mac up at first. I felt a little strange about it myself, but as usual Mac made the decision for himself. When he saw me he jumped up and gave me a big hug, he really did. He put his arms around me and lay his head on my chest and just squeezed. He wouldn't leave my side. We all sat and talked for a while. Then Mac went to the little girl and sat with her for about five minutes and did the same thing with her mother. Then he came back to me and went to the door, as if he were saying, 'It's OK now. I've said good-bye. Let's go home.' "

Normally I take clients' stories about their pets with a grain of salt. Scratch a pet owner, and you usually find a proud parent. But Sandy seemed different. I suppose you could say that Mac had hooked me, too, but what I found most appealing was Sandy's attitude toward him. A lot of owners regard their pets as people but, as with their children, they see them primarily as extensions of themselves, not as separate beings with their own unique personalities. Sandy struck me as unusual in that she loved Mac but at the same time gave him a lot of freedom to let him be, as she put it, his own dog. At any rate, since she felt like talking and I felt like listening, I got her permission to tape our conversation that day. Here is the story she told me:

"Buying a dog was the last thing on my mind the day I met Mac. I have a little Alfa Romeo convertible I love to drive on twisty mountain roads, and one morning I was tooling around the mountains behind Half Moon Bay and ended up at a kennel. I started talking to the owner in a general way, and he asked me to describe my ideal dog. I said I would want a dog that would be good protection as well as a good pet, since my work sometimes keeps me out late at night. He said, 'I've got just the dog for you,' and out trots Mac, this enormous Doberman, two and a half years old, over ninety pounds—and he just lays his head in my lap. He'd had obedience training and some protection training—the kennel ships protection dogs all over the country—but didn't work out. The guy said Mac was really good at climbing over fences and all that stuff, but that when the trainer put on all his padding for the attack training, Mac just laughed at him. I certainly hadn't planned on buying a dog, but there he was with his head in my lap—and he did fit my description—so half an hour later I'm driving back down the mountain with a huge dog hanging out of my car. And I'm starting to get a little scared. You know all those stories you hear about Dobermans? And here was this enormous dog, and we really didn't know each other at all.

"The first night I was actually afraid of him. He kept making these funny growling sounds. The kennel owner had said that Mac was used to dog food but that he could also eat whatever I was eating. Dinner that night happened to be spaghetti, and since I didn't have any dog food, that's what I fed Mac. Do you have any idea what tomatoes do to a dog's intestines? That's what all the growling was about. That first night he completely ruined my white flokati rug.

"I started taking him to my studio with me. I really had no choice. At first I'd say, 'Good-bye, Mac, you stay here,' but by the time I got to my car he'd be sprawled in front of it as if he'd been lying there for hours. He thought it was a big joke. That was when I realized he knew how to unlock and open sliding doors. I still don't know how he manages to get where he does. I've come home from the store with him, and I'm fumbling with bags of groceries trying to get the front door to the apartment building open. By the time I make it down the hallway to my apartment, he's already inside. He must climb through drainpipes.

"He's a terrific manipulator. If he wants to get out of the building, he'll go up and down the hall knocking on doors. At first he scratches, and if no one answers he shoulders the door—thud, thud. My neighbor was a Christian Science healer and Mac knew there were always a lot of people there who weren't wise to his tricks. So he'd knock on the door, pick out some sucker, grab his hand with his teeth, and actually lead him to the front door. He could always get out that way.

"There isn't anything he won't do to get a laugh. I think that's why he liked to go to work with me. Everyone at the studio likes to do crazy things, and we're an appreciative audience. He'll grab a towel or a rag and wrap it around his head and just stand there until people stop laughing at him. At Christmas I had this little wreath for him to wear around his neck, and it got to the point where he wouldn't go out of the house if he didn't have his wreath on. He's also got an incredible range of facial expressions. Once a guy who works for me drew some big Groucho Marx eyebrows on him, and stuck a Pentel in his mouth. Every time he moved his face his eyebrows went up. He had us rolling on the floor. Well, that afternoon I had an appointment and had to take a cab. Mac was with me, and when the driver looked in the rearview mirror and saw Mac, he freaked out. I'd forgotten all about the eyebrows.

"You know, taxis won't stop if they see you've got a dog, so he's learned to hide behind a bush or parked car until I can flag one down. Then he just sort of sneaks in. That's a useful trick. Once I ran out of gas on a freeway and had to hitchhike to a gas station. I was standing by the side of the road, but Mac had disappeared. I found him crouching behind my car, hiding from the traffic. Now, you've got to admit that's pretty smart.

"He has a strange relationship with cars. Maybe he thinks they're other animals. Once he was playing with another dog on the Marina green, having a great time, and when the dog's owner called it back to her car, Mac got mad. He wanted the dog to stay. So the woman is in her car—a VW—with her dog, and Mac is barking furiously. If she tried to go forward Mac would stand in the way and bark and nip at the wheels. When she backed up he'd run around to the rear and bark some more. It took her forty-five minutes to get from the Marina green to the Presidio. By this time Mac is frothing at the mouth because of all his running around, and when the military police at the Presidio see him they assume they've got a mad dog on their hands, right? They don't have any ropes or gloves, so while they are waiting for reinforcements to arrive, Mac has more time to really get into it. By now he's bitten off a big chunk of the rubber bumper and demolished both taillights—really—before they managed to capture him. But the best part is, the policeman who called me up told me Mac was one of the nicest dogs he'd ever met. Apparently as soon as he was caught he immediately turned into the most docile, charming pet. He completely snowed the policeman in just a matter of minutes.

"One of the reasons I don't worry about him now is that he simply will not stay where he doesn't want to. Take the story with the bone. My kitchen is on the floor above the dining room, and

Mac knows he's supposed to chew on his bones in the kitchen. One night we were having steaks. I gave him a bone, and he took it halfway up the stairs and started chewing. I told him to get upstairs, and he went up a few more steps and then started in again. So I gave him a whack. I assumed he was in the kitchen, but about an hour later I got a call from a friend who lives at least two miles away. Mac had climbed up his fire escape and jumped in his bedroom window. Things just got too heavy at home for him, apparently, so he ducked out for a while.

"By the way, that shows you what a navigator he is. He'd only been to my friend's apartment once before, and that was in my car. He used to find his way to my studio, on the other side of town. He'd show up at quitting time, and if I started to leave and then got sidetracked with a phone call or something, he'd start to get impatient. He used to go to the closet and get my coat out for me. The only problem with that was we all laughed so much that he'd start taking everything out of the closet just to keep his act going. One day I got a call from a pet-store owner in Belmont. God knows how Mac had found his way down there —he must have hitchhiked—but he was having a ball entertaining the customers. He'd found this white rat and would gently pick him up in his teeth and carry him around the store, showing him to everyone.

"He does all these outrageous things, and no one ever gets mad at him. I had him tied up outside a restaurant in Santa Cruz where I could watch him through the window. He would bark and spring at people—I think he was trained to spring when he was on a leash—and they were all giving him a wide berth. Then he would just sit there and smile—that's one of his expressions, by the way—and within half an hour he was getting about three out of every five passersby to pet him. That's a pretty good trick for a Doberman, don't you think? He still loves to terrify people, though. He used to lie in my car pretending to be asleep, and when people would get close he'd let out this ferocious bark. It was just to get a reaction, though. He'd never hurt anybody; he's even gentle in a dogfight. I've seen him in fights, and he always manages to dominate the other dog without actually hurting him. What he does is bite down on the other dog's ear just enough to control him.

"He's great with kids, too. One time he was snoozing at a party, and a three-year-old girl hit him on the head with an ax handle. Everyone thought he would attack the girl, but you know what he did? He licked the ax right out of her hand, just licked her hand right down to the ground until she dropped the ax.

"I know why he's gone now. I mean, he used to take little jaunts, but he always came home. But recently I got a horse and moved down to the beach. I know Mac needs a lot of attention, so I took him to the stables to see the horse, and I was very careful about being impartial. If I gave the horse an apple or a carrot, I'd give Mac one, too. Plus the fact I couldn't always take him to work since he'd be too wet from running on the beach. I thought he'd enjoy spending time there, but I guess he got bored.

"The last night he was home was very strange. A friend and I were having dinner, and I made a point of including Mac. He always joins in the conversation, of course, but I made sure his favorite mat was pulled up right next to us. He was acting very strangely, though. He'd go and sit in the corner and then turn around and look at me as if to say, 'Hey, don't you see I'm acting strange?' Then he'd go outside to this really windy point, right by a telephone pole, and stare back at us through the window. It really was sad. I was doing everything I could to make it a nice evening for him, but it wasn't what he wanted.

"The next day I didn't take him to work with me. He stopped by the stable during the day, and the last person I know who saw him was the old cowboy who works there. I figure Mac must have stopped to talk to some people and maybe got in their car—a lot of people pass through the area. He's got tags with my name and phone number and everything, so I guess someone must have stolen him. If whoever took him left his tags on, I'm sure I'll get him back. But if they took them off, I'm not so sure."

At the time Sandy called me, the sum total of my pet-finding activities consisted of making my "pound rounds," and Mac never turned up. When I began writing this book, I wanted to know if Mac had ever returned. Normally, I would assume that after the passing of so much time, he would not, but then Mac is obviously not your run-of-the-mill dog.

"No," Sandy said, "he hasn't come back. Maybe he won't. I know I still miss him, though, because I dream about him sometimes, and several times I've gotten out of my car to go after a Doberman I thought might be Mac. I do miss him, but there's not a lot of pain. It's sort of the way you miss a good friend who's moved away. He's much too smart to get hit by a car, and he's too good an escape artist to stick around people who are abusing him. I'm sure that wherever he is, he's having a good time. He just wouldn't have it any other way."

10
Notes from a
Pet Detective's Journal
(II)

IN THE MIDDLE of the night, crazed Spanish gypsies dance across my wooden floor, castanets working furiously. Clicketa-clicketa-click, scrabble, scrabble. Scrabble? Wait a minute. Spanish gypsies don't scrabble, even when crazed. I fight my way up through several layers of sleep, crack one eye, and there at the door is my Castilian rhythm section, looking for all the world like a turned-on Old English sheepdog just itching for a little action. It's Paco. Somewhere under all that hair I know he's got his big black eyes glued to my sleeping form, receptive as a radar station to my slightest move. One more sign of life from me, and what looks like a quietly quivering pile of fur will be all over me like a sweat. Carefully, so as not to make a sound, I slowly slide my eyelid closed, and in a few seconds I hear the slip of toenails, the thump on the floor, and the disappointed "hmph" that tell me he has given up his attempt at a midnight frolic. Nice try, Pac, I think as I drop back to sleep, but I win this round.

Talked to an old man today who wants me to find his black chow. The man was crippled and didn't have much money. I told him I wouldn't charge him.

"Now, don't give me that," he said. "I don't want no charity. I don't want that."

I told him it was my business and I could run it any way I wanted, and if I chose not to charge him, I wouldn't charge him.

"Well, it would be nice to have Blackie back," he said, "even though she keeps biting me. I wish she were biting me right now, in fact."

Another horror story from the animal shelter: a cocker spaniel was brought in with tags. The shelter called its owner, who promised to come down right away. Two days later he still hadn't come. They called again. He promised again. Four days later they put the dog up for adoption. Five days after that he hadn't been claimed, so they destroyed him. The next day the owner showed up, furious.

"It happens a lot," the attendant said. "What can we do? We can't keep a dog forever. Sometimes people won't come in to get their pet. They think it'll be cheaper to wait until it's put up for adoption. Then they won't have to pay boarding fees and fines—they think."

I'm beginning to understand why so many shelter people have such a cynical view of the "pet-loving" public.

Am disturbed by something that happened today. A woman called for help in finding her boxer. She said we'd met several months ago, walking our dogs in Golden Gate Park, but I had no recollection of any such encounter. This morning she showed up, and was she ever gorgeous! Long blond hair, blue eyes, great figure, nice tan—but I still didn't remember meeting her. Then she showed me the pictures of Sam, and *then* I remembered! Sam was the biggest boxer I'd ever seen, a truly striking animal with a gait like a thoroughbred racehorse and the bearing of a king. But how could I not have remembered his gorgeous owner? I must be getting entirely too wrapped up in this business.

Today a guy at the pound told me that every so often a Chinese sailor just off some ship will come in looking for a puppy —a nice, fat puppy. This guy says they're looking not for pets but for meals, because dog meat is considered a delicacy in China. I try to take a cross-cultural perspective on this practice—after all, what if I found myself spending the Thanksgiving holidays in a country where turkeys were pets?—but it isn't easy.

This business can get bizarre. Today I spotted a bus that matched the description of a vehicle a gang of petnappers is said to drive. So I followed it. When it stopped at a gas station I called the cops from a phone booth across the street. Within ninety seconds, what appeared to be an unmarked police car pulled up, and a really fat guy got out and handed me his card. A cop? No, a photographer who listens in on the police radio and chases down interesting reports. A few minutes later two police cars pull up.

"Why two?" I ask.

"Oh," a cop says, "the other guy read an article about you and just wanted to see what Sherlock Bones looks like."

The bus turned out not to be the one I thought it was.

Turned down an interesting payment today for finding a pit bull belonging to a pimp.

"Tell you what," he said, "how would you like a date with one of my girls?"

"Frankly, I'd rather have the money," I told him.

"What's the matter?" he teased. "Don't you like the ladies?"

"Yes, I like the ladies," I replied, "but my landlord likes the rent money, so I get paid up front in cash just like the ladies."

Dear old Paco, what a conversation piece. Yesterday evening I'm driving into San Francisco. The toll-taker on the bridge takes one look at Paco sitting next to me and says, "Is that the best you can do for Saturday night?"

11
The Case of the
Stolen Guard Dog

ONE LOOK AT MRS. GARVER was all I needed to know
that Ma's Royal Café had not been the best choice of meeting
places. There could be no mistaking her. She stood just inside
the front door, next to the notices for parent-effectiveness training and workshops in the world's most ancient healing art. Not
a hair on her well-coiffed head was out of place, which was more
than I could say for Mrs. Garver herself, an island of elegant
respectability in a noisy sea of tank-topped, tie-dyed countercul-
ture. She clutched an expensive leather handbag close to a navy-
blue suit that bore the unmistakable aura of tailored money, and
she smiled vaguely at the people brushing past her. She looked
like the lady of the manor who had come down to see how the
peasants spent their free time and was determined not to appear
shocked.

"How do you do, Mrs. Garver," I intoned with all the gra-
ciousness I could muster. "I'm Sherlock Bones. Sorry if I've kept
you waiting."

"Oh, hello there," she replied, extending her hand with
visible relief. "I'm so glad to see you. I was afraid I was in the
wrong place."

"No, this is Ma's, all right," I said. "But it seems even more
crowded than usual today. Perhaps you'd rather go somewhere
else."

"Not at all. You're busy and I'm busy and this is just fine.

It's rather . . . interesting, isn't it? I don't think I've ever seen a restaurant quite like this one."

I didn't doubt her for a minute. Ma's is an institution around Oakland among students, student types, laid-back members of the Consciousness III generation, and all those double-knit folk who like to observe the aforementioned species in their natural habitat. On weekends the lines go around the block, and no wonder. Ma's serves great food—wonderful omelets, home fries, natural-grain breads, and an assortment of dishes with bean sprouts, avocados, mushrooms, and raw vegetables that adds up to down-home organic cooking in the best California tradition. My waistline looms as more-than-ample testimony to its culinary expertise, but Ma's uniqueness lies in its decor. Hovering somewhere between a bus-station lunch counter and your crazy Aunt Tillie's attic, the atmosphere in Ma's is like no other. I'd been coming here so often I no longer noticed it, but Mrs. Garver's presence caused me to take a new look.

What gives Ma's its special flavor is its layered look. Over the years each new owner has simply added his own stamp without bothering to remove what was there before. The result looks like the inside of a time capsule. Jukeboxes and Coca-Cola pinup girls are left over from its days as a soda fountain. An ornately carved oriental mirror frame, corners tilted up like the roof on a pagoda, remains as evidence of its long history as a Chinese restaurant. The cultural schizophrenia of the last two decades is reflected in the collection of "found art" that is glued to, hanging from, or resting on almost every surface: a small American flag, a Halloween mask, a dusty pocket watch, a ventriloquist's dummy, and, gazing down from the rear wall, a huge buffalo head, its glassy-eyed serenity topped off by a woman's wide-brimmed green hat balanced on the point of one horn.

As soon as I spotted an empty booth, I hustled Mrs. Garver into it and snagged two menus from a passing waitress. The waitress was wearing a well-filled yellow T-shirt with *I'm Expensive* emblazoned across her very mobile chest and *But I'm Worth It* imprinted across her shoulder blades. I sneaked a look at Mrs.

Garver to see how she was taking all this, but she had forestalled the need for any explanations by busying herself with the menu. Just as well, I thought, I'll have a minute to collect my thoughts.

Mrs. Garver had called me that morning to ask if I could help locate Tony, a Saint Bernard–German shepherd that had been stolen from her husband's lumberyard. I had started asking about the dog's disappearance, but she had even more questions about me and how I worked. When every answer from me provoked another question from her, I decided the only way to allay her suspicions was for us to meet face to face. After checking our schedules, we decided that lunch was best, and I suggested Ma's. It happens to be right next door to my apartment, and I do a lot of business there, especially when my place is a mess—which it usually is.

The bouncing yellow T-shirt passed by again, this time with a tray of food.

"Oh, my," said Mrs. Garver, "doesn't that look tempting?"

Doesn't it, indeed, I thought, glancing at my client. Did I catch a glimmer in her eye?

Apparently not. "Yes, I'll have one of those omelets. They look simply delicious. And see the fresh carnations on all the tables. What a lovely touch!"

Feeling much better about Ma's now that she seemed to like the place, I placed our order and took the time before it arrived to fill Mrs. Garver in on myself. I then proceeded to ask about her dog.

"You said something about Tony being stolen," I began. About half the people who call me are convinced their dogs have been stolen, when in fact they simply wandered off, and I was fully expecting to hear the usual ". . . and the next time I looked out he was gone." Instead, Mrs. Garver began the story of a most curious theft.

"You see," she said, "as I told you, my husband owns a very large lumber business, and for several years we've used guard dogs to help keep down losses from theft. They're German shepherd–Saint Bernard mixes, really lovely dogs."

My mind stopped at the words *guard dogs.* I've got a thing about guard dogs. I've heard of too many owners who have deliberately underfed and underloved guard dogs in an effort to make them mean. I've always thought it was unfair for people to exploit a dog's natural instinct to protect his territory at the expense of his equally natural instincts for companionship and affection. An image of half-starved, desperate animals drifted into my head, and I suddenly didn't know if I wanted to take this case or not. I had no stomach for returning an animal to a life like that.

"... and we've just got to get Tony back," she was saying. "He's the cutest little puppy."

Puppy? Weren't we talking about guard dogs? "You'll have to excuse me, Mrs. Garver," I apologized. "I was thinking about something else."

"I can't really blame you," she replied. "It's not a very pretty story, a little puppy stolen right from under his parents' noses. And absolutely nothing they could do about it. It just makes me sick."

"I don't understand. How could that happen?"

"There is a double cyclone fence around the big yard where my husband stores lumber. The two fences are separated by about five feet. That way, if someone cuts through or climbs over the first fence, the dogs have time to get to him before he can get over the second fence. Well, Tony was between the two fences, and Sophie and Buck were behind the inner fence. Someone cut a hole in the outer fence and caught Tony. Or else Tony ran out through the hole. Anyway, he's gone."

"But if Tony's just a puppy—"

"I know," she interrupted, "why was a four-month-old puppy between the fences all by himself instead of with his parents? That's what you were going to ask, wasn't it?"

"Well, yes, something like that," I admitted.

"I'm afraid you'd have to know my husband to understand," she said carefully. "My husband is a . . . he's a strong man. He built his business from scratch, with no help from anybody. He's a firm believer in self-reliance. That's how he's raised our son,

Buddy. Buddy's twenty-one now and works in the yard, but even as a little boy his father made him work for every penny he got, even making him contribute for room and board. If it were up to me—but that's another story. The point is, my husband decided about three weeks ago that Tony should start earning his keep, so he began putting him between the fences at night to learn how to be a guard dog. You probably think that sounds cruel, don't you?"

"It's hard to say," I waffled, but I thought it did. I thought she did too, although she was far too loyal to come right out and say so.

"But I know he's just as upset as I am about Tony. He's not the kind of man to admit it, but I know he is."

I would have liked to share her conviction, but it sounded like wishful thinking to me. Her husband might be upset, all right, but probably more because of his wife's feelings than for any other reason. This wasn't shaping up into something I wanted to get involved in. I wasn't sure Tony's owner deserved to get him back. As a professional, I probably shouldn't have concerned myself with a moral judgment like that, but there it was. I hadn't gotten out of the insurance business to return innocent puppies to slave-labor conditions.

"How long has Tony been gone?" I asked, stalling for time.

"Two weeks," Mrs. Garver said.

"Two weeks!" I replied. "Why—"

"I know, I know," she interrupted. "I wanted to call you right away, but my husband wouldn't hear of it. But before you turn me down, there's one more thing."

"I didn't say I was going to turn you down," I objected.

"Not yet, but you were about to. I told you, I can tell what you're thinking. If I were in your position, I might think the same way. But just let me tell you about Sophie."

"That's Tony's mother, right?"

"That's right. Poor dear, I can tell she's feeling awful. She doesn't eat, just runs around sniffing the ground. It just kills me to see her like that."

I fixed Mrs. Garver with my most piercing stare, but she looked right back, her face a perfect picture of guileless concern for the distraught Sophie. I had heard of dogs grieving over their lost puppies but—well, didn't all puppies sooner or later grow up and leave home? Mrs. Garver, I said to myself, you sure know how to push my buttons.

"OK," I said finally. "I'll tell you what. Why don't I visit the lumberyard, take a look around, and see if there's anything I can do? I can't promise anything, but at least I'll take a look."

"Thank you so much," she said sweetly, permitting herself a slight smile. "I do appreciate it. I'll tell my son Buddy to expect you there—shall we say this afternoon?"

Having got the better of me, in her own ladylike way, Mrs. Garver proceeded to tuck into her omelet with great gusto, leaving me to wonder how I had been so easily trapped in a case I said I didn't want to take. Well, what the hell. I hadn't made any promises, had I?

Later in the afternoon, driving out to the lumberyard with Paco in the back seat, my mind turned to the case itself. The part that had me puzzled was motive. It's not so unusual for someone to pick up a mutt on the street or even to pluck a dog out of someone's yard. This kind of easy theft appeals to all types of petnappers, from the hardened professional to the little kid who contrives to make some pooch "follow" him home. But cutting through a cyclone fence to snatch a mongrel puppy? That didn't make sense to me. It requires a degree of premeditation, and besides, you also run the risk of getting caught breaking and entering. I just couldn't see anyone going to that kind of trouble over a dog that had very little market value, unless some other motive were involved. Maybe it was revenge. I made a mental note to ask Buddy about disgruntled employees or dissatisfied customers.

The lumberyard was located in a drab industrial section of town—lots of low buildings and sheds, big empty areas for trucks to park and turn around, a few billboards, a squat bar every so often—not really run-down, just sort of bleak, the kind of place you would notice someone on foot. The Garvers' lumberyard was doing a good business. In front of the main building people were struggling to fit planks of varying sizes into cars, station wagons, and trucks.

Before I went in, I decided to drive around the block to get a look at the yard in back. As soon as I turned the corner, I could see the double fence. It began at one corner of the building and formed three sides of a square before it reached the main building at its other rear corner. Inside the inner fence were stacks and stacks of all kinds of lumber raised off the ground on pallets and partially covered with flapping black plastic. Opposite the main building, the fences were interrupted by a double set of closed gates that I assumed were used for deliveries. I still hadn't spotted the hole in the fence, but no sooner had I pulled up at the gates than I saw the two dogs, Buck and Sophie, rushing toward me from between the two fences, barking and snarling. Paco took one look and decided to stay in the van, but I climbed out and approached the fence. I could see the worn path on the ground the dogs had paced in their fierce and lonely vigil, and once again I thought of all the stories I had heard about guard dogs. I couldn't imagine anyone who really loved dogs subjecting them to such a solitary way of life.

Suddenly the dogs stopped barking. A young man was crossing the yard toward me.

"Hello," I said. "I'm Sherlock Bones. Are you Buddy?"

"Bud," he answered briefly, busying himself with opening the gates. The two dogs stayed between the fences, no longer barking but keeping a close eye on us. They were both big bruisers. One seemed to be almost all German shepherd except for its floppy ears and a thickness around the face, while the other had the spots, the bulk, and the drooping muzzle that gave evidence of closer ties to the Saint Bernard side of the family.

"Hi, Bud," I said, sticking out my hand.

He ignored it pointedly. "So you're the guy my mother said would stop by. I hear you're going to get Tony back." His tone of voice made his estimate of my chance for success abundantly clear.

"Not exactly," I replied. "I just told your mother I'd come out and—"

"I don't suppose she told you what I've already done, like putting up signs. I'll bet that's all *you* do, isn't it?"

"Well, that's part of it," I said. Oh boy, I thought, what a welcome. How did I get into this, anyway—a case I wasn't sure I wanted and a kid with his nose out of joint who didn't want me around at all?

Buddy looked at me for a moment. "Well, as long as you're here, what can I do for you? I'm pretty busy, so let's get going."

"Fine," I agreed. "Why don't you show me the hole in the fence?"

Buddy shrugged and walked around to the side of the yard I hadn't seen yet. "There it is," he said laconically. "Just a little hole."

It certainly was small. The fence had been cut back at ground level, leaving an opening big enough for a dog to climb out—or a very small person to climb in. I studied the ground.

"Do people ever walk along the outside of this fence?" I asked.

"No, there's no reason to," he said. "You can see it's more of an alley on this side than a real street. Why?"

"That would explain why they picked this part of the fence."

"They? How do you know it was more than one?"

"The footprints." I pointed to the ground around the hole, where I had spotted several different impressions. Two or three were smaller and looked like they had been made by kids' sneakers, and one was adult-size. Buddy was peering closely at the ground—probably, I thought, for the first time. "That big one," I continued. "Could it be yours?"

"No way." I thought I detected a trace of respect in his voice. "I always wear these work boots, just like my father's."

"And see the tire tracks?" I went on. "It looks as if they pulled the car up real close to the fence, so no one could see them."

Buddy was torn between trying not to seem impressed and

wanting to hear more. "So OK," he needled, "who did it?"

"Hard to say for sure, of course," I said, wishing I had a pipe to pull on. Buddy's hostility was bringing out my professional detective rap. "Of course, I'll have to check things more thoroughly, but off the top of my head, I'd guess it's a group of kids and an adult, or maybe two adults."

Buddy kept giving me the old fish-eye. "Yeah," he said, "but why would they want Tony? He's just a mutt."

I wasn't about to give this kid the satisfaction of agreeing with him, so I changed the subject. "Can you think of anyone who might have a grudge against you or your family? An employee, maybe, or some irate customer?"

"Not that I know of, but you'd have to ask Dad to be sure. There he is now. Hey, Dad, Sherlock Bones wants to talk to you!" His voice was heavy with sarcasm.

"Sherlock *who?*"

A big, burly man dressed in khaki pants and work shirt and carrying a clipboard full of papers walked toward us. He had a full head of white hair, a luxurious mustache, and the weathered face of a man who spends a lot of time outdoors. I couldn't imagine a less likely husband for the elegant matron I had met just a few hours earlier. This man looked rough—crude even—yet he also carried himself with an easy authority. I suddenly wished I had adopted a more serious-sounding professional handle.

"Actually, my real name is John Keane," I said in my deepest, most sincere tones, "and I'm in the business of finding lost or stolen pets. Your wife tells me you might be able to use my help locating Tony."

He managed a smile and stuck out a huge, calloused hand. "Bob Garver, John, pleased to meet you. So you're the fellow Ada has been bending my ear about. Well, she's got you here, so what can we do for you?"

Buddy filled his father in on what we'd been talking about. I noticed that, while he wasn't quite so hostile as before, he wasn't about to endorse my findings until he'd gotten his father's reaction. Bob Garver was obviously a strong person. Two hours ago

I'd been wondering if I would take this case, and suddenly I was hoping he would approve of me. Actually, I found myself liking the guy. He radiated an aura of fairness and solidity I found appealing.

He looked interested when he heard about the footprints, and made some remark to Buddy about having told him to check for that sort of thing two weeks ago. The last thing I needed was for Buddy to feel any more competitive with me than he already did, so I interjected my question about any employees or customers who might have taken Tony in revenge for a real or imagined slight. He couldn't think of anyone who fit that bill. He asked me a few questions about how I worked and what my fee would be. Then, after a moment's pause, he smiled. "OK, Sherlock, or whatever your name is, you're in business. Let's go up to my office and I'll write you a check."

As we made our way along the fence back to the office, the two dogs followed us closely—or rather, they followed Bob Garver. He'd reach down absentmindedly through the fence, and they would give his hand a nuzzle and a lick.

"Great dogs," he said. "I got them at the animal shelter. We've had Sophie for eight years and Buck for four. They both would have been destroyed, more than likely, because they were too aggressive to make good pets, but they're perfect for here. They've got no use for strangers, but once they get to know you they're pussycats. Don't let that get around, though. I'd hate to ruin their reputation."

I was getting a totally new viewpoint on guard dogs—and their owners.

"What about Tony?" I asked. "Your wife said you were training him to be a watchdog, too."

"Yeah, but just between you and me, he was a dead loss. I promised her that if we get him back she can keep him at home, but to tell you the God's honest truth, I was about to give him to her when he was stolen. Don't tell her, though, or I'll never hear the end of it."

That reminded me of something else. "Mrs. Garver tells me

Sophie's really been off her feed since Tony was taken."

He stopped and gave me a quizzical look, then shook his head and smiled. "Oh, Ada told you that, did she? Well, see for yourself. She looks OK to me. Of course, my wife's more sensitive to things like that than I am."

Sophie didn't look to me as if she were pining away, and despite Bob's gruff exterior, he didn't seem all that insensitive to his two dogs either. Ada Garver, I decided, was a woman who knew how to get what she wanted. And she had gotten me on this case.

"So," I said, when all the formalities were taken care of, "if you've got a snapshot of Tony, I'll take it to get some posters made. I think about seven hundred should do it."

"Buddy," Bob said, "get that picture your mother took last month. I think it's out by the cash register."

"But, Dad," Buddy complained, "we've already offered a three-hundred-dollar reward. I don't see why we—"

"You don't have to see why," his father interrupted. "Just do as you're told. And when those posters are ready, you're going to help put them up. That's a lot of posters, and I want John free for more important things. How'd you like an assistant, John?"

The last thing I wanted was to ruffle Buddy's feathers any more than was absolutely necessary, but I agreed to drop off half the posters for him to put up in the immediate neighborhood; I would take the outlying districts and the area's schools. Without ever making a conscious decision, I was on the case, and with a clear conscience. Bob Garver might make his son's life miserable, but he seemed to treat his animals well, and I had no fears that Tony would be returning to an intolerable life—if he returned at all, that is.

As I was walking out the front door to go back to my van, I caught sight of the reward notice Buddy had posted on the front gate. On a tiny four-by-five-inch card he had lettered: $300 RE-WARD FOR RETURN OF DOG STOLEN FROM THIS PROPERTY. It sure wasn't going to be hard to top *that* advertising campaign.

The next day I picked up the posters, dropped half off at the lumberyard, and swung around to several pounds—more from force of habit than from any real hope of success. I couldn't seem to get a fix on this case. I had known of adults and kids working together in dognapping rings, but this seemed different. If the dog had been taken for the reward money, whoever did it would have made some kind of contact with the Garvers by now, and if it had been stolen to sell—but that didn't make sense either. For all Tony's puppy appeal, there were too many dogs loose for the taking to go to all that trouble to snatch Tony through a fence. Maybe the smaller footprints were made by women, I thought, but that didn't ring true, either. In my experience women don't get involved in escapades like this—although these days anything is possible.

On the third day I hit the schools and started plastering posters near playgrounds, in front of stores where I could see kids hanging out, and on nearby telephone poles. I hated this floundering phase, just going through the motions without having any real idea what I was looking for, but I had no choice. I talked with several kids. No one knew anything about Tony or had any idea who might have taken him, but everyone thought the reward was a swell idea and promised to get busy on the case. I'd heard *that* before.

By lunchtime I had affixed one of my last posters to a telephone pole near a playground and was wondering if I should get some more from my friend Buddy when I noticed a kid hanging back against the playground wall watching me. He looked to be maybe thirteen or fourteen—on the pudgy side, with glasses, jeans, sneakers, and a T-shirt. He looked as if he had something to say but was waiting for an opening, so I gave him one.

"Hello," I said. "You didn't happen to see this missing puppy, did you?"

"Which one?" he asked. "Oh, that one. Why?"

"I don't know, just thought I'd ask."

"Not me," the kid said. "Hey, what are you, a cop or something?"

This kid was not too swift. I had a mental image of a policeman spending hours plastering posters of missing dogs all over town. "No, I'm Sherlock Bones. See my name on the poster? I find people's missing pets."

The boy's eyes grew wide. "You mean, they're *paying* you to find their dog?"

"That's right, and they're also offering a three-hundred-dollar reward. So keep your eyes open. You may earn some quick money."

This kid didn't tumble. "You're sort of like a private detective, right?"

"Yeah, I guess you could say that—except I just work on animal cases."

"Boy," the kid said, obviously intent on his own train of thought, "*I'd* never steal that dog. I'd never do something like that."

"Glad to hear it," I responded.

Steal that dog? I hadn't said anything about the dog's being stolen, and I never mention that fact on a poster. That's a good way to turn people off who may have valuable information but who don't want to inform on someone who may have committed a crime. Nor does it leave any face-saving room for the petnapper. Of course, the boy could have jumped to that conclusion on his own. I took another good look at him. He was getting more nervous by the minute and seemed just about ready to bolt. I could see it was time for an appearance by Dr. Bones, the old armchair psychologist, and his trusty sidekick Paco, that canine confidant to boys in distress.

"Look," I said, "would you do me a favor? I've got to get something from that grocery store across the street, but I don't want to leave my dog in the van. Would you mind just holding his leash while I make a quick dash?"

Before he had time to refuse, I got Paco out, snapped on his leash, and handed it to the kid. I hurried across the street, picked up a couple of cans of soft drinks, and by the time I came back the boy was sitting on the low wall scratching Paco's ears. As I had hoped, Paco had worked his special magic, and the boy already seemed a lot calmer. I offered him a soft drink and joined him on the wall. Neither of us said anything for a moment.

"This is a neat dog," the boy said finally. "What's his name?"

"Paco," I replied. "You seem to have a way with dogs. I can tell he really likes you."

The boy squirmed at the compliment. "Yeah, I guess so. We used to have a dog, but he died."

"That's too bad," I said. After another long pause, I decided it was time to draw him out. "Hey, what do you think of that three hundred bucks? That's a lot of money, don't you think?"

"Yeah, I guess so."

"You know," I went on, "you don't have to actually find the dog to get the reward. Anybody that's got information leading to the dog's whereabouts will get the money."

He shrugged and stared at his feet.

"Of course," I continued, "all the owner wants is to get the dog back, no questions asked. No one wants to make problems for anyone."

No response.

"And it's all confidential, just between me and the other person—and Paco, of course. He helps me on all my cases."

Paco, bless his heart, chose that moment to stick his furry face in the boy's lap for another ear scratch.

"So if you think you might have seen something," I wound up, "Paco and I would sure like to know, even if it's just a hunch. Every little clue helps."

The boy was massaging Paco's head. "Well, there's this kid I know, sort of," he began, "but he didn't actually do anything. I mean he did, but it wasn't his fault. See, this other kid made him."

"Other kid?" I restrained myself from coming on too strong.

"Well, not a kid exactly, more like an older guy, maybe eighteen or nineteen. Larry. Anyway, it was his idea."

"What was?"

"I don't know, the whole thing. I mean, the way it happened

was they were just riding around with this guy Larry, in his car, see, and they saw these dogs behind this huge fence, and he stopped, and . . . but my friend didn't know they were going to do that." His voice trailed off.

I picked up my cue. "I certainly agree that it doesn't seem to be your friend's fault, not if it wasn't his idea. The main thing is to find the dog and get him back home. Did you know the other dogs were the puppy's mother and father?"

"Really?" The news seemed to stun him.

Treading carefully so as not to back him into a corner, I asked, "Do you think your friend knows where the dog is?"

"He doesn't have the dog. Larry kept him in his car."

"Oh, I see. Well, maybe your friend knows where Larry lives."

"Yeah, well, he might know where Larry's mother lives. I . . . I could ask him."

"You could," I replied. "Of course, that would take time. If you'd like to take care of this right away . . . well, I was thinking, maybe you might have some idea yourself of where she lives. Maybe we could just drive around and it might come to you."

He looked at me closely. "Yeah. OK, let's go." We both knew the facade of "his friend" had just about collapsed, but neither of us acknowledged it. He directed me down a thoroughfare and then slumped in the seat without saying another word, a picture of dejection and tormented guilt.

I knew just how he felt. Twenty years earlier the same thing had happened to me. It was a hot Saturday night in Queens, and I was thirteen years old. Some of my friends and I were riding around with Bob Schultz in his falling-apart Cadillac convertible, the latest in the string of beat-up cars he always drove, drinking beer and feeling like tough guys. Bob Schultz must have been about twenty, the kind of kid any mother would warn her children to stay away from. I'd been warned too, but the temptation of playing with the big boys was too strong to resist, so here I was cruising the streets and throwing beer cans out the windows. I suppose even then I must have wondered why anyone Bob's age would hang out with kids so much younger, but we were too flattered by his attention to ask questions.

On this particular night, Bob had had a fight with his girl friend, who had gone out with someone else. He decided to visit her parents' house, where she lived, and make their lives miserable. When we drove up the house was dark, and Bob instructed us to take all the old empty beer cans in the car—there must have been dozens—and build a pyramid right in front of the front door.

"Can't you see her old man going off to church tomorrow morning and knocking beer cans all over the front lawn?" he chortled.

I was terrified of such a stunt—pranks were pranks, but in my family you didn't mess around with adults—but I was afraid to say so for fear of being left out of future adventures. Even in my beery state, however, I managed to stay in the car with Bob while my friends took the cans and started to carry out his orders. They had just gotten started when a car rounded the corner.

"Jesus!" Bob swore. "That's Kathy and that creep she went out with!" Without waiting for my friends, he tore down the street like a maniac. I was too scared to say anything.

In a few minutes we pulled into a secluded spot underneath the Whitestone Bridge. Bob got out of the car, jacked up the rear end, and put a snow chain on one of the tires.

"Hey!" I shouted. "What's going on?"

"You'll see soon enough," was his answer, and off we tore, this time to Malba, a then-lovely neighborhood with larger homes and beautiful lawns. Suddenly, without warning, he wheeled the car up onto a lawn and floored the accelerator, and the car leaped forward, leaving a long ugly gash in the grass.

"Are you crazy?" I shouted. "What do you have against those people?"

"I don't even know the rich bastards," he snarled, "but when I'm mad, the world pays."

"Well, you can leave me out," I said.

His response was to tear up another lawn, and then another.

At the end of the block, he lurched back on the street, took a corner too fast, and sideswiped a couple of parked cars.

Now I was truly terrified. This, I knew, was out-and-out crime. All fears of chickening out vanished. I wanted to go home. At the first stoplight, I leaped out of the car.

"See you later, candy-ass," he laughed, and with that he took off down the street, his chain striking a stream of sparks against the pavement.

My mother met me at the front door, quickly took in my flushed face and beery breath, and grabbed my shirt. "You've been out with that Schultz boy, haven't you?" she shouted. "After everything we've told you!"

I wriggled out of her grasp and ran up the stairs.

"You just wait till your father gets home," she shouted after me. "He's going to take care of you good!"

The funny thing is, I don't remember my punishment, although I'm sure it must have been severe. I always wished there had been someone I could have told about what happened, someone who could have helped me put the events of that summer evening in perspective, but there was no one. What lasted over the years was a suffocating sense of guilt and a feeling I'd done something so terrible that I could never atone for it, no matter how hard I tried or how good I was.

The boy pushing my arm brought me back to the present. "Hey, I said turn here," he repeated.

He pointed me down a street of Spanish-style stucco bungalows set close together. I knew we must be getting close because he had slumped so far down in the seat as to be almost invisible from the outside. I realized the risk he was taking.

"Don't stop," he said, "but I think that's her house. He doesn't live there, though. She kicked him out a couple of months ago."

I made a note of the address and kept on going. At the end of the street I turned and headed back to the playground. I thought he would be relieved to have it over and done with, but he still seemed upset. For obvious reasons, neither of us had mentioned the three hundred dollars. When I pulled over to the curb he started to get out, but I held him by the arm.

"Listen, there's something I want you to tell your friend," I said.

"I know, I know," the kid said. "That he did a really bad thing."

"Well, yes, but I think he knows that already. Actually, there are a couple of things. First, tell him to stay away from that guy Larry. Larry should be hanging out with people his own age, not getting little kids in trouble."

"I know." My friend nodded vigorously.

"But you know the most important thing?"

"What?"

"The most important thing is to tell him this isn't the end of the world for him. Tell him what's important now is to learn from what he did. If he's smart, this whole experience will help him get his act together. In fact, maybe this is exactly what he needed to shape up. Tell him—but I don't have to tell you what to say. You've got the picture, haven't you?"

"Yeah," he replied, suddenly happier and more animated. "I'll really tell him." He opened the door and stepped down. "And thanks a lot."

"Don't thank me," I said. "You were a big help, and we appreciate it—Paco and me."

"OK," the boy said, grinning broadly now. "Well, I've got to go. So long—and so long, Paco." And he ran off.

Things started happening more quickly after that. In my reverse directory—which lists an area's residents by address rather than by name—I discovered that the woman who lived in the house the boy had pointed out was a Mrs. Ethel Stovak. Feeling a little like Sergeant Friday on an old "Dragnet" show, I returned to her house and rang the bell. A timid, gray-haired woman in a neat dark skirt and white blouse answered the door.

"Mrs. Stovak?"

"Yes, I'm Mrs. Stovak. Is something wrong?"

With a son like hers, that seemed a logical opening line. "I'd like to see Larry, please."

"Larry? He's not here. I mean, he's not living here at the moment. Is something . . . is there something I can do?"

"It's about my client's missing dog. I have reason to believe your son may know its whereabouts." I was trying to sound as official as possible.

"Your client? Oh dear. Well, won't you please come in?"

She never should have let a strange man in her house without demanding proper identification, but as I was beginning to see, Mrs. Stovak was the type of person who not only expected the worst but also seemed to think she deserved it. She ushered me into a shabby living room.

I sat on the couch and told her briefly who I was and what had happened. She listened impassively, and I couldn't help but feel sorry for her. The details might be new, but I'm sure the story was an old one for her.

"I don't know what to say," she sighed. "The dog isn't here. You can look around if you like."

I assured her that wouldn't be necessary.

"Larry has such bad luck," she said. "About two months ago someone gave us a dog, and Larry became very attached to her. About a week later she disappeared. I'm sure she must have been hit by a car, but Larry was convinced someone stole her. I don't know what put that idea into his head. You know, he's really not a bad boy, he just has such bad luck."

It was a mother's classic line. I didn't want to make Mrs. Stovak's life any more difficult than I had to, but my first responsibility was to my client, and I could see Mrs. Stovak needed a little spine-stiffening.

"Here's the situation," I said. "My client is a woman who just wants the dog back, period, no questions asked. Her husband wants to prosecute, but so far his wife has the upper hand, and I think if the dog were returned immediately, they'd let the whole matter drop. I'm sure you agree that with your son's bad luck, the last thing he needs is a run-in with the law. So why don't you tell me where he is and I'll have a talk with him."

"Oh dear," she said. "You see, I don't actually know where he is. He comes around, but I never know when."

"In that case," I replied, "perhaps the best thing is to turn it all over to the police and let them find him."

"No," she said, with a hint of firmness in her voice, "please don't do that. I . . . let me call my brother. Ever since my husband died, he's been trying to help me with Larry. He's the one who told me I shouldn't have him around the house any more. He's been awfully tough on Larry, I think, but he might know where he is. Please, let me call him before you do anything."

Somewhat reluctantly, I agreed to wait another day, but by the next afternoon I had heard nothing and was getting nervous. I was wondering if Mrs. Stovak hadn't been fooling me with her helpless downtrodden act when the phone rang.

"Sherlock, this is Bud, out at the lumberyard. You'll never guess what just happened!"

"Probably not," I said. "Give me a hint."

"Tony's back! I guess we didn't need your services after all."

"Well, what do you know! Tell me, did a kid about nineteen or twenty bring him back?"

"Uh—yeah," he said, surprised. "How did you know?"

"That's the guy who stole him."

"You mean, you—" he began. "How did you find him?"

"It's a long story," I replied. So Mrs. Stovak had done her duty. "How's Tony?"

"He's fine. You should have seen the happy reunion. It even got to Dad, and he's the original great stone face." Poor Buddy was so impressed he lost his cool altogether. "So it was you that put the fear of God into him. That was a great idea. He was a nervous wreck, babbling about having done what he was supposed to and now he wouldn't have to go to jail. The guy was really a basket case."

Larry's uncle must have really put the heat on, I thought. I told Buddy I'd try to get out to see Tony in the next few days. The biggest reward in my job comes from seeing the object of all my labors happily reunited with his owners, but I suddenly got busy that week and never made it to the lumberyard. My real interest in this particular case, however, lay not so much with Tony and his family as with that boy at the playground wall. I wanted to let him know everything had turned out all right. I also wanted to tell him something I had remembered about Bob Schultz, the guy who had gotten me into so much trouble when I was a kid. Years later, when I had just gotten out of the marines and was back visiting my old neighborhood, someone told me that Bob had finally straightened himself out and found a career—as a New York City cop. I appreciated the irony, but I thought the boy would appreciate the fact that even the really bad kids can change. I realized, though, that I didn't know his name and had no way of finding him. A couple of times I drove by the playground, and even sat on the wall with Paco, but I never saw him again.

12
A Different Kind
of Caring

ELI'S INITIAL PHONE CALL caught me at a down point in my career as Sherlock Bones. I think that may be why I misread him so badly over the phone, and why I later got so involved with him and his dog, Cal—too involved, I'm tempted to say, although in the end I came to a new acceptance of my evolving feelings for animals.

For a change, this particular down point was more emotional than financial. I had more work than I could handle—mostly consultations, one-shot deals in which I designed a poster and laid out a search plan for the client to follow. I much preferred full-time cases where I assumed total responsibility, but I hadn't had any for several weeks. Doing consultations made it possible to help more people, but it took me out of the action and placed me in the role of adviser. I could feel myself going stale. Although I still cared deeply about animals, it bothered me to realize I was not the same person who had stood in the back room of the Oakland Animal Shelter and heard for the first time the fate that awaited unclaimed pets. The white-hot zeal of the convert was beginning to fade. Even my relationship with Paco seemed different somehow. Those initial fantasies of me and my trusty dog against the world no longer held the meaning they once had. I still loved him. He was still important to me, but it wasn't the same as it had been at first.

What I thought I needed to snap myself out of my slump

was a case I could really sink my teeth into, but all I got were consultations. Perhaps it was just my mood, but most of these clients seemed to be just going through the motions. The one I did for the couple on Russian Hill the morning of Eli's call was a typical example of how things had been going. The friend's dog they were caring for had gotten lost, the woman told me on the phone, and they were frantic—more, apparently, because of what the dog's owner would think of them than out of any concern for the animal itself. She'd seen me on the Johnny Carson show and wanted to know how I worked. I explained my two types of services and my fees: $30 for a consultation, $100 a day plus expenses for a full-time effort.

"Oh, I think thirty dollars is quite enough," she had said, and so there I was in their elegant drawing room, sitting across from them with my notes spread out on a pink marble coffee table.

"So in this way," I was saying, filling in a diagram, "by putting posters here, at an angle on the poles, you catch drivers who stop for the light. Then put some on the other side of the poles, higher up, where pedestrians will spot them. Any questions so far?" I looked up to see them staring at me blankly.

"Yeah," the man said, rousing himself from his obvious boredom. "What's Johnny Carson really like, anyway?"

To their great relief, I wound up my session with them as quickly as I could and beat it back home to check my messages and go over the mail. Surely there was someone who really needed my help. Among the letters was a newspaper clipping a friend had sent me about a woman who had mortgaged her home, quit her job, and was now devoting every waking hour to a search for her missing Irish setter. After almost a year she was still looking and still hopeful. Now that's dedication, I said to myself, that's real determination and gallantry. But at the same time a small voice in my head piped up: Yes, but at what cost to the rest of her life? Where do you draw the line between determination and obsession? Shouldn't she think about letting go? I tried to put these thoughts out of my mind, but they refused to go. What was the matter with me? If anyone should champion her cause, it was Sherlock Bones. Was I becoming calloused just like the employees at the animal shelters?

So, a few minutes later when Eli called, my spirits were none too good—and he didn't do much to raise them. In heavily accented English he told me that his golden retriever had been stolen three days ago from in front of the library on the Berkeley campus, where he had tied it while he was inside doing some research. He was traveling through Berkeley, living out of his van, and someone he had met yesterday had given him my name. Could I please tell him something about myself?

I mentioned my two types of services and my fees.

There was a long pause, and then he told me he couldn't afford me full time, and as for a consultation, he was sure he had already done everything I would tell him to do.

There was an arrogant curtness in his voice that turned me off. In my present frame of mind, I couldn't resist giving him the business. "I assume, then," I said, equally curt, "that you've put up posters? Several hundred?"

"Posters?" he repeated, obviously taken aback. "No, I . . . what should these posters say?"

This was not one of the times I felt like passing out free advice. "That all depends on the circumstances," I said. "I cover all that in my consultation."

"Well, how much would you charge to make posters for me?" His tone had softened somewhat.

"Look," I said, regretting my initial antagonism, "if it's just the posters you want, and not any advice, it would be cheaper for you to go directly to the printer. That's what I do, anyway, and I'll be happy to give you a couple of names."

I heard him say something in a language I couldn't understand. "I beg your pardon?" I asked.

He laughed briefly. "I said, *Hoo yavo in pajama.* That's a saying I remember from my family in Israel. It means, He will come with pajamas."

"I'm afraid I don't follow you."

"Well, in other words, someone coming for advice who already thinks he knows everything should be prepared to stay a long time to get what he came for. Please forgive me. I see now you are an honest man, and I would like a consultation with you as soon as possible. And I promise not to bring my pajamas."

We agreed to meet in an hour at a nearby coffee shop he was familiar with, but I still had some serious misgivings. He had changed his tune so quickly I was afraid he might now change his mind about keeping our appointment. And as for having to work the area around the Berkeley campus—well, maybe it was colorful and politically important ten years ago, but today there are so many street vendors, panhandlers, and soapbox orators you can barely make your way down Telegraph Avenue. And there are dogs running loose everywhere. In short, it's not the easiest place to track down a missing pet.

Eli had described himself as having red hair and a beard, and I had no trouble picking him out. He was sitting in a booth, an open notebook on the table before him. He was short and thin, wearing jeans, a T-shirt, and running shoes. I pegged him as somewhere in his early thirties, about my age.

I introduced myself and sat down. We began chatting, and it didn't take long to realize that Eli really needed my help. He presented a much more vulnerable, desperate quality in person than he had over the phone. No wonder his cocky facade had crumpled so quickly. This guy was a bundle of emotion strung out so tight I thought he might snap.

Before we got into the consultation, I wanted to get him more relaxed so he would be able to hear what I had to say. In response to my promptings, he told me he had come to this country at the age of twenty-two from a tiny village in Israel. His purpose was to get the high-school education he hadn't qualified for at home, but, having attained it here with honors, he then went on through college and two graduate degrees, supporting himself with scholarships and a heavy schedule of part-time jobs. Now he was living in Massachusetts, where he continued to explore different fields in education and mental health. There was undoubtedly something of the professional student about Eli, a way of life I'm not ordinarily too keen on, but I admired his courage. In fact, as he began loosening up, I found myself liking the guy.

His dog, Cal, was the most important thing in his life. Eli had gotten him three years ago, right after his girl friend had walked out on their five-year relationship. "I needed a friend," he said, "someone who wouldn't leave me. A dog just seemed the natural thing."

It soon became apparent that Eli lived for Cal (short for California). They did everything together, including taking long runs through the Massachusetts countryside. In fact, he told me, he'd dropped out of rabbinical college because it had taken time he preferred to spend with Cal. On the trip he was making across the country, Cal had been his only traveling companion. "I wasn't lonely," he said. "With Cal I had all I needed."

It was one of those occasions when two total strangers achieve instant rapport. True to his promise, Eli placed himself totally in my hands. I had the know-how and the levelheadedness he needed right now. He had an openness to the feelings that had gotten me into this business in the first place, feelings that I was still not always at ease with. Most compelling to me, however, was the totally involving relationship with his dog that fit the fantasies I wanted to recapture for myself.

After we'd talked for a while, he paused and looked down at the notebook in front of him. "You know," he said, looking up at me, "when I'm distressed it often helps me feel better to put my feelings into words." He shifted in his seat. "I've written a farewell letter to my dog. Would you like to hear it?"

I was stunned. A farewell letter? What could I say? "Sure, go ahead."

"To my son, Cal," he began. "Peace and shalom. This is perhaps the last letter I will write to you, but I will always remember you. You were such a wonderful dog, such a pal, so intelligent, so free, and so strong. You brought light to my life. When I went to sleep at night you kissed me, you really kissed me. When I drove my van you sat beside me and kissed me again. There will never be another dog like you.

"When you were stolen from me, I cried and cried on the streets of Berkeley. Please, please know I did not sell you or give you away, and I never would. You were more important to me than anything else I had, and for all the water in the Jordan River I wouldn't have given you away. I hope your new home will be a loving and caring one. I look for the reason you were taken from me, for I believe there must be some purpose, but the streets of Berkeley are wet with my tears, and still I cannot find it."

The words began to catch in Eli's throat. "Maybe some day I'll get another dog, another golden retriever, but he'll never be like you." Tears began to flow from his eyes. "You were"—he breathed heavily in an effort to remain in control—"you were my pal, my friend, part of me. Good-bye, good luck, and please, *please* don't forget me." His hands went to his face and he gave in to helpless sobbing, oblivious to anyone around him. I sat across the table, wanting to reach out but not knowing what to do or say.

After a moment I pulled a napkin from the holder and handed it to him. "That was beautiful," I said.

"So was Cal," he cried, "but he's gone now." He fell again into broken sobbing.

I could feel the tears in my eyes as well. Wait a minute, Eli, I wanted to say, he's not gone yet, we'll find him. It's not fair that your dog should have been taken from you. He was your mainstay in life.

For the first time in weeks I felt a surge of the old feelings of outrage, of wanting to *do* something. This was a case I had to take—and solve, no matter how long it took. I knew I would be asking Eli to reopen a wound—his letter truly had been a farewell message—but I couldn't let him give up.

"Eli," I said, "you know what? We're going to find Cal. The two of us. Together."

He put his hands to his face. "Find Cal? But what about your fee? I can't—"

"Let me worry about that," I interrupted. He shook his head

in disbelief and brushed his eyes with his hands. Before he started to cry again, I reached into my briefcase and pulled out a blank poster. "Let's get going," I said. "Do you have any photographs of Cal?"

"Back in Massachusetts. Maybe I could—"

"No time for that." I took out my book of charcoal dog drawings. "How about this one?" I asked, pointing to a sketch of a golden retriever. "Does that look like Cal?"

"Yes," he said, sitting up. "It really does."

"OK," I said, cutting it out of the book. "Why don't you paste it here, on the poster, and then we'll decide what we want it to say." I wanted to get him involved.

By the time we had decided on the wording his mood had brightened considerably. I convinced him to offer a reward of $100, even though he didn't have that much money immediately available. Once he got his dog back, I told him, he could always arrange a series of payments for whoever had found it.

"You know," he said, as we left the restaurant and headed for the printer's, "I feel really good. You think we'll find him, don't you?"

"You're darned right," I said. I could feel the adrenaline flowing. It could have been my dog we were looking for. "But we've got our work cut out for us."

Indeed we did. Armed with a thousand posters, tape, and a staple gun, we marched forward to do battle on the streets of Berkeley.

Finding space for a poster in Berkeley is a cutthroat business. In the commercial blocks surrounding the campus, every wall, every pole, every tree is aflutter with paper. Women's poetry readings, aikido classes, underground films, protest meetings, psychic readings, lecture series—they're all there from years back, new posters stapled over old and sometimes over the new. We worked without stopping until seven thirty that evening, and then again the next morning until noon. We must have made a study in contrasts—the big, burly, dark-haired Irishman and the small, wiry, redheaded Israeli, but we were a good team. After lunch we placed an ad in the *Berkeley Gazette* and then parted company.

Now came the waiting part. I had given Eli a list of the pounds to check each day. Since I couldn't reach him in his van, which he parked in a different part of town every night, we arranged to meet at the coffee shop for breakfast each morning to exchange progress reports. By the time I got home there were already several messages from my service about Cal, but none of them panned out. There were apparently a lot of golden retrievers roaming around Berkeley, but none of them so far was Cal. Eli had said Cal was wearing Massachusetts tags. If he still had them on, they would be the quickest means of making a positive identification.

The next morning I had just returned from our breakfast when Flo called. "A guy just called who said he knew where Cal was," she said.

"Great. Give me his number, and I'll check it out."

"He didn't leave one. He said he'd be at the Villa Hermosa Restaurant, across from Cody's Bookstore on Telegraph Avenue, for the next hour at least."

"I better get going, then," I said.

"I guess so," she replied. "I don't know, though. He said you'd recognize him because he had a long ponytail and would be wearing a big gray hat. Sounds like one of those hippies to me."

"Well, hippies like dogs, don't they?"

"Yeah, except he sounded pretty flaky. Oh, and one more thing."

"What's that?"

"His name is Meatloaf."

After I shouldered my way first through the street vendors and then the pack of dogs lounging at the restaurant's front door, I immediately spotted Meatloaf, sitting at a table and staring into the middle distance. Despite his ponytail, he looked more like a bum than a hippie. Except for his red eyes and nose, everything else was gray, as if he'd been sprayed with a very thin layer of dust. He was, I decided with a sinking heart, someone who was seriously committed to substance abuse.

"Meatloaf?" I said. "I'm Sherlock Bones."

"Have a seat," he replied, smiling a row of yellow teeth and sticking out his hand. "Watcha got for me?"

"Not so fast, friend," I said. "Suppose you tell me first what you know about the golden retriever I'm looking for."

"Don't trust me, huh?" he said amiably. "OK, well this guy I buy dope from had this beautiful golden retriever in his car yesterday. Said somebody traded it to him for a couple of lids night before last."

"Are you sure you know what a golden retriever looks like?"

"Hey, man," he said, "give me a break. I'm a real dog freak. You don't believe me? See those dogs outside? They're all mine. Hey, Toke! That's the leader. I named him after my favorite hobby. See the one with the red bandanna?"

Sure enough, a big black hound with a red rag around his neck stood up and started wagging his tail expectantly.

"OK," I said, "but how do you know it's the dog I'm looking for?"

"Don't for sure, but I seen it had out-of-state tags."

"Massachusetts?"

"Can't remember."

"So what's the dealer's name?" I asked, getting out my notebook. This appeared to be the best lead I'd run across so far.

"Like I said before, whatcha got for me?"

What the hell, I thought, handing him twenty bucks. At least he loves dogs. "So tell me, what's this guy's name?"

"Don't know. We just call him the dealer."

"I don't suppose you know where he lives?"

"Are you kidding? When I want to get ahold of him, I call this number," he said, fishing a crumpled piece of paper out of his pocket and handing it to me. "He sets up a place, and I meet him there. Drives a green Mercedes with a paint job like glass."

"Isn't that a lot of trouble just to sell grass?"

"Yeah, well, who knows what else he's into? He's got good stuff, so I don't ask questions." He stood up from the table and started to leave.

"One more thing," I asked, as we got to the front door. "Why are you telling me all this? Aside from the money, I mean." He gave me a wounded look. "Oh, right," I said. "You're a dog freak."

"I told you, man," he said. "It's just not right, ripping off someone's dog."

As we hit the sidewalk, his dogs got up and Meatloaf ambled down the street, his canine entourage fanned out in loose formation, leaving me to wonder just how far I could trust the word of a dog-loving junkie.

I stopped at the first pay phone I saw and called my contact at the phone company. Five minutes later he called back to say that the number was unlisted but the billing department had it registered to a Ralph Ottman in the Berkeley hills above the university.

In a very short time I found myself in peaceful suburbia, cultural light-years away from the chaotic street scene I had just left behind. I was hard pressed to imagine that a drug dealer would inhabit this well-tended domestic neighborhood, even though in the last few years a lot of people on further reaches from the law had sought refuge in equally respectable areas, including liberation armies, kidnap victims, and militant religious groups.

The house was a nondescript one-story ranch-style, set on a corner lot up close to one street. Shutting the side yard off from view was an old unpainted fence consisting of vertical planks about seven feet high that formed a smooth if somewhat worn wall. I parked around the corner next to the fence, and as I walked back to the house I tried the gate. It was locked. Suddenly I heard the familiar sound of dog tags jingling on the other side of the fence. Maybe that's Cal, I thought—or maybe it's a well-trained guard dog, the kind that lunges first and barks later. I knew a lot of dealers kept dogs like that to discourage unwelcome callers.

I rang the doorbell three times, but no one answered. Nor was there any sign of a green Mercedes. I was walking back along the fence to the van when I noticed a board that had rotted away at the bottom. By lying flat on the ground I could peek through and see the yard. I whistled once, and a beautiful golden retriever sprang into view. He stood uncertainly, tail wagging slightly, head cocked the way dogs have when they can't figure out a sound they've heard.

"Cal!" I called out.

He moved toward me a few steps and then stopped. Was that a response to his name or just simple curiosity?

"Cal!" I called again, but he didn't move. I got up and dusted myself off. I had a strong suspicion this was Cal, but to be sure I had to get a look at those dog tags.

Now, I am not normally given to strenuous—much less dangerous—physical activity. If you stop to think, there is almost always a smarter way to solve the problem at hand. I can only explain what I did next by saying I was so caught up in my born-again zeal, and so determined to keep the momentum going, that I just bulled my way ahead.

There was a big tree growing between the fence and the street, and its lower limbs hung over the fence into the yard. With a show of enthusiasm that would have pleased even my old drill instructor in boot camp, I jumped up, grabbed a limb with both hands, and walked my feet up the trunk until I was able to clasp my ankles together around the branch. There I hung, like an overfed three-toed sloth, certain that every housewife on the block was peering at me from behind her chintz kitchen curtains. Inch by abrasive inch I twisted around until I caught the branch in the crook of one knee and heaved myself astride it. Before I had time to change my mind, I grabbed a sturdier branch above me and began working my way toward the fence, hand over hand. To clear the fence, I had to pull up my feet, and for a split second I rested them on the fence. Wondering how well I could navigate with two broken ankles, I gave a final lurch to pull myself upright and then pushed off from the fence into the yard below.

I remember hearing a series of loud cracks like rifle fire, and the next thing I knew I had landed on my right side directly on top of the fence, the entire length of which had collapsed under the insult of my weight thrusting against it. I looked up just in time to see a large golden retriever leap over the fallen fence and take off down the block, tail between his legs. I scrambled back to the van, winced at the pain in my right arm as I threw the engine into gear, and took off after the dog, convinced that at that very moment I was being reported to the Berkeley police as a suspicious character. I must have driven down every street in the Berkeley hills, but there was no sign of Cal. Cursing rickety fences and the pain in my arm, I gave up and headed home.

Once inside my apartment, I threw some Epsom salts into a tub of hot water and climbed right in after them. In about half an hour my aching body seemed grudgingly ready to play the game again, but my brain refused to cooperate. I had wanted so desperately to get Cal back I had blown it. I was sure now it was Cal, or at least not a dog who lived in that house. Had he belonged there, he would have barked at me—and he probably wouldn't have made such a beeline for parts unknown. But now we were in worse shape than when we began. At least Cal had been safe in that yard. God only knew what had happened to him by this time.

Eli was right, though. Cal was a beautiful dog, with his regal bearing and thick burnished-gold coat. Even from my brief look at him, I fancied I saw the same dignity and quiet strength that I found so comforting in Paco. I lay back in the tub and pictured him again in my mind's eye as I had seen him, head cocked and tail wagging slowly—except that in my image he wasn't in that backyard any more, he was standing in front of the library. I suddenly sat up. The library! Why not? I thought. Wasn't the library the last place he had seen Eli? Wouldn't he try to get back there if he possibly could?

I was dressed and halfway down the stairs on the way to check out my hunch when the phone rang. Eli? I didn't want to talk to him now. Maybe it was a lead, though. Better check it.

"Sherlock Bones," I said impatiently.

"Oh hi," a young man's voice responded. "I think I've got a dog you're looking for. Golden retriever, Massachusetts tags?"

"Cal!" I shouted. "Where was he?"

"Right in front of the library. I—"

"No kidding!" I laughed. "Well, how about that?"

"Yeah, I was jogging around the campus, and I must have passed thousands of your posters. When I stopped by the library to take a breather, there he was. He walked right up to me. He's real friendly."

I found out where he was calling from and told him I'd be right over. "And for God's sake, don't let him get away!"

Funny, I thought as I raced toward Berkeley, I'm always telling my clients to trust their hunches. I should listen to my own advice more often.

When I swung the van into the curb by the pay phone he'd described on Bancroft Way, there was no sign of a golden retriever. Oh no, I thought, not again. Leaving the motor running, I climbed out and stood looking up and down the sidewalk. I was about to give up hope when around the corner ran a shirtless young man in green shorts and running shoes, with a golden retriever loping easily at his side.

"You must be Sherlock Bones," he said, not even breathing hard. "This is one great dog. We took a lap around the block while we were waiting. You said not to let him loose, so I used my shirt as a leash, but I don't think he really needed it. He sure loves to run."

"That's right," I said. I knelt down beside Cal. It was the same dog I had seen in the yard, but just to be sure I checked his tags. "Cal," I said, "I could kiss you," and I did, right on his cold, wet nose. I got a big lick in response.

I could hardly wait to tell Eli the good news. However, it was already getting dark. If he hadn't already called me, chances were I'd have to wait until we got together for breakfast at the coffee shop the next morning.

And that's how things turned out. I took the student's name, promised we'd send him the reward, and brought Cal home in my van. I felt like a million bucks. He sat right next to me, as he had with Eli, and from time to time he put his paw on my arm in a friendly gesture. Paco wasn't nearly so happy to see Cal as I had been, but after a few minutes of territorial hostilities, he agreed to an armed truce and subsided, his nose only slightly out of joint.

I was so excited I had a hard time getting to sleep that night. Cal slept at the foot of the bed, although I could hear him getting up and moving around during the night, in the way dogs have when they're in a strange house and can't find a place that feels right. At dawn I got up, dressed, and checked the dish of food I'd given him the night before. It didn't look like he'd touched it. While I waited for eight thirty to roll around, I gave Cal a good brushing to make him look as good as possible for his reunion with Eli. He stood patiently as I went over his thick, silky coat. I had no trouble understanding how Eli had grown so attached to him. He reminded me a lot of my own canine security blanket.

When I could wait no longer, I took Cal and made the short drive to the coffee shop. He rode with his head out the window, relishing the cool morning air in his face. I arrived just as Eli was getting out of his van. He'd said he hadn't slept well since Cal had disappeared, and it was beginning to show. Fatigue and discouragement had taken the bounce out of his step. He was too preoccupied to notice us, so I stepped down from the van and shouted, "Hey, Eli! Over here! Look who I found!"

He turned, started to say something, and then stopped, unable to register what he was seeing. "Oh my God!" he shouted. "That's my dog! That's my dog!" He ran toward us, and to my great surprise threw his arms around not Cal but me. "It's my dog!" he shouted, beginning to sob. "You found my dog! Oh my God!" He clung to me as if he would never let go, pouring forth all his tears of joy, releasing the tension he had lived with for the last five days. He was sobbing hysterically now, unable to speak at all. Cal stood on the seat with his head out the window, tail going furiously.

"Everything's OK," I said after a moment. "It's all over now." I was so caught up in his feelings I forgot to be embarrassed at the idea of embracing another man in broad daylight. "Hey, why don't you say hello to Cal?"

Eli drew back from me and, with tears streaming down his

face, turned to his dog. "Oh, Cal," he cried, hugging him through the window as Cal licked his face greedily. "Where have you been? Where have you been?" He opened the door, and Cal jumped out. Eli knelt next to him, running his hands all over his body, as if to restore a tactile memory of the dog he hadn't laid eyes on in almost a week. "Let's see how you are. Have you lost weight? Yes, you have. You're so thin. Come on, Cal, let's find something for you to eat." He rummaged around in his van and came out with a dog dish and some dry food, which Cal devoured. I could tell Eli was still in a daze. As for me, I was so caught up in Eli's feelings of joy I couldn't tell where his ended and mine began. I tried to tell him what had happened, but he was too keyed up to listen. What he needed now was time to get reacquainted with his pal. I knew that, in order to look for Cal, he'd postponed a trip to visit a friend in Big Sur. I suggested we have lunch before he took off to see her. He agreed. I think we both wanted to do something to seal our friendship, since we would probably not be seeing each other again.

Three hours later we were sitting at a picnic table in a park, watching Paco and Cal tear around on the grass.

"Well, Eli," I said, after we had finished rehashing the events of the last two days, "how do you feel, now that's all over and you've got your dog back?"

He assumed a thoughtful expression. "Oh, I feel great," he replied. "I never thought I'd see him again. You know, when I first met you I had given up."

"I know. I thought maybe I shouldn't have asked you to try again."

"No," he said quickly, "you did the right thing. It was very generous of you. But . . ."

"But what?" For a man who had just gotten his dog back, he wasn't as elated as I had anticipated. In fact, all through lunch he'd seemed preoccupied.

"Well, you know, it's a little different now with me and Cal."

"Oh, that. Well, after dogs have been lost, they always act strange for a few days."

"No, it's not that. It's more . . . remember I said I knew there must be a purpose to Cal's getting stolen? Now I think I know what it is. You see, I never thought I could live without him, really I didn't. But I could. I did. I even wrote him a farewell letter."

"I know. It was really beautiful."

"And now that he's back . . . I mean, he's the same dog, and I still love him, but . . . when I got Cal, I was so alone, he was the only thing in my life. Really, it's true. And now, well, he'll always be my dog, but I don't think it will ever be like that again."

Something in what he said hit me hard. For a long moment I looked at Paco and Cal playing. "Maybe that's not such a bad thing," I said finally.

"No, it's not," he agreed. "But it's still a little sad. Do you know what I mean?"

I flashed back to my original fantasies of Paco and me, those all-engrossing images of eternal companionship that I had found so nurturing. "Yes," I said, "I know exactly what you mean."

He whistled for Cal and stood up to leave. This time it was I who hugged him. "Take care," I said, "and enjoy yourself."

"Thanks," he replied, as he held the door for Cal and climbed into his van. "I think I'm ready to."

13
How to Find
Your Missing Pet

WHAT IF YOU WERE to lose your pet?

I know, I know. You never would. That's what ninety-nine percent of my clients tell me. "I never thought it could happen," they cry. "He never gets out of the yard" or "He's always on a leash" or "He always comes home." I get the same story even from clients I've worked with before. "I never dreamed it would happen *again*," they say. "I thought lightning wasn't supposed to strike in the same place twice."

But pets do get lost, even the most beloved homebodies. A delivery person leaves the gate ajar, some kids want a temporary playmate, a tantalizing feline sashays by, a car window is rolled down a shade too far—and before you know it, your pet has vanished. I think I've heard every reason from the predictable to the ridiculous. "I always assumed my six-foot fence kept Pepper in my backyard," one woman told me, "until the dog next door came into heat. He cleared that fence with a standing jump!" Another owner blamed her dog's disappearance on peer-group pressure. "I'm sure he never would have left on his own," she confided, "but he fell in with a bad bunch of dogs, and the next thing I knew he was on the other side of town."

Pets get lost while traveling with their owners or while in the care of others while their owners are out of town. They disappear during the course of a move to a new home with their owners. They bolt from cars involved in highway accidents. They disappear under truly bizarre circumstances. One client's dog took off in terror when it caught sight of the Goodyear blimp floating overhead. Another escaped from a garage when a passing police car with its siren screaming triggered the automatic door-opener. Some pets (fewer than most people believe, however) are stolen. More get lost and only later fall into the hands of opportunists. So believe me, even *your* pet can get lost. It *can* happen to you.

This chapter is a guide to help you find your pet, should it ever disappear. It contains much of the advice I would give you if you hired me for a private consultation: my theory of pet-finding tips on what you can do right now *before* your pet is lost, my ten-step method for recovering a pet, answers to the questions I am most frequently asked, and, finally, a proposal I believe will help reduce the growing numbers of stray and unwanted pets in the nation today.

MY THEORY OF PET-FINDING

When I began my career as Sherlock Bones, I had no idea I would ever be calling upon my background in sales and marketing to help me find missing pets. What I needed, I thought, were investigative skills and a knowledge of animal behavior. Although in the course of my work I have learned a great deal about "detecting" and animals, I have found my experience in communications and human behavior much more valuable. That's because the secret to finding a missing pet lies not so much in the looking as in letting others *know* you are looking. You can spend eight hours in a solitary search for your pet—whistling on corners, driving up and down streets, tramping through fields and back alleys—and if you don't find it, you probably know nothing more than when you started. Those eight hours have been wasted. If, on the other hand, you spend the same amount of time spreading the word of Fido's disappearance, you have established a cadre of people who, to varying degrees, are aware of Fido's existence and will keep their eyes open for him. How well you spread the word —and how easy and attractive you make it for others to respond

—is eighty percent of a successful search. The remaining twenty percent consists of your personal visits to animal shelters.

Who are you trying to reach? Everyone. Your audience is the general public—men, women, and especially children; people who know and love animals, as well as those who can't tell a cocker spaniel from an Irish wolfhound; the good samaritans and the money-hungry; people who will go out of their way to perform an act of kindness and those who can't be bothered—all those, in short, who in the course of going about their daily lives could conceivably have picked up your pet or learned something of its whereabouts.

While some pet owners assume their missing pet is running loose, others make a basic miscalculation that fatally misdirects their efforts: They assume they are looking for the person who has their pet, either because they think it has been stolen or because they imagine that someone has picked it up and is now desperately trying to find its owner. The thing to do, they decide, is either find that person or let him know where they can be found. So they limit their efforts to running ads in newspapers—spending sometimes upward of fifty dollars—in the belief that whoever has their pet will read the lost-and-found ads every day and give them a call. Sometimes they may even sit back and wait for this "other person" to run a found-pet ad of his own.

There are several errors in this line of thinking. In the first place, by assuming the existence of another person you are prematurely narrowing your focus. No matter what your suspicions are, there may be no other person—your pet may simply be running loose. Besides, even if your pet is in someone's possession, he or she may not want to give it back, may not read the paper, or bother to check the lost-and-found ads. A more fundamental error, however, is the assumption underlying these and other limited efforts that people in general care enough about your plight to go out of their way to help you. In my experience, a search based on this premise will reach about two percent of the population—and that's a generous estimate. It's not that most people are uncaring, only that they're busy and preoccupied with their own affairs.

To be effective, your search must allow for all possible motivations and circumstances, and you should therefore direct your message to as broad an audience as possible. Every time I go out looking for someone's pet, I'm mounting a mini-advertising campaign to sell a disinterested public on being alert to the existence of a particular animal. Although it may look as if I'm just slapping up a lot of posters, I am in fact carrying out a carefully planned and thoroughly tested effort in communications, each element of which is designed to get the broadest possible range of people to heed and respond to my message. It's a broad-brush appeal to petnappers, informants, concerned citizens and the idly curious. Any one of them could have—or later come across—the piece of information I am looking for. I have no way of knowing at the outset, however, what that information may be or who has it and is willing to come forward, so I direct my message to as many people as possible. Every element of my campaign, therefore, is designed and assembled in such a way as to appeal to all these groups and offend none of them.

What should your message say? Given the fact that your audience is made up of busy people who are by and large not interested in what you have to say, the most important component in your message should be something that makes them pay attention. "Hey! Look at me!" you are saying. If you remember how often we are bombarded with claims for our attention and how adept we have become at ignoring these claims, you can understand that for any message to get through it must be simple, clear, and frequently repeated. If it doesn't register the first time, perhaps it will by the fourth or fifth. It must also include some motivation to respond, some benefit—tangible or intangible—to the person who takes the time to give you a call. Although we would all like to think that the simple act of reuniting an owner with his pet is motivation enough, the fact is you can't depend on it. You need something more.

Thus the reward. A reward is not only a motivator, it is also an attention-grabber. The fact that you are offering a reward should be the most prominent part of your message—along with the amount of the reward. I know the arguments against specifying the amount: you commit yourself to paying more than you might have to, you encourage petnapping by indicating exactly how profitable it can be, and you provide a baseline for bargaining by someone interested in upping the ante. On balance, however, I believe the following advantages outweigh the arguments:

- A specific reward is tangible proof of exactly how much you care for your pet, and it counters the claim many people make that "if the owner cares all that much, why did he let his pet get loose in the first place?"
- A reward indicates your seriousness of purpose. Offering $100, say, might make some people think twice about keeping a pet that they could otherwise rationalize had just "wandered into their yard."
- People seeing a specific reward will quickly translate it into something they would like to have. Fifty dollars to a child might mean the bicycle he's always wanted; for an adult it could mean a gift for someone else, new clothes, or a night on the town.
- A stated reward, if substantial enough, makes it clear from the outset that whoever has your pet can probably get more money, and more easily, by returning the pet than by selling it.
- A specified reward speaks to people whose behavior is indeed influenced by money but who may not want to admit that fact by calling you up and asking the amount. It may also make retrieving the pet (if the finder gave it away) worth the effort involved.

Equally as important as the reward is the critical phrase "for information leading to the return of." I would estimate that as many as half my clients' pets are found because someone called with information about the pet, rather than the pet itself. Even calls like "I think I saw your dog at the corner of Fifth and Market" can be all you need to focus your search and track down your pet. Offering the reward for information rather than possession of the pet itself motivates people who might otherwise think there is nothing in it for them unless they have your pet in hand. It also motivates people with the knowledge of who has your pet but who don't want to get personally involved in any potentially unpleasant or dangerous confrontations—or who are just too lazy to make a phone call to you.

Next, of course, your message should include a clear description of your pet and the time and place of its disappearance. Nothing beats a clear photograph that shows up any identifying features. It attracts attention and depicts your pet better and faster than any written description, especially where kids are concerned. A drawing is good if no photograph is available. If your pet is a purebred, there are drawings in books and magazines you can use. Generally, they're clearer than most snapshots and will attract more attention, even if they don't look exactly like your pet (you can mention differences in the caption). A written description alone is less desirable; it takes too much time to read and can mislead people. However, it's generally better to go with a written description than wait several days to find a photo or a drawing. Simply mentioning the name of the breed is no good at all. To the surprise of many pet owners, the vast majority of the American public has no clear concept of what a Persian cat looks like, or an English setter, or even a golden retriever.

Finally, in order to make it as easy as possible for a person to respond to your message, you should do two things:

First, prominently display a telephone number (or numbers) where you can be reached at any hour of the day or night, and make sure someone is there to take calls. You can't bank on someone calling back a second time. If it is impossible for you to sit by a phone all the time, and if you have no answering machine or service, consider asking a friend to receive calls. In my experience, twenty-four-hour availability works better than saying "evenings only" or "between ten and four." That's a schedule dictated by your convenience, not the other person's. If someone spots your pet in the afternoon, but is instructed not to call until evening, he may forget about it—or assume the pet to be long gone from the area by that time and therefore not worth calling about. Also, if that person is informing on someone else, he or she may have a change of heart.

And, second, avoid any reference to your pet's being stolen, even if you are absolutely certain it was taken. Publicizing your suspicion will serve only to scare off people who might know your pet's whereabouts but don't want to get involved with anything smacking of criminal activity, police questioning, and subsequent court trials. It will also make the thief (or someone else who might have picked up your pet) more leery about coming forward.

What is the best medium for your message? Posters. Although a series of television ads would reach more people, posters are the fastest, easiest, and least expensive means at your disposal. Properly designed and placed, they will reach the people most likely to have information about your pet. The type of poster I use (see page 221) is on white 8½-by-14-inch paper (legal size). I advise putting up as many as one thousand in an area within a radius of twenty blocks from the point of your pet's disappearance, so that anyone passing through the area will see dozens of posters in a short period of time and presumably will begin to get your message without having to try very hard. That's the purpose of your entire campaign: to put your message in the lap of the public.

BE PREPARED

What can you do right now to be prepared for that day when your pet might be lost? I won't lecture you about obeying your community's leash laws or keeping your pet in a fenced-in area. You know you should, but perhaps you're one of the many people who feel that if animals can't have a certain amount of freedom, it's not worth keeping them. I will ask you, though, how well prepared you are to institute an effective search for your pet, should it disappear. The following checklist won't guarantee its return, of course, but it will increase your chances of getting it back quickly and safely. (Although, except for specified sections, this chapter is written primarily with dogs in mind, it applies with slight modifications to cats as well—and, for that matter, to birds and more exotic pets.)

1. *Is your pet wearing a collar?* The excuses I've heard for someone's animal's not wearing a collar are endless: "He's outgrown it and we haven't gotten around to buying a new one"; "The dye in the leather ran, so we took it off"; "We washed him and didn't put it back on"; "It gave him a rash"; "He scratched all night and his jingling tags drove us crazy; he sounded like the rhythm section in a rock band." Your pet's collar, even without tags, is at least some evidence of ownership, although not conclusive. Many shelters treat pets with collars (even if there are no tags) differently from the way they treat collarless pets, which they sometimes assume to be strays that no one will claim. (By the way, if your pet's tags jingle too much, try taping them.)

2. *Does your pet have up-to-date license and identification tags?* The need for a dog license is self-evident. It is not only required by law but is the best link between your pet and the public pet-finding machinery in your community. The number on your dog's tag, like the license number on your car, is on file with your city or county. If your dog ends up in the animal shelter, this number is the means through which you will be contacted. If someone finds your dog, he or she will usually (although not always) be able to get your name by calling the pound and giving the number on the license. Keep your dog's license number on file where you can find it quickly. It is an important means of identification.

Identification tags connect your pet directly to you. Your dog should have one and so should your cat. The most critical piece of information is your phone number, including the area code. I also recommend including the pet's name. Some people disagree, on the theory that it gives a petnapper greater control over your animal, but I feel that if someone has stolen your pet, knowing or not knowing its name won't make much of a difference. On the other hand, if your dog has wandered into someone's yard, that person stands a greater chance of keeping it around if he or she can yell "Hey, Carlos!" whenever it wanders away. Besides, if someone has taken your pet and decides to keep it, I somehow think it would be easier if it were called by its proper name in its new home.

Your name and address are not crucial. It has happened that a pet has been stolen, the owners notified to come and get it, and while they are gone their house is robbed. This is not a common occurrence, but if you feel hesitant about having your name and address on the ID tag, you can safely leave them off. Telephone numbers are more important. In fact, if your vet—or a relative or a good friend—will agree, I recommend adding their number as well.

Two final notes on ID: It's a good idea to have a new tag made *before* you move to a new home, since many pets get lost during the move. And, although it seems unnecessary to say so, be sure your pet is always *wearing* its ID and license tags. More than one client has told me, "Tags? Oh, yes, my pet has tags. I've got them right here. Would you like me to read you what they say?"

3. *Do you have clear, up-to-date black-and-white photographs of your pet?* Most people have pictures of their pets, but not usually in black-and-white or clear enough to reproduce well on posters. If you don't have any, buy a roll of black-and-white film and take some. Get good close-ups, against a contrasting solid background, that show your pet's body shape and any distinguishing features. Take some with your pet groomed and *ungroomed*, since that may be its condition during the time it is lost. Think of them less as portraits than as mug shots. If you can't get a camera, find an accurate drawing and put it away on file. If your pet is a purebred, you can find one in many books on pets. If you've got a mixed breed (and an artistic bent), try your hand at making a drawing of your own, in charcoal or black ink, in a size that will show up well on a poster.

While you're at it, take a look at your pet and try describing it. How much does it weigh? How tall is it? Make a note of any distinguishing features such as scars, lumps, or unusual markings. If it has one blue eye, is it the right or the left? Even if these features aren't readily visible, they can help you separate real leads from false alarms.

4. *Do you know your local animal shelters and pounds?* Many pet owners assume that by calling their local pound they have exhausted all possibilities. If you live in a large metropolitan area with overlapping county and town jurisdictions, however, there may be several public shelters—and a few private shelters as well. Pets are often picked up in one area and turned in to shelters in another town or county. It behooves you to have a list of all the shelters in your area, including the private ones. Although most of the latter do not accept lost pets but deal instead in what they call owner-surrendered animals (pets that their owners are giving up for adoption), slipups do occur. I have known many people who find pets and turn them in to private shelters, claiming to be their owners, in the belief that the pet stands a better chance of finding a good home than if it were given over to the public pound.

So look in the Yellow Pages under "animal shelters" and "humane societies." Record their numbers on a piece of paper. Call the public shelter that serves you and ask them for the names of other shelters. Don't assume that there's much communication among them; there isn't, at least formally. Note their hours of operation and their policies concerning how long they keep animals before they are destroyed or put up for adoption. (And check them again if your pet is lost; they may have been changed.)

MY TEN-STEP METHOD FOR RECOVERING A MISSING PET

Now, suppose your pet gets lost. What is the first step you should take? Actually, the first thing is to decide that your pet is lost. If it normally roams the neighborhood for several hours at a stretch, this decision may take a few hours, but if—after a quick check of favorite haunts and a trip around the neighborhood— you begin to get a gnawing feeling in your stomach, it's time to start looking in earnest. Don't give it a few days, even if your pet has been gone for a few days before. If it's been picked up by a shelter, a few days is all it has.

1. *Call your local animal shelter, police department, and emergency after-hours veterinary hospitals.* Smaller police departments often have holding cages where they keep animals overnight until they are turned over to the public shelter. If the shelter claims to have your pet, your search is over—almost. Pick up your animal immediately. Not only will you save on boarding fees, but only when you actually have it in your possession can you be sure it's safe. Mistakes are rare, but they do occur. Several pet owners have told me they waited a day or two to pick up their pets, only to discover that they had been destroyed "by mistake." Shelters are frightening places for animals and are also good places to pick up diseases. Finally, by retrieving your pet quickly, you may make it possible for another animal to be adopted rather than destroyed, for many shelters will extend the period of time they keep animals if there are cages available for them.

If the shelter or police department says it doesn't have your pet or can't make a positive identification, visit them anyway. Follow the procedures listed under step 5, below. *Don't* rely on any assurances that you will be called "if anything turns up." Many shelters promise to notify you if your pet was wearing tags, but you can't be sure its tags are still on. Finding your pet is your responsibility. The police have other matters to worry about, and the shelters have many animals to deal with and cannot be expected to devote the time and energy required to find your pet. Filing a lost-pet report is not enough. You must be prepared to follow through.

2. *Determine a reward.* To arrive at this step you must first face the fact that your pet is lost and prepare yourself to mount a full-fledged search. Many pet owners make the mistake of starting out small ("Well, maybe it really isn't lost"), escalating efforts and rewards only as the days go by and their pets still haven't

turned up. This approach wastes valuable time. It may feel like overkill, but I've learned that you've got to go all out from the very beginning in order to allow for all possible circumstances. Of the many things you do, only one may pay off, but there is no way of knowing when you start which it will be.

Determine at the outset the maximum reward you are prepared to pay. Escalating the amount as the days go by will require extensive repostering. Anyone seeing your first poster who has information about your pet is not likely to read one again. The size of the reward should depend first, of course, on your pocketbook (although remember that, even if you are short of cash, it may be possible to work out some arrangement for payment later). I generally advise clients to offer a minimum of $50 and a maximum of $300, with the average being about $100. Your purpose is to fix the reward at a figure that will outbid any competition for your pet. Factors that indicate a higher reward are suspicion that a pet has been stolen, a young pet (because they're easier to sell and/or fall in love with), an expensive or especially beautiful pet, and a pet that's been missing for some time. For an average-looking mixed-breed dog, for example, I'd offer a $50 reward if it had just gotten lost and perhaps a $100 reward if it had already been gone a week or more (on the assumption someone had taken it in and was thinking of keeping it). I'd offer a minimum of $100 for a purebred, and even more if it had been gone some time *and* was obviously of show quality or had special training. I have gone as high as $300 for truly outstanding animals, and in rare instances even higher.

3. *Design a poster.* You will be designing a master that a printer will reproduce. The sample poster shows the format I have found most successful: REWARD and the amount in large letters, a large photograph or drawing, circumstances and written description in block form with "bullets." Standard- or legal-size paper is best. Anything smaller gets overlooked and anything bigger is hard to handle and objectionable to many merchants, who don't want their stores cluttered up with large signs.

As to what to include:

- *Don't* include your name and address.
- *Do* include the pet's name, along with a phonetic spelling if it is difficult to pronounce as written.
- *Do* mention any familiar landmarks near where your pet was lost, along with cross streets and the name of the area, if any, plus the warning that it could well be outside this area.
- *Do* include the time, date, and *day* it was lost or, if you are *absolutely certain,* the same information for when it was last spotted—by, for example, a neighbor who knows your pet well.
- *Do* include a brief description, including color and any identifying features (scar on nose, floppy ear). Give size in weight rather than "small," "medium," or "large," unless your pet is *very* small or *very* large.
- *Do* say so if your pet was wearing tags, but add "possibly," since for all you know they could have been removed.
- *Don't* say your pet needs medication unless it does. Some people believe this will heighten the urgency of the search or will put people off from keeping a sick pet. Too many people have used this emotional appeal for it to be effective. On the other hand, if your pet does need medication, name the medication and give the symptoms likely to occur without it.

If there is time and you can afford it, have this information set in type—either by the instant printer, if he has the equipment, or, more likely, by a typesetter. There are also rub-off lettering kits available in stationery and office-supply stores. If time and money are short, you can do it yourself. Letter it first in pencil, leaving space for the photograph or drawing, and then go over your work with a black felt-tip pen. Don't paste the photograph down yet; there's one more process first (see step 4).

4. *Have one thousand copies of your poster printed.* Look in the Yellow Pages under "copying and duplicating services" for an

- REWARD -
$150

FOR INFORMATION LEADING TO THE RETURN OF THIS DOG

NAME: "PACO"

TYPE: OLD ENGLISH SHEEPDOG

SEX: MALE

AGE: 4 MONTHS

WEIGHT: APPROX. 20 LBS.

COLOR: BLACK BODY, WHITE FACE, CHEST AND FRONT LEGS

IDENTIFYING FEATURES: NO TAIL, RIGHT EAR IS BLACK, LEFT EAR IS WHITE WITH BLACK SPOTS

COLLAR: POSSIBLY WEARING SILVER CHOKE CHAIN WITH OAKLAND TAGS AND NAME TAG

LOST: TUES., OCTOBER 4 AT 9 a.m., FROM BROADWAY AND 51st ST., NEAR ROCK-RIDGE SHOPPING CENTER, OAKLAND

1977 JOHN KEANE

Sherlock Bones

(a.k.a. John Keane, the country's first and only
professional pet detective)
(415) 655-9666

instant printer or copy center. These establishments are geared up to turn out small orders quickly (as against regular printers, who deal in larger orders and take more time). The photo-offset method instant printers use produces sharper, clearer, more fade-resistant copies than those you can run off on most office copying machines. Instant printers can usually do the job for you the same day, perhaps even while you wait. Call several to see who is fastest, and plan on spending about $20 for one thousand copies.

If you are using a photograph (or two—one for the body and one for the face), crop out any confusing background. You will need to have a Velox halftone reproduction made before the posters can be run off; the printer cannot work directly from a photograph. A halftone is the result of turning a photograph into a series of little dots, like the photographs we see in newspapers. (Color photographs can be used for this purpose, although with a loss in clarity.) If your instant printer doesn't do halftones (most don't) and doesn't know someone who can, check in the Yellow Pages under "typesetting." The cost is approximately $7. (Sometimes a photograph from a book or magazine can be reproduced without another halftone having to be made. Ask your printer's advice.)

Be sure to find out how much time will be required to make a halftone. There's a trade-off between immediacy and clarity, and you don't want to wait two days to get a halftone done, for example, when you have a perfectly good drawing that looks much like your pet.

Incidentally, I always have my posters printed on white paper. White stands out and shows a fuzzy photograph off to its best advantage.

5. *Visit all the shelters in your area.* If you must wait a few hours for your posters, use the time to begin canvassing shelters. Start with the public shelter that serves your community. Tell them your problem and become familiar with their procedures and policies. If you haven't already done so, ask them for the names of other shelters. Visit them too. If you don't find your pet on the first go-round, plan on returning every other day, if possi-

ble, depending on your time and how long they hold animals.

Although each shelter will take you through its own procedures, there are some guidelines for dealing with animal shelters that you should know:

- Always visit the rooms where the animals are kept and look at each animal very closely. Many distraught owners walk right by their pets without even recognizing them.
- Most shelters have a quarantine area for animals who have bitten people, are suspected of having rabies or other communicable diseases, or are injured. Make sure you check out any animals in this area and visit it, if possible. Even if your pet was healthy when you last saw it, it could be sick (or appear to be sick) now—or it could have been placed in quarantine through human error.
- Most shelters also keep lists of "found" animals reported by people who prefer to keep them until they are reclaimed by their owners. Sometimes, however, these "found" pets get placed in the "lost" category (on bulletin boards or in logbooks) by mistake. What is "lost" to one person, after all, is "found" to another. Be sure to check both lists.
- By the same token, some shelters segregate records of pets by sex. Check both male and female listings. Mistakes in gender are not infrequent; many people are too reticent to make a positive determination.
- Once again, don't assume that your pet is still wearing its tags.
- On subsequent visits, put one of your posters on each shelter's bulletin board, if it is permitted.
- If you're looking for a small dog, check the cat cages as well. On rare occasions, overcrowded shelters have been known to put small dogs there.

6. *Distribute the posters.* Now your work begins in earnest. With a detailed map of your area, mark out an area twenty blocks from your house (or wherever the pet was lost) in all directions. If there's a shopping center or other public gathering place (in-

cluding schools) just outside this area, include it. (If you've recently moved across town, include your old neighborhood. That's where many pets are headed when they get loose in the first place.) In my experience most pets are found within a twenty-block area. Furthermore, that's where anyone having information on a missing pet is likely to work or live. Concentrating the posters therefore has the greatest impact. If you have the time and the manpower, you can expand your efforts, of course.

Lay aside about 150 posters; you may need them later (see below). With the remainder, your map, a roll of Scotch tape and a heavy-duty staple gun (you can rent one for about $2 a day), you are ready to set forth. Begin closest to the center of your area and work out; most pets are actually found within ten blocks of where they were lost. You might find yours before you reach the outer perimeters. If you can arrange it, take a friend along to drive the car so you won't have to worry about parking. Besides, two people working together can get more than twice the amount of work done.

The first place to staple your posters are telephone and utility poles. Although, strictly speaking, this is against city ordinance, few towns have given me or my clients a hard time. Poles are very effective display areas. Drive down the street, putting two posters on every other pole, hitting the alternate pole across the street on your way back in a zigzag, shoelace pattern. How you place the posters is critical. Remember, you are trying to get people to read your poster without having to exert more than the absolute minimum of effort. So angle the two posters so that pedestrians walking in either direction can spot them as they approach the pole without having to turn their heads. Keep them at *low* eye level, since you want to attract children as well. If the pole is wood, staple the poster at each corner. If it's concrete, you may have to wrap two pieces of tape all the way around the pole, one at the top of the poster and another at the bottom.

When seeking to attract motorists' attention, choose an area where cars are likely to slow down, as at a stoplight, and put up a poster on each of four preceding poles. Place them low enough so that the driver can see them by looking through the windows on the passenger side of the car. Your intention is to arouse his curiosity enough for him to pull over at the third or fourth poster to find out what this photograph and reward business is all about. You're using the same technique as roadside-stand owners who place a series of signs along the highway immediately preceding their place of business.

Be sure to put up posters on poles near areas where people congregate: bus stops, newspaper stands or vending machines, school grounds, park entrances, pools, and other recreational facilities.

Next, put your posters in stores. The best ones are high-traffic, long-hours operations: supermarkets, drugstores, beauty parlors and barbershops, Laundromats, liquor stores, all-night convenience stores. Pet stores, obviously, are good bets, as are hobby shops that attract kids who may be especially susceptible to the lure of a reward to buy the model-airplane kit they've had their eye on. By all means, get the owner's or manager's permission first, if possible; don't just leave a poster with a clerk. Try to speak with someone in authority, and put up the poster yourself. The best location is just to the right of the front door at eye level, inside the glass and facing out. It gets more attention than a community-announcement bulletin board that supermarkets and Laundromats sometimes have. Most store owners and managers will be cooperative, once they know your purpose. In general, I get better results when I couch my request in terms of a problem I need help with rather than a favor I'm asking for.

Schools are good poster locations. Kids are great animal-spotters. They like animals, tend to spend a lot of time outside, and usually can spot a strange animal in the neighborhood. It's worth a visit to the school office to ask if you can put a poster inside on a bulletin board. And remember, keep the posters low so children can see them—both inside the school and on poles outside.

If there are veterinarians in the area, I always drop off posters for their bulletin boards and ask the receptionist to keep her eyes open for the pet, on the chance that someone will bring it in for treatment. I also suggest mailing posters to veterinarians throughout the area. Include a covering letter explaining that your sole interest is to recover your pet and not to make a legal issue for the veterinarian. If you show that you respect his or her professional responsibilities to patients, you stand a better chance of gaining the cooperation you need.

Although eighty percent of my leads come from posters placed on poles and in stores and given to children, it is also a good idea to cover groomers, boarding kennels, and the airlines' animal-transportation departments. If you mail posters to these people, also include a covering letter emphasizing that your interest is in getting your pet back, not in creating problems for them.

Don't be afraid to blanket the area. Your intention is to create a cumulative impact so that someone passing through will see several posters in a short period of time and, without having to put out a lot of effort, will gradually become aware of your missing pet. This information may suddenly trigger an association with an animal he has just seen. Or he may later see your pet, recall the posters, and give you a call.

While you're putting up posters, tell as many people as possible that you're looking for your pet, and give them a poster as a concrete reminder. Be sure to contact the service people—postmen, milkmen, garbagemen, paperboys (or girls), cops on the beat, utility meter readers (and meter maids), delivery people—anyone who spends time outdoors making the rounds.

Give several to your postman so he can distribute them to his colleagues. (You can't put them in mailboxes, by the way—it's a federal offense—but you can put them near mailboxes.) If you can locate the drop-off points where several newsboys pick up and fold newspapers for their routes, make a point of being there to give each newsboy a poster.

Also, make a point of giving posters to any children you see. Kids will make an adventure out of looking for your pet, and a personal poster is a great motivator. It also keeps them from tearing down posters you have already put up.

Check your posters every few days to be sure they are still up and visible. And don't forget to take them down once you have ended your search. Don't add unnecessarily to visual litter.

7. *Run newspaper ads.* Although ads are usually the first thing owners think of, their impact is limited to those people with a reason for reading the lost-and-found section of the paper. Ads are also one of the ways to reach people outside the postered area. Generally, an ad is most effective when your tagless pet has been found by someone who has taken it in and wants to find the owner rather than turning it over to an animal shelter. This is only one of many eventualities, however, and since ads are not inexpensive, I advise clients who can't afford posters *and* ads to concentrate on posters.

There is also a problem with timing. Let's say you lose your pet on a Saturday but don't get around to placing an ad until Monday that doesn't appear in the paper until Wednesday or Thursday. In the meantime, someone could have found your pet hours after you lost it (not knowing, of course, how long it had been lost), checked the paper for four or five days, and, seeing no ad, assumed no one was looking.

If you do run an ad, however, be sure you make it sufficiently clear and easy to read to justify the cost. Abbreviations and omissions can be too confusing to justify the savings in space. Begin with REWARD and the amount. Mention the breed, but also include a description and indicate the time and place it was lost. A sample ad might look something like this:

REWARD: $100 for information about Buck. German shepherd mix, gold color, big ears, white tip on tail. Possibly wearing brown leather collar with ID tags and Marin license #3034. Lost Tuesday, August 29, Mill Valley. 388–5002 or 456–6622.

Unlike posters, ads reach a wider geographic audience, so keep the location of your pet's disappearance fairly general. It could be miles away, and you don't want to discourage readers who may have spotted it, but who don't believe it could be the same animal. I'd suggest running the ad in the major morning and evening dailies, since they have a widespread readership. Local weeklies can also be effective, especially if you can get an ad in an issue coming out immediately after your pet is lost. Quarter-page ads are good and are often not too expensive.

Don't forget to *read* the lost-and-found ads. Someone may have found your pet and be looking for *you*. Be sure to check all back issues (your library will have them if you don't) to within a day or two of your pet's disappearance.

8. *Wait for the leads to come in.* It is critical that you be prepared to deal with leads, for they may start coming in almost immediately. It is often difficult to sit and wait during this time. Many owners want to drive around and look for their pet, but if there is no one to take messages, all your earlier efforts will have been wasted. Children, by the way, don't make very good phone-sitters.

There are some techniques, both practical and psychological, for dealing with people claiming to have information about your pet:

- Keep a map by your phone to pinpoint areas where people spot your pet. A pattern to its movements may emerge. When investigating a lead, take some of the remaining posters and put up a few where your pet was spotted. Others may see it there.
- Always try to get a caller's phone number and address as soon as possible, in case he or she gets cold feet halfway through the conversation. Then ask them for their information.
- Be casual and low-key. Try not to make the caller feel defensive. By the same token, don't be so over-anxious that you sound like a sitting duck for an extortion scheme.
- Avoid asking children leading questions. They get so ex-

cited they'll agree with anything. Instead of asking, "Did the dog have a big tail that curled over his back?" ("Yeah! Sure!"), ask them what the dog looked like. Get *them* to volunteer the information.

· If you suspect a caller is pulling a prank, get the number and call back.

9. *Try some "positive imaging."* Clients are often surprised at this suggestion, especially coming from an ex-marine, but many later claim it worked for them—enough so that I'm convinced its results cannot be explained by chance alone. At the very least it will give you the energy you need to complete your task and can keep you from spinning your wheels and unnecessarily increasing your anxiety.

Here's how it works: Five times a day (including especially right before you drop off to sleep) visualize a happy reunion with your pet. Don't force the circumstances; just let the images appear. Feel the emotion behind the image, be it joy, relief, anger, or surprise. Tune up the volume, so to speak, on any intuitive feelings as to where your pet is, whom to talk to, or where to put a poster. Act on these intuitions. The more we listen to our subconscious, the stronger and more available it will become to our conscious mind. If, for example, you are driving down the street and suddenly get the feeling you should put a poster in a certain store, do it. It may be the poster that returns your pet to you.

I'm convinced that positive imaging can play an important part in your search for your missing pet, but I'm not interested in making converts. As I tell my clients, "You ask me what steps I find effective. I find positive imaging effective. The decision of whether or not to use it is up to you."

10. *Exercise caution and common sense when recovering your pet.* In nine out of ten cases, a person calling to say he has found your pet has done just that—he has not stolen it, nor has he concocted a scheme to burglarize your home or extort money

from you. Just in case, however, I recommend the following precautions:

- Arrange to meet at the person's home, unless something sounds fishy, in which case you should get together at a public place. Don't have him or her come to your home. If you feel the least bit nervous, take a friend along.
- Be prepared to pay the reward in cash or with a cashier's check, rather than a personal check that has your address on it. Remember, you might be called on to pay at any time, evenings and weekends included.
- Make sure you have your pet in your possession before you part with any money. Don't buy lines like, "He's just in the backyard. Why don't you give me the money and I'll go get him?"
- There's nothing wrong with insisting on sitting in your car (with the doors locked, if need be) and asking the person to bring your pet to you.
- If the person calling tells you your pet is in someone else's possession, I recommend going immediately to pick up your pet without phoning first, just in case whoever has it does not want to give it up. Take a friend along. Adopt a no-questions-asked attitude. "I understand you've found my dog" is a good opening line, followed by an immediate offer of half the reward (the other half going to your informant, but do not mention his or her name). Start out friendly, but be prepared to be firm. If you suspect the person of having stolen your pet, I'd suggest keeping your suspicions to yourself until you have your pet back and both of you are safe. If the person seems hostile and uncooperative, don't make threats or risk physical violence. Simply mention the fact that you have registered your loss with the proper authorities. If you see you're getting nowhere, leave and ask your friend to watch the house while you notify the police.

If more than one person has been instrumental in helping you recover your pet, let your conscience be your guide in dividing the reward. I've rarely had any problem. Most people are more than willing to be fair.

Following these ten steps may sometimes make you feel as if you're going after a tiny rock with a steam shovel. You may end up like one of my clients, whom I had convinced to have all the posters printed and go through the full procedure. She had just started putting them up when she noticed her dog, sitting about five feet away, staring blankly down the street. "Gretchen!" she cried, and the dog ran to her, evidently not having noticed her before.

"Well, you were right," she told me later, "putting up posters is certainly the best way to get your dog back."

Her search was over quickly. Most take longer, depending of course on the circumstances. Jennifer, a recent client, had a more typical experience, one that illustrates the fact that there's just no predicting what can happen to your dog. She was driving to her mother's house with her dog in the back seat and the window open, and when she arrived the dog was gone. She put up posters and eventually got her dog back in the following way: A taxi driver picked up the dog (apparently it had jumped out the car window) and left it at a gas station. An eighteen-year-old boy found the dog and took it home. A ten-year-old neighbor kid who played with the dog once or twice saw a poster and gave his sister the owner's number. She called Jennifer and told her where the dog was. Jennifer and her father went to the eighteen-year-old's house to pick up the dog. The boy was gone. His mother was at first reluctant to let them see the dog, and Jennifer's father's belligerence didn't help. Finally, however, Jennifer was able to convince the mother to let them see the dog, and its reaction was proof enough of ownership. They left the reward with the mother, even though she didn't want to take it. Later, when her son came home, he divided it between himself and the ten-year-old that had seen the poster.

ANSWERS TO SOME FREQUENTLY ASKED QUESTIONS

I'm surprised you don't talk more about animal behavior, and especially about how animals navigate. Isn't it important?

Yes, but in my opinion not so important as some people think. Many of my clients, having read stories of pets that performed extraordinary feats of navigation to find their way home, assume their pets can do the same. Leaving it all to Mother Nature, however, is a mistake. In the first place, some pets are so thoroughly domesticated and dependent on their owners (the very attributes that make them delightful companions) that they don't know how to survive on their own. Faced with a choice of finding their old owner or adopting a new one, many will choose the latter out of a need to survive. Second, the world "out there" includes hazards Mother Nature never thought of: highways, bridges, heavy industry, dense urban areas, and dogcatchers—to name just a few.

In my experience, finding a pet requires more knowledge of human behavior than of animal behavior. Still, there are circumstances when knowing how animals behave can help. We know that animals find their way around their immediate vicinity by leaving scents on trees, fire hydrants, and so forth. (Farther away, some experts suggest, they use the sun to find their way home, moving in the direction that will put them in their accustomed relation to the sun at any given time of day.) If your pet was lost away from home—or if it bolted from your car during an accident —it's a good idea to leave an article of clothing carrying your scent (something worn close to the body, like a sock or shirt) at the scene to encourage your pet to hang around once it returns to the point of its disappearance, as it may well do.

Also, studies have shown that stray dogs sometimes stay in quiet, sheltered places during the busiest parts of the day, coming out between five and eight in the morning, after six in the evening, and very late at night. The early morning hours are especially good times to look for your pet, since most other animals will be inside, the streets are quiet and your voice will carry farther, and there aren't many people out to frighten your dog back into its temporary lair.

What should we do if we lose our pet while traveling?

It's hardest to find your pet in an area where both of you are strangers—and also expensive and inconvenient in terms of un-planned hotel bills and changes in itineraries. In general, the same ten-step method applies, with the following additions:

- Be sure to leave an article of clothing where your pet was last seen, and return to the area frequently to check for its return.
- Notify your phone company to forward calls from your home number (if your house is empty), in case someone finds your pet and calls the number on its tag. On posters, list your local contact number *and* another number where you can be reached (collect), in case you must leave the area before you find your pet.
- Consider getting a humane animal trap from the local animal shelter, if your pet was lost in the country. Actually a small cage that closes once the animal is inside, it can be baited with a favorite food and placed where you lost your pet. You may end up with a raccoon or someone else's pet, but it's worth a try. Check the cage at least once a day.
- Contact the local newspaper and radio and television stations and tell them your plight. The circumstances of your loss might appeal to them as a human-interest story, and you can't beat the coverage they can give you.

Above all, be sure your pet is wearing up-to-date tags every moment you are away, even if you leave your pet at home. This is the best insurance that it will be recovered.

Do you have any special tips for finding a missing cat?

Cats are harder to find than dogs. In the first place, most cats form a stronger attachment to their home than to their owners. That's why you should keep your cat inside your new house right after you move; otherwise it might return to your former residence. Also, cats are independent and quite capable of adopting a new owner—or owners—none of whom may realize they are sharing a pet. If your cat is lost, follow the ten-step method, with the following additions:

- Be sure to check garages, closets, sheds, trunks, boxes, basements—any place your cat could have inadvertently gotten shut in by someone not knowing it was there.
- Examine any lairs or hidden places around your house. Many injured cats hide near their home.
- Even though your cat may have wandered off before, don't assume it has safely done so again. You may not want to mount a full-fledged search yet, but at least check the shelters. They don't pick up cats off the street, but many people drop cats off there. Shelters will also pick up cats if they have been put in a box. I have known people to dispose of a neighbor's bothersome feline in this way.

I know my cat should wear a collar and an ID tag, but I worry that she will get it caught on a branch or a nail and not be able to free herself. Is a collar worth the risk?

Far more cats perish at animal shelters because their owners cannot be located than from being strangled or trapped by a collar. I recommend you buy a "pull-away" collar designed especially for cats. It's a regular leather collar, one section of which is elastic. If the cat gets caught, the elastic will expand and allow the cat to wriggle free. Even if you're strongly anti-collar, it's a good idea for your cat to wear a collar and tags for a few weeks after you move to a new house. (If your cat wears a flea collar, try this trick: with an indelible pen, write your phone number on the collar.)

What about TV and radio "lost pet" features? Do they bring results?

Yes, sometimes. Many radio and TV news programs announce lost and found pets as part of their community service.

If there are some unusual circumstances surrounding your pet's loss, or if your pet is special in any way, you might call your local stations and see if they will run the story as a human-interest feature. It's worth a try. They're always looking for news stories, especially those they can help bring to a happy conclusion. It's good public relations for them and an excellent way for you to get some free publicity.

What should I do if I find a stray pet? How can I return it?

First, if you are sure it is lost, take it in and keep it secure so it won't wander off. Don't let it back on the street. If it's wearing an ID tag, call the owner. If it's wearing only a license, call the public shelter in the community that issued the tag. If it's impossible for you to keep it, return it to the shelter. If you prefer to keep it until its owner claims it, call the shelter anyway and have them register the pet as found, together with your name and address. If the owner checks the shelter's found-pet registry, he or she will find your name there.

If the pet is tagless or collarless, don't automatically assume it is also ownerless. Don't adopt it as your own or give it to someone else before you do everything you can to find its owner. If you cannot keep it, return it to the public shelter in the vicinity you found it. If you can keep it temporarily, notify all the public and private shelters in the general area. Run an ad in the newspaper. Read the lost-and-found ads, including as many back issues as possible (once again, your local library should keep copies of the papers in your area). Keep your eyes open for posters. Ask around —paperboys, mailmen, delivery people. If you are so inclined, you can take a photo of the pet (or a drawing) and make some "found" posters of your own. Contact vets and groomers.

Clearly, the pet stands a better chance of surviving if you keep it in your possession rather than turn it in to a shelter. Although some shelters will say they will call you before they destroy the animal, they don't always follow through. Also, by keeping the pet you are creating one more free cage at the shelter that can house one more animal, perhaps long enough to find its owner—or a new home.

Our dog was lost recently. Unfortunately, he was wearing tags with our previous telephone number. Is there anything we can do?

If your number has been disconnected and your new number listed as a forwarding number, calls will be referred to your new home. In most cities, however, this service is discontinued after a few months; to have it temporarily reinstated will require a call to the phone company, perhaps several. If you don't get satisfaction at first, try calling someone in the president's office. The higher up you go, the greater the chance for bending the rules.

If your pet is lost wearing an old license, inform the animal shelters and follow up with a poster for their bulletin boards. If someone calls in, they can refer him or her to you.

What can be done about organized rings of dognappers? Isn't the whole business of offering a reward just playing into their hands?

I don't think so. There is little real information on the prevalence of professional dognappers. In my experience, however, for every professional there are hundreds of opportunists and crank thieves. Professionals usually have a well-oiled system for selling animals and do not rely on returning them to their owners for a reward. I have a gut feeling, at least in the San Francisco area, that there is less professional dognapping than most people think—or perhaps it's just because it's a subject that's hard to get a handle on. Certainly there are few arrests and even fewer convictions.

If your pet is lost, I believe your first priority is to get it back. This is not to say that I advocate a laissez-faire approach to petnapping. It is an extremely difficult offense to prosecute successfully, however, despite the existing laws requiring various certificates of sale when pets are bought and sold by labs, breeders, and pet stores. My experience in trying to secure police cooperation on cases I've had has been disappointing. Citizen action is one answer. There is a citizen's group made up of people living along Interstate 81 in Virginia who, having experienced a rash of dognappings along that highway, banded together to form a vigilante committee to watch out for instances of petnapping and to seek the cooperation of all those people—breeders, labs, attack-training schools, animal-control agencies—who might unwittingly receive stolen pets. If you think your community needs such a group, write Action 81 for further information at Route 2, Box 151, Berryville, Virginia 22611.

Do you think tattooing your dog is a good idea?

Yes, although by itself it's not a final answer. Tattooing is a permanent stamp of ownership that keeps most people from palming your dog off as their own. Usually done on the inner thigh or inside the ear, it is relatively painless.

There are problems with tattooing, however. First, it is a relatively unknown procedure, and many people (including shelters) don't always check lost dogs for tattoos. Second, and more critical, is the problem of what number to tattoo. The number should be as permanent as the tattoo and quickly identifiable as to type. Everyone knows what a phone number looks like, but for most of us it is too likely to change to be useful. Americans move once every seven years, on the average, and Californians once every five. Most owners think their Social Security number is the best choice, but in fact it is difficult, if not impossible, to trace someone through that number. Try asking your Social Security office for the name of the person with your number and you will be told that it is privileged information they cannot divulge.

There are also private businesses called pet registries that, for a fee, will register your animal with its own number and act as a twenty-four-hour clearinghouse for lost pets. You could have this number tattooed on your pet. However, there are problems. The number alone won't mean anything to most people. Furthermore, it's difficult to know how extensive and well-established these registries are. Like many small, private concerns, they can go out of business at any time.

I recommend tattooing your driver's-license number, since it is relatively permanent (so long as you stay in your state). Someone finding your pet also has a better chance of getting your name from the department of motor vehicles, or whatever state office maintains these records. If he or she can't, the police or animal-control officers usually can. Don't assume, though, that just because your pet has been tattooed it doesn't also need an ID tag.

Our dog was lost for a week before we recovered it. The vet says he's OK, but he doesn't seem his old self. Is this unusual?

Not at all. Lots of recovered pets sleep a lot or seem a little quiet, even withdrawn and unfriendly, when they first get home. Partly it's exhaustion from the nervous tension that they, like you, have lived with. Sometimes they're just tired—and maybe angry with you for "letting them get away." I'm glad you had your vet look your pet over. That's always a good idea.

You go into great detail about finding a missing pet. What can I do to keep my pet from getting lost in the first place?

I believe most pet owners know what they should do; it's just a question of how motivated they are. If you have recently recovered your pet, take a moment to recall how you felt while it was gone, and consider the following steps you can take to save yourself (and your pet) further anguish:

- If you keep your pet in a fenced-in yard, inspect it for escape hatches. With sufficient motivation, a dog can get through incredibly small openings.
- Make sure all outside gates swing shut. You can't rely on people to close them. Locks will keep unwanted visitors out. Many pets are lost because kids let them out of yards.
- Discuss spaying or neutering your pet with your veterinarian. Not only will you be helping to reduce the numbers of unwanted dogs and cats, but you will keep your pet

from wandering off in pursuit of romance. When the mating urge strikes, old Rover suddenly turns into a twenty-four-hour Lothario. Not only will he leave home, but he might get into serious fights with other dogs that can result in serious injury, death, and/or getting impounded.

- If you have a new dog, give him a tour of the neighborhood so that he can familiarize himself with his new turf and leave "sign posts" that will help him return home should he later wander off.

- If you choose not to fence your dog in or keep him on a leash in public (two procedures I recommend highly), make sure he is obedient. Enroll in an obedience-training class or buy a good book and train him yourself. There are procedures for training a dog to stay on your property, even if you have no fence. They won't keep the dog from bolting in every instance, but they will help keep him home most of the time. If your pet is a neighborhood nuisance, it's not his fault. It's yours. If a neighbor decides he's had enough and calls the pound (or takes more drastic steps to get rid of your pet), you will ultimately have no one to blame but yourself.

A FINAL WORD FROM A NON-CRUSADER

If I've had some wild adventures as Sherlock Bones, they are nothing compared to the inner roller-coaster ride I've been on for the past few years. I came into this business as an adventurer with an eye toward a fast buck, a couple of laughs, and some good stories to tell at parties. What I found turned me almost immediately into a heavy-breathing animal lover—at first overwhelmed by the dimensions of the stray- and unwanted-pet problem and determined single-handedly to wipe it out. I flailed about looking for someone to blame—shelters, owners, the pet industry—but slowly realized the situation was far too complicated to lay at any one doorstep. I lapsed into moments of discouragement and disillusionment when I realized I was not equipped by temperament or inclination to be a knight in shining armor, at least not to the extent that seemed to be required. Any crusading I do will have to be done in a way that suits me best—and that seems to be through sharing my experiences and doing what I can to help people find their pets and keep them safe.

I think there is, however, a larger solution to the problem—one that would, by fixing responsibility for pets with the people who own them, reduce the number of unwanted animals, save taxpayers' money (over $500 million of which is spent each year to destroy unwanted animals), simplify the tracing of missing pets, and reduce the incidence of petnapping. I would like to see each state introduce statewide dog registration, much the same as the present registration of automobiles. Each dog would be tattooed with a number, to be kept on file in a central state office, which would charge a fee large enough to make the program self-supporting. Each time a dog changed hands, this fact would be recorded in the central file. Anyone finding a dog could call a state office and find the name of the owner. Any emergency veterinary fees, boarding costs, and other expenses incurred while the animal was in the care of a public facility would be charged to whoever was listed as the pet's last registered owner.

Such a program will no doubt strike some people as unduly burdensome or as an unwanted governmental intrusion in their lives. Faced with such an eventuality, they might choose not to own a pet—to which I say, Fine. There are too many well-meaning people who take on the ownership of a pet without thinking through the responsibility to the pet and to the community that such a decision entails. I think the nature and duration of this responsibility needs to be spelled out and underscored by state law. The result could well be fewer pets, but those that remained would be healthier, happier, and more assured of ending their days with owners who can give them the love and care all pets deserve.